Recycling

for

dummies®

A Wiley Brand

Recycling

by Sarah Winkler

Recycling For Dummies®

Published by: **John Wiley & Sons, Inc.,** 111 River Street, Hoboken, NJ 07030-5774, www.wiley.com

Copyright © 2023 by John Wiley & Sons, Inc., Hoboken, New Jersey

Published simultaneously in Canada

For general information on our other products and services, please contact our Customer Care Department within the U.S. at 877-762-2974, outside the U.S. at 317-572-3993, or fax 317-572-4002. For technical support, please visit https://hub.wiley.com/community/support/dummies.

Wiley publishes in a variety of print and electronic formats and by print-on-demand. Some material included with standard print versions of this book may not be included in ebooks or in print-on-demand. If this book refers to media such as a CD or DVD that is not included in the version you purchased, you may download this material at http://booksupport.wiley.com. For more information about Wiley products, visit www.wiley.com.

Library of Congress Control Number: 2023933120

ISBN 978-1-394-15954-3 (pbk); ISBN 978-1-394-15955-0 (ebk); ISBN 978-1-394-15956-7 (ebk)

SKY10044341_031423

Contents at a Glance

Table of Contents

Introduction

Recycling is one of the most accessible environmental actions you can take that will have an immediate and positive outcome. It also plays a vital role in waste management and addressing the distressing impacts of waste on our planet. It's not just about recycling that piece of plastic you hold in your hand; it's about protecting our wildlife, cleaning up our planet, and reducing pollution and climate change impacts.

The issue is that we create too much waste, and we're struggling to get control of it. We currently produce 2 billion tons of waste worldwide annually, and that number is growing. Seeing the impact this waste has on our environment, our precious wildlife, and the climate is enough to get your attention. Recycling is a great way to address these issues, but sadly, as I write this book, worldwide recycling rates are still very pitiful. The average recycling rate worldwide sits at around 30 percent. Although the rate varies depending on the material, for plastics — the most harmful — it can be as low as 9 percent. Let's see if we can fix that.

About This Book

Welcome to *Recycling For Dummies*. This hands-on guide is full of practical information and advice to help you figure out what goes in your recycling bin and how to develop better recycling habits. Plus, this book goes beyond helping you know what to recycle and explains *why* you should recycle, giving you an appreciation of the energy and resources invested in making products so you can realize their value and prevent them from wasting away in landfills.

You'll get an understanding of how the recycling industry operates and discover ways you can help support it. That means focusing our efforts on reducing contamination, saving recyclables from landfills, and buying back our recycling. The ultimate goal is to build a sustainable recycling industry where recyclables are collected and turned into new products.

First, I've broken recycling into two main groups: curbside and specialist recycling. Curbside covers paper, plastic, glass, and metal packaging, materials often picked up at your curbside. But whether or not you have access to a curbside service, the information you find in these chapters will be helpful.

Next, to help you wrap your head around how to recycle, I've broken down the recycling rules into three categories: what you can recycle, what you can't, and what you need to check. Rules across states and countries vary depending on the availability of services, so you'll need to do a little homework and check guidelines in your local area. To assist, I've provided some easy-to-use worksheets for these main recyclables.

Specialist recycling covers all the other services available for things like e-waste, food waste, or more specialist items like mattresses or batteries. Many of these have drop-off locations and mail-in options, or can be taken to your nearest recycling center or transfer station.

This book is full of actionable content that enables you to become the best recycler you can be and play your part in solving our waste crisis. And with a focus on the waste hierarchy, you'll also get plenty of tips and tricks to help you reduce your waste, look after what you have, reuse and repurpose what you no longer need, and generally lighten your impact.

A quick note: Sidebars (shaded boxes of text) dig into the details of a given topic, but they aren't crucial to understanding it. Feel free to read them or skip them. You can pass over the text accompanied by the Technical Stuff icon, too. The text marked with this icon gives some interesting but nonessential information about recycling.

One last thing: Within this book, you may note that some web addresses break across two lines of text. If you're reading this book in print and want to visit one of these web pages, simply key in the web address exactly as it's noted in the text, pretending as though the line break doesn't exist. If you're reading this as an e-book, you've got it easy — just click the web address to be taken directly to the web page.

Foolish Assumptions

Here are some assumptions about you, dear reader, and why you're picking up this book:

>> You're concerned about the impact our waste is having on the environment and want to do more.

>> You want to feel like you're contributing to a better world for future generations.

>> You don't have time to search through all the information available on how to recycle and are looking for a single, comprehensive reference guide to help find the answers you need.

>> You're curious about what happens to your recycling after you place it in your bin.

>> You want to know how to make better decisions at the store and switch to recycled products.

It doesn't matter if you've been recycling for years or if you're just starting your journey; there is something inside this book for everyone.

Icons Used in This Book

Like all *For Dummies* books, this book features icons to help you navigate the information. Here's what they mean.

REMEMBER

If you take away anything about recycling from this book, it should be the information marked with this icon.

TECHNICAL STUFF

This icon flags information that delves a little deeper than usual into a particular recycling-related topic.

TIP

This icon highlights especially helpful advice about how to improve your recycling habits and applying the principles of "reduce, reuse, and recycle."

WARNING

This icon points out situations and actions to avoid when recycling so you don't unknowingly create contamination, a safety issue at the recycling plant or elsewhere.

Beyond the Book

In addition to the material in the print or e-book you're reading right now, this product comes with some access-anywhere goodies on the web. Check out the free Cheat Sheet for essential recycling tips and tools, guidelines on how to cut contamination, and ways to reduce how much waste you create. To get this Cheat Sheet, simply go to www.dummies.com and search for "*Recycling For Dummies* Cheat Sheet" in the Search box.

Where to Go from Here

You don't have to read this book from cover to cover, but if you're an especially thorough person, feel free to do so! If you just want to find specific information about recycling and then get back to work, take a look at the table of contents or the index, and then dive into the chapter or section that interests you.

For example, if you simply want to check whether an item can be recycled, you can search for that item and read the appropriate section to find out. But if you want to understand what resources are needed to make it and how the recycling process works, then I recommend you read each chapter in full.

If you're looking for tips to improve your recycling habits, head straight to Chapter 5. But if you're pretty comfortable with your local rules, then you might be interested in reading Part 3 to discover more specialist recycling programs. If you're as eager as I am to find out about all the recycled products available, go directly to Chapter 16.

It's completely up to you where you start, stop, and return. But no matter where you start, I recommend that you keep this book handy so you can refer to it whenever you have a question. I hope you'll find the answers to most of your recycling questions in this book and gain enough knowledge and confidence to become a recycling superstar.

P.S. When you've finished with this book, please remember to keep it in use as long as possible and pass it on to someone else.

1
Getting Started with Recycling

Discover the essential skills to help you contribute to a successful and thriving recycling industry.

Rummage in your bins to better understand waste and how to manage it.

Realize the damage that too much waste inflicts on our parks and nature reserves, waterways and oceans, the air we breathe, and the animals with which we share the planet.

Explore the recycling processes to discover what happens to our waste and whether it really does get recycled.

Chapter **1**

Reviewing the Elements of Recycling

A ccording to the World Bank, more than 2 billion tons of municipal solid waste is produced worldwide every year, and this number is expected to grow to 3.4 billion by 2050. Clearly, we have a waste issue that we need to start addressing. I don't think anyone would disagree with that. Our waste management practices impact the air, land, rivers, oceans, wildlife, and quality of life for both present and future generations. The Earth cannot sustain the amount of trash we create.

Meeting the challenges posed by our waste isn't simple. But we have to start somewhere, and recycling is a good place. Maybe you're already an avid recycler, or perhaps you want to get started but don't know how. Either way, I'm sure you'll find this book useful, whether you're digging deeper into why recycling is important, understanding how the recycling industry works, or finding specialist recycling opportunities to complement your curbside recycling.

This chapter gives you a high-level view of why recycling is vital, where it sits in the grand scheme of environmental protection, and your role in ensuring its effectiveness. It gives you a basic understanding of recycling and the key take-aways of being a good recycler. There are many great reasons to recycle, and hopefully some of the tips and examples I provide in this chapter and the rest of this book will show you how you can master it.

Understanding the Recycling Cycle

When we dispose of our waste, there are four possible destinations: recycling, composting, going to a landfill, or going to a waste-to-energy facility. Recycling, the focus of this book, is the process of collecting material and turning it into something new. More often, recycling is associated with local government curbside pickup services. However, that's not the only type of recycling available. Fortunately, for those who don't have access to a curbside recycling program, there are recycling centers or drop-off locations available. Plus, there are many other specialist and commercial recycling services that are unrelated to your curbside pickup.

REMEMBER

The following are the main steps in the recycling process:

1. **To recycle an item, it must first be collected.**

   As mentioned earlier, there are two main services for collecting recyclables:

   - Curbside collection is where recycling gets picked up from your curbside weekly or fortnightly. This service may look different when you live in an apartment complex, but it's generally the same.

   - Specialist recycling includes recycling centers, transfer stations, and services where you're required to drop off your waste at a collection point like an in-store drop-off or sometimes even send it by mail. Fortunately for those without access to curbside recycling, the centers and transfer stations will usually accept the same materials.

   Once the waste is collected, it's usually delivered to a materials recovery facility or a specialist recycling facility.

2. **Items must be sorted and separated into different categories.**

   Most curbside services use a combination of machines and manual labor to sort the material. For specialist recycling, items are often sorted already and may require minimal sorting.

3. **After sorting, the material is bound up into bales and sold to a reprocessor or manufacturer.**

4. **The reprocessor or manufacturer cleans the material to remove remaining contaminants, then uses it in a new product.**

Recycling is an effective process for turning waste material into new products; you'll discover many success stories in this book. Although recycling may seem simple, there are many factors to consider when determining if and how a material is recycled. Not all items bound for recycling actually make it into new products. Sometimes the quality is too low, or there are no manufacturers who want to use it. But by following the rules, we can help increase the likelihood that these materials make it into a new product.

Making the Case for Recycling

We're using the planet's resources at an alarming rate with no sign of things slowing down. And we're using those resources in the most wasteful way possible: extracting minerals, metals, oil, and gas; making them into products that we use for a short time, sometimes only minutes; and then tossing that precious material into a hole in the ground to slowly rot away. These actions endanger the environment, endanger human health, harm wildlife, threaten ecosystems and biodiversity, and jeopardize the planet's future.

It sounds pretty grim, doesn't it? The truth is, it actually is pretty terrible when you start digging into the details.

The first step in solving these problems is to become aware of how much harm we're causing. Then we need to start taking action to lessen our impacts. Reducing our waste is one of the fundamental ways that we can make a difference. And even though the purpose of this book is to show you how to recycle, activities like reducing and reusing are so important and intertwined with recycling that I couldn't help but include them throughout.

REMEMBER

As for recycling, it's one of the easiest things you can do to help reduce waste. Plus, the benefits go beyond making use of discarded materials. Recycling helps to

>> Minimize how much material is sent to landfills.

>> Reduce the risk of environmental damage to ecosystems and animals.

>> Lower our reliance on raw resources and reduce the negative impacts of extracting them.

>> Save energy and reduce greenhouse gas emissions.

>> Decrease the effects of plastic and other litter on ecosystems.

>> Supply important raw materials to manufacturers for new products, supporting innovation, boosting the economy, and creating jobs.

>> Protect the planet for future generations.

REMEMBER

It takes only a moment to think: Am I putting this in the right bin? Will it get recycled, or will it cause contamination and result in recyclables being sent to a landfill?

Protecting our parks, oceans, and wildlife

Let's be straight: One of the main reasons we're talking about recycling is the devastating impact waste is inflicting on our environment. Our excessive waste issues are impacting every corner of the globe. It's just not possible for us to continue down this path. We must make some changes and soon.

Some of the ways our waste is harming the environment include these:

>> Greenhouse gases, toxic chemicals, and other harmful substances are released from landfills.

>> Plastic is filling our oceans. In fact, the Ellen MacArthur Foundation predicts there will be more plastic in the ocean by weight than fish by 2050.

>> The animals with whom we share the Earth are getting tangled and caught up in our waste or consuming it unknowingly. This is leading to devastating impacts on individual animals and more widespread issues on ecosystems and biodiversity.

>> Microplastics have been found in every corner of the planet. They're present in the air, the ocean, and the soil. They have even been found in the human body (see the next section). We're yet to understand the irreversible damage of this prevalent pollutant. The sooner we start addressing it, the better.

By recycling, we can reduce this pressure on the environment and minimize the risk of pollution.

Reducing risks to communities

The impacts of waste are often focused on the environment and wildlife, and rightfully so: It's extremely important. But there are many ways waste and the associated pollution affect humans. More often, these impacts are felt by minority or low-income communities, and many developed nations still export their waste to developing countries where waste management practices aren't as advanced and communities and the environment aren't as well protected.

Some of the issues poor waste management can cause include the following:

>> Pollution can negatively affect people's livelihoods, like the loss of tourism or reductions in local fish populations disrupting businesses.

>> The spread of disease from waste practices or emissions of toxic compounds can impact people's health and the health of communities.

>> The value of land in areas with poor waste management or pollution can drop.

One of the more concerning issues is that of microplastics, those tiny pieces of plastic less than 5 millimeters (0.2 inches) long. They've already been discovered in human lungs, blood, and even breast milk. Estimates suggest that we could consume up to 100,000 pieces every year. These particles enter the human body through the food and water we consume or even through the air we breathe. At this point, research is ongoing to help us truly understand the full impact on humans. Find out more about this and other environmental issues in Chapter 3.

Minimizing our carbon footprint

Increasingly people are thinking about how to live more sustainably to reduce their carbon footprint. Most people are unaware of how recycling and waste reduction can help combat climate change and reduce greenhouse gas emissions. Energy savings are one of the reasons recycling is so good for the environment. But we can also reduce our reliance on fossil fuels and stop trees from being harvested.

REMEMBER

A great deal of energy is lost in the current linear model where we take from the planet, make products, and then toss them away once we're finished with them. Recycling aims to preserve some of this energy by keeping materials in use and reducing our reliance on new resources.

The positive benefits of recycling on climate change are as follows:

>> It reduces our reliance on fossil fuels. For example, recycling one ton of plastic can save up to 16.3 barrels of oil.

>> It saves trees from being harvested. Recycling one ton of paper can save 17 trees from being cut down. This has the added benefit of increasing carbon storage.

>> Minimizing the amount of material that ends up in landfills decreases the production of greenhouse gases and the risk of them escaping into the atmosphere.

TIP

Reducing your food waste and keeping it out of landfills is one of the easiest things you can do to help tackle climate change. Discover ways to reduce your food waste in Chapter 12.

>> It lowers energy use by keeping materials in use for longer. By replacing raw materials with recycled content, manufacturers can cut the amount of energy required to make products. Here are some great examples of how recycling can result in energy savings:

• Recycling one glass jar can save enough electricity to light an 11-watt compact fluorescent light (CFL) bulb for 20 hours.

- Recycling just one aluminum can saves enough power to run your TV for three hours.

- Recycling a plastic bottle can save two-thirds of the energy required to make a new plastic bottle.

REMEMBER

Recycling can help slow down climate change, but reduction and reuse concepts can go a step further in minimizing our carbon footprint. Find more on this topic in Chapter 3.

Securing the future for our children

REMEMBER

Recycling helps us conserve energy and resources so that we can leave some behind for our kids and our kids' kids. Recycling isn't just about turning the glass jar or the plastic water bottle into something new. It's about preserving the basic materials required to make a new jar or bottle and using the recycled material in its place. It's sometimes easy to forget that the planet has only a finite amount of resources.

Recycling lowers our reliance on raw resources, reducing the impacts associated with mining minerals or fossil fuels, processing them, and manufacturing them. Impacts include ecosystem disruption, deforestation, biodiversity loss, water and soil pollution, and the release of greenhouse gases. It also keeps materials that have already been extracted in use instead of them rotting away in landfills or incinerating them. The more we recycle today, the more these raw resources will be available in the future.

CONSIDERING THE BIGGER PICTURE

Recycling is only one aspect of waste management, not a stand-alone activity. It plays a crucial role in the waste hierarchy, a framework for waste management practices that helps minimize environmental and human health impacts. The waste hierarchy is the source of the well-known phrase "reduce, reuse, and recycle." It's presented as an inverted pyramid with reduce at the very top, illustrating that this should be where we place most of our efforts. Next down is reuse and then recycle. The last item on the pyramid is to send materials to a landfill. This is the least favorable outcome and should be avoided as much as possible. Find out more about the waste hierarchy and its application in Chapter 2.

Recycling also plays a crucial role in a circular economy. In contrast to the existing linear economy, where items are manufactured, consumed, and thrown away, a circular economy is built on keeping resources in use by reusing, repairing, refurbishing, and recycling them. Recycling helps bring the two ends of a linear economy together to create a circle where your waste can rejoin the process, keeping the materials in use for longer.

Getting Started with Recycling

Taking an extra moment to ensure you're putting the right thing into your recycling bin makes a huge difference in the effectiveness of recycling. Many resources are at your disposal, but familiarizing yourself with your local rules is one of the most crucial first steps. Throughout this book, I'll help you find other resources and make sense of what is sometimes conflicting information.

The easiest approach to getting started is to set small achievable goals and accept that you and the recycling system aren't always perfect.

Appreciating your role in the solution

Teamwork is the key to building a resilient recycling industry. Everybody has a part to play, including brand owners and manufacturers, retailers, recyclers, governments, and, of course, people like you and me.

REMEMBER

As consumers, you and I can help change how we buy, use, and discard products, and in doing so, we can be a part of the recycling success story. We can

>> Know the recycling rules and stick to them.

>> Unlearn poor recycling habits.

>> Recognize the importance of preventing contamination.

>> Work to reduce our waste overall.

>> Choose to buy recyclable products over ones that can't be recycled.

>> Support products made with recycled content.

Knowing how to get started

It can sometimes be hard to know where or how to get started. All the information can seem a bit daunting. Here are some tips to help you succeed.

Taking small steps

We've all been there; whether it's getting fit, learning a new skill, or some other goal, you give it everything you have and set really high goals for yourself, only to give up after a short time. Recycling is just like any of these tasks. If we set goals that are too demanding, we may give up on them after only a short time. Figure 1-1 illustrates this concept. The person on the right struggles to reach the first step because it's too big, but on the left, the steps are smaller, so the person has almost reached the top.

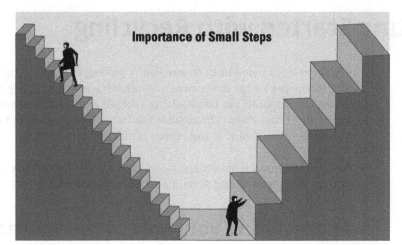

Importance of Small Steps

© John Wiley & Sons, Inc.

FIGURE 1-1:
You get much
further when
you take
small steps.

Breaking your recycling goals into smaller steps can

>> Make it easier to give things a go.

>> Give you less to focus on at one time.

>> Make it less likely you'll be overwhelmed and more likely you'll succeed.

Small steps add up. Initially, you might feel like you are not making much of a difference but believe me, it won't be long, and you'll be looking back at all the changes you've made. Once you've mastered each small change, you will feel ready for the next one.

TIP

Choose one type of material to work on first. Start with curbside recycling of paper, for example. Then start by reading the relevant chapter, Chapter 7. Use the worksheet provided to check your local recycling rules and place it near your bin. Whenever you have a paper or cardboard product to recycle, check the worksheet or head back to the chapter to see whether it's recyclable. Then keep doing that for a few weeks. Once you feel comfortable that you know that material well enough, move on to the next one, like plastic or metal.

TIP

Don't be afraid if you mess up. Just keep trying and do what you can. Every bit helps. And keep in mind that not everyone has access to the same resources and recycling services, so try not to compare yourself to others.

Accepting that things aren't perfect

Throughout this book, I explain the recycling process in detail. Since you probably haven't read the whole book yet, let me explain one of the problems: Recycling is a complex process with many working parts, from all the different groups involved to the complex mix of materials that must be sorted and processed. Plus, things are constantly changing and developing.

REMEMBER

Don't be discouraged from recycling when you hear that one type of material doesn't necessarily get recycled. There may be a good reason why it's not, like there is too much contamination, it's too expensive to process, or there is no market for the material. It may also be a rogue company; they exist in every industry, but remember the phrase "don't paint everyone with the same brush." Many hardworking people in the recycling industry are trying to make things work. It's good to focus on doing what we can do through reducing and reusing, recycling right, keeping contamination low, and buying recycled products.

Uncovering the life cycle of everyday items

Throughout this book, you'll see many instances where instead of discussing what goes in the recycling bin, I explain what materials and resources go into making items and what their environmental impacts are. You might wonder what this has to do with recycling. One of the most important changes we need to make is to start appreciating the inherent value of items around us and to understand the environmental impacts to date.

Every item we own or use is made using energy and resources. It's not just at its end of life that a product has an impact. For example, to make a plastic water bottle, first oil must be extracted from the Earth, processed at a refinery, and then converted into plastic pellets. These are transported to a manufacturer, molded into plastic bottles, then filled with product, packaged, and transported to a retail store. Finally, a consumer like you or me purchases it, drinks the contents, and tosses it away. All these steps require energy and resources and also cause damage to the environment.

We need to start considering these impacts not only when figuring out how to dispose of an item but earlier when deciding whether to buy something. Plus, when recognizing their value, we can better understand the importance of recycling them and keeping the materials in use.

A great way to do this is to apply life cycle analysis, which is a way to quantify the environmental impacts associated with a product's entire lifecycle from creation to disposal. Chapter 3 provides further information on this process and how recycling can lessen the effects.

Recognizing recyclable materials

Key to the success of recycling is collecting the right stuff. For us, this means putting the correct things into our curbside recycling bins or the bins at a drop-off center. It seems easy but can become overwhelming with all the different types of packaging materials we encounter daily.

TIP

Here are some tips to help get you started on identifying recyclables from nonrecyclables:

>> **Starting from the beginning:** Reminding yourself what belongs in your curbside container is a fantastic approach to improving your recycling. Generally, curbside recycling is limited to paper and cardboard, glass, plastic, and metals. Did you know it's also limited to packaging material? For example, a glass vase, metal coat hanger, or plastic toy typically doesn't belong in a curbside recycling bin. You can find more tips on what doesn't belong throughout Chapters 6 to 9.

>> **Recycling labels and guides:** A number of countries are revamping the recycling information provided on packaging, and where available, these can make things much easier. Head over to Chapter 5 to get familiar with these new labels and how they can help.

>> **Plastic by numbers:** The plastic number system (see Chapter 6) is a handy tool for working out which type of plastic an item is made from. You can then match that to the types of plastic your local area accepts.

>> **Recycling check sheets:** Throughout this book, I provide a number of worksheets to help you navigate the rules on recycling. I encourage you to keep a copy of these worksheets near your bins to make checking what can and can't go in much easier. A good place to start is Chapters 6 to 9.

REMEMBER

If you're unsure if you can recycle an item, sometimes it's better to put it into the general waste bin instead of putting it into your recycling bin in the hope it will get recycled.

Throughout this book, I've broken items into three groups:

>> Things you can recycle no matter where you live

>> Things you can't recycle in any curbside service

>> And the things you should check to see what the rules say for your local area

Recycling rules differ depending on where you live, so it would be impossible for me to list every specific rule for every local area in every country. I hope that by listing the rules this way, I've made it simpler for you to work out what can and cannot be recycled where you live.

Despite that, one of the most important things to do is check your local town or city government's rules. In fact, I recommend that you recheck them from time to time. Recycling is constantly changing as technology advances or markets change, so it's good to stay abreast of any updates.

Keeping contamination low

One of the most important things that will help improve recycling is to reduce contamination. When incorrect items are placed in recycling bins, they can lead to issues at the recycling plants and can result in a lot of recycling being sent to landfills. You can minimize contamination by

>> Getting to know what is and isn't accepted in your local curbside or other services

>> Following the rules when you're asked to separate materials before collection

>> Avoiding wishcycling (see Chapter 5) — when you're unsure whether something can be recycled but you place it in the recycling bin anyway

>> Keeping food waste out of your recycling bin

>> Emptying leftover liquids or foods from bottles and containers and giving them a quick rinse

Your efforts will be rewarded with clean recyclables that are more likely to get made into new products.

Finding specialist recyclers

The recycling sector is expanding, and many entrepreneurs are making great efforts to find solutions to our waste issues. In addition to curbside recycling services or drop-off locations for typical packaging like paper, plastic, glass, and metal, there are many additional services for items you may want to throw away. I encourage you to seek these out and take advantage of them if you can.

Some of the most common specialist recycling services available include food waste or composting, e-waste, soft plastics, and batteries. These materials contribute to today's rising waste issues and the resulting environmental harm. Yet solutions are available to help you minimize your impact and recycle them. You can discover more about these and many other exciting programs in Part 3.

Buying back your waste

Recycling must come full circle in order to be successful. This means that the materials we toss in our recycling bin must be reprocessed into brand-new products that are purchased, used, and, ideally, recycled again. That's when recycling is most effective and has the biggest impact.

Buying products with recycled content also decreases our reliance on fossil fuel and metal extraction, cuts water usage, lowers the number of trees harvested, and saves energy, reducing our carbon impact. Finally, it keeps the material from wasting away in a landfill.

There are too many recycled products to list here, but you can find a long list of examples in Chapter 16. Items range from sportswear to kitchen utensils to consumables. In the past, recycled goods were frequently considered to be of low quality or overly expensive. But nowadays, it's not only difficult to see any physical difference, but quality and price are comparable.

REMEMBER

If you're serious about recycling, it's time to rethink your purchasing habits and buy recycled. Who knows, you might even be using some already.

Chapter 2

Getting to Know Your Waste

There's no doubt that we continue to produce a staggering amount of rubbish. For most of us, tossing our rubbish into a bin is second nature. You put the trash in your garbage bin or recycling bin and take it out to your curb or drop it off at a center, then someone comes along and takes it away. But have you ever stopped to wonder what happens to all that waste you create?

In this chapter, I start at the beginning and help you understand what waste is and how much you create before taking a closer look at what's inside your bin. After outlining the available waste treatment options, I explain how applying the waste hierarchy can improve how we manage our waste.

Defining "Waste"

Every individual and business generates waste, except for those amazing "zero wasters" that we aspire to be more like. In this book, I focus on what's referred to as municipal solid waste, which is the waste you and I generate in our households, schools, and small businesses. Other waste categories, such as industrial, agricultural, construction, mining, and medical waste, are outside the scope of this book.

We use the word "waste" in many ways, so to be clear, in this book I'm referring to unwanted and no longer useful material. However, there's still a problem with this definition. Something defined as no longer useful to one person may still be very useful to someone else, like the old saying "One person's trash is another person's treasure." Anytime I refer to "waste" in this book, I want you to think "resource" instead.

REMEMBER

The best philosophy is to consider that everything you no longer want has value, treat your waste with respect, and remember how much energy and resources went into creating the item. Try to make a mental effort to stop throwing away the things you don't want and instead put them where they will do some good and be used again and again.

Exploring the Types of Waste

You generate many types of waste in your home, from everyday items like food scraps and product packaging to more irregular household items like appliances or furniture. It might include hazardous items, recyclable items, compostable items, or items that currently have no other option but to be sent to a landfill.

It makes sense to group the waste we produce into categories that match their next stage of life. In Table 2-1, I list the major groups of waste we regularly produce in our homes: organic waste, recyclable materials, other household waste, and hazardous waste.

TECHNICAL
STUFF

You may be shocked that according to the World Bank, an average person living in a high-income country discards about 3.5 pounds (1.6 kilograms) of garbage every day. This equates to almost 1,300 pounds per person per year.

The same report reveals that, despite having access to advanced waste services, developed countries such as the United States and Canada are among the top waste-producing nations in the world. In fact, Americans are the worst offenders, producing almost 4.9 pounds (2.2 kilograms) per day; that's almost 2,000 pounds of trash per year per person.

So what are we throwing away? Undoubtedly you glance inside whenever you drop something in there, but have you ever taken the time to examine what's inside? Figure 2-1 illustrates what you'll find in the average bin across developed nations.

TABLE 2-1

The Categories of Waste People Generate

Organic Waste	Recyclable Materials (Curbside)
Food scraps	Glass bottles and jars
Yard trimmings or garden waste	Aluminum or steel cans
	Plastic bottles and containers
	Cardboard and paper
Other Household Waste	**Hazardous Waste**
Soft plastics	Paints, paint removers, stains, and finishes
Furniture	Glues and adhesives
Toys	Cleaning chemicals
Textiles	Herbicides and insecticides
Other household items	Batteries
	Electronic waste

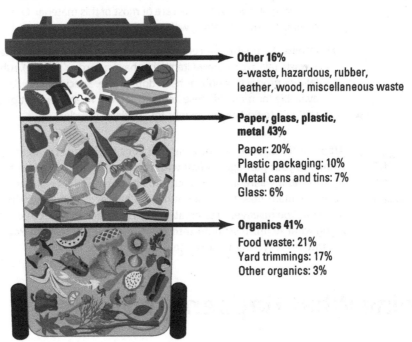

Other 16%
e-waste, hazardous, rubber, leather, wood, miscellaneous waste

Paper, glass, plastic, metal 43%
Paper: 20%
Plastic packaging: 10%
Metal cans and tins: 7%
Glass: 6%

Organics 41%
Food waste: 21%
Yard trimmings: 17%
Other organics: 3%

FIGURE 2-1:
The average percentage by weight of the different types of waste found in your bin.

Let's take a closer look at each of these categories.

>> **Recyclable waste (including paper, glass, plastic, and metal):** Recyclables make up 43 percent of what goes in our bins. Much of it is paper and paperboard, around 20 percent, one of the easiest materials to recycle. About 10 percent is plastics, mostly plastic packaging from our daily food shopping. The remaining is half glass, half metal, again generally food packaging but may include other metals and glassware. A sizable chunk of this 43 percent should be reasonably easy to recycle, depending on where you live. Hopefully you're already putting it into your recycling bin or taking it to a recycling center.

>> **Food and organics:** Based on weight, about 41 percent of the contents of our bins is made up of organic matter. This is great news because there is a lot we can do with organics instead of landfilling them. Food scraps and other discarded food items make up more than 20 to 30 percent of the waste we generate. And by taking action, you can reduce how much you create. Head to Chapter 12 to find out more.

The remaining amount is yard trimmings, garden waste, and materials like pet waste. If you have access to a garden organics bin or yard waste collection service, that is a way to take care of most of this material. Otherwise, you can compost some of it along with your food waste if you have a home compost.

>> **Other:** The final 16 percent of our bins contains other items like textiles, e-waste (electronic waste items that have a cord or battery), rubber and leather products, wood, or hazardous waste. Specialist recycling services are available for many of these items so you can keep them out of landfills. Head to Part 3 to find all the options for specialist recyclers.

After you're more aware of what's in your trash can, the next step is to find ways to ensure your garbage is dealt with responsibly and has the least impact. You may want to do a waste audit of your bins to uncover more about the waste you produce. I explain how to run an audit in Chapter 17. When you've finished, you can use what you discovered to create a plan of attack to reduce your waste. Otherwise, if you want to jump straight into recycling, you can head to Parts 2 and 3 to get all the info on recycling your waste.

Seeing What Happens to Waste

We diligently place items into our different bins, put them on the curb at the scheduled time for emptying, or take them to designated drop-off centers. But what happens after that can seem a bit of a mystery. The primary purpose of waste management across the globe is to reduce the impact of waste on humans and the environment. And depending on the type of waste and the facilities nearby, the waste we produce can head in a few different directions. These include

>> Recycling facilities

>> Composting facilities

>> Incineration plants or waste-to-energy plants

>> Landfills

Unfortunately, waste can also end up littering the environment, but that is not the intended outcome.

Recycling

Recycling is the process of transforming waste into materials that can be used to manufacture new products. It conserves resources, cuts carbon dioxide (CO_2) emissions, and keeps garbage out of landfills and the environment. The most common method is mechanical recycling. In this method, the waste is collected, sorted, cleaned, and baled, ready to be sold to a manufacturer and made into a new product. Most curbside services and recycling facilities rely on this method.

Another method you might have heard about is chemical recycling. This process uses chemicals to break materials into their original components and then rebuilds plastics or other compounds to make new products. There's been a great deal of research into this type of recycling recently, but most of these processes are still under development. You can discover more about this topic in Chapter 18.

Composting

The goal of composting (covered in Chapter 12) is similar to recycling, to turn waste into a useful product. It uses organisms that break down organic waste, like food scraps and garden waste, into their basic parts. The resultant decomposed matter is nutrient-rich and has the potential to improve soil quality while reducing our reliance on synthetic fertilizers. It may potentially result in higher agricultural crop yields by assisting in the rehabilitation of polluted soils. Additionally, it substantially lowers the methane emissions produced when food waste is left to decompose in landfills.

Methods for composting can range from simple home composts to industrial composting plants that can process large amounts of material at once. These industrial plants can achieve a higher temperature and, therefore, a faster breakdown than home composts.

Waste to energy

The waste-to-energy process converts waste products into heat, electricity, or fuel that can then be reused. This transformation occurs via several methods, including incineration, gasification, or pyrolization. The most common waste-to-energy process, incineration, is where waste is burned at very high temperatures, and the resulting heat is used to fuel a power station. The burning waste is used to heat water, creating steam that then powers a turbine and produces electricity. The volume of trash can be reduced by more than 90 percent, leaving behind a mix of materials, including metals, glass, and other solids, called bottom ash.

WARNING

One of the biggest concerns regarding incineration is air pollution. In developed countries, many regulations are placed on waste incineration. Control systems remove the pollutants from the resulting gas, and the remaining ash is either sent to a landfill or used in roadbeds or rail embankments. Unfortunately, in countries without strong regulations, burning waste may release toxic gases that are dangerous to both humans and the environment.

Another method for turning waste into energy is anaerobic digestion. In this process, an anaerobic digester uses microorganisms to turn organic materials into either energy or other products. The process produces biogas, a gas made up primarily of methane. Similar to landfills (see the next section), this gas can be captured and converted into energy. Anaerobic digestion is commonly used on a small scale to process organic waste from industries such as farming.

Landfill

A landfill is a site where waste is buried in a hole in the ground. But it's important to differentiate between landfills and dumps. Dumps are uncontrolled sites, often illegal, where waste piles up without any control measures. As a result, dumps can pose a significant risk to the environment.

Modern landfills aren't the same as dumps. They're well-designed sites quite different from what you might expect. Waste is compacted in layers with a covering of organic and inorganic material soil in between. A liner protects the surrounding soil and groundwater by keeping the garbage and its by-products contained. Most sites will use a clay liner, but many also use plastic liners.

Landfills are designed to store waste, not to let it break down (uncover why they're designed this way in the nearby sidebar "A landfill isn't a compost"). However, inevitably the material does break down in some manner. Decomposing organic matter in landfills creates methane (CH_4) and carbon dioxide (CO_2) greenhouse gases. Many landfill sites mitigate this issue by collecting the gas via pipes installed throughout the landfill. Once captured, the methane may be converted into energy and used to help run the facility or even fed back into the power grid.

WARNING

Despite this process, landfills are still one of the biggest sources of methane emissions resulting from human activity. And there's always a risk of toxic leachates (water that's percolated through the landfill) escaping into the surrounding environment.

A LANDFILL ISN'T A COMPOST

Many people think it's okay to throw rubbish into landfills because it will break down anyway. But that is not actually the case. Landfills are intended to store waste, not to let it break down. In fact, they're designed to keep air and sunshine out to stop the waste from decomposing, although they have the effect of slowing down decomposition rather than completely stopping it. Landfills are designed in this way for several reasons:

- If left open to the elements, the heat produced by the decomposing waste can spontaneously combust.
- When waste biodegrades quickly, it can reduce in size, causing areas to become unstable.
- The slower waste decomposes in landfills, the lower the risk of groundwater pollution.
- Controlled conditions allow for careful monitoring of leachate and emissions.

How long does it take for things to decompose in a landfill? Check out these examples:

- Apple core: 6 months to 2 years
- Paper waste: 2 to 6 weeks
- Biodegradable plastic: 3 to 6 months
- Plastic bag: 10 to 100 years
- Plastic bottle: 450 years or more
- Nylon fabric: 30 to 40 years
- Aluminum cans: 80 to 200 years
- Glass bottles: up to 1 million years

Applying the Waste Hierarchy

Waste management is an important service that protects public health and the environment, but it's a very complex business. The waste hierarchy was developed to address this difficulty. It's a tool or framework for waste minimization that incorporates the protection of the environment and human health. Through an inverted pyramid, it emphasizes reduction at the source through reducing, reusing, and recycling. It puts decreasing focus on energy recovery, waste treatment, and the least preferred option, landfilling. You can see the waste hierarchy in Figure 2-2.

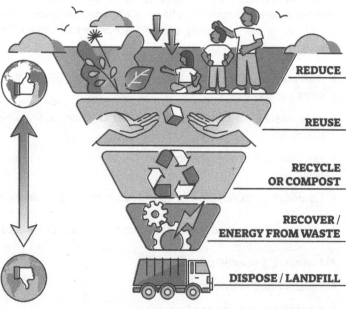

FIGURE 2-2:
The waste hierarchy framework for waste minimization.

VectorMine/Adobe Stock

Around the world, this framework is implemented into policies, plans, and programs for waste management. Introducing the waste hierarchy helps guide governments, businesses, and even individuals in making more sustainable decisions. In the following sections, I describe each of the levels of the waste hierarchy and how they apply to you.

Avoiding as a way to reduce waste

The top level of the waste hierarchy pyramid in Figure 2-2 is all about prevention. Reduce refers to changing how we design and consume products. Simply choosing not to buy something has the most impact and the added bonus that you'll save some money too. Reducing is also about rethinking and redesigning the products we need, so they don't result in waste: using recycled and sustainable materials, keeping toxins out, and making sure items can be recycled at the end of their life.

TIP

The best way for us as individuals to avoid and reduce waste is to think before we buy. Ask yourself, "Do I really need this product?" or "Can I get the desired result some other way?" The choice to buy single-use plastics is a perfect example. Next time you're out and want to buy a coffee, why not take a reusable coffee cup with you instead of buying a single-use cup that goes straight to the landfill?

Reusing things before they become waste

If it's not possible to reduce, then the next best thing to do is reuse. Keeping products in use for as long as possible is the best way to make sure the energy and resources that went into creating them aren't wasted. You can reuse products in many different ways. You might keep using a product instead of buying a new one, like continuing to use your mobile phone and delaying upgrading it until you really need to. You might find someone else who needs or wants an item you no longer have a use for.

TIP

Another way to reuse is to extend the life of existing items. You can do this by caring for them and repairing them when necessary. Most of us are conditioned to believe that when something breaks, we should toss it away and get a new one, but this isn't the case. My husband and I are getting better at looking for ways to repair and reuse things instead of tossing them. My husband is more skilled with tools than I am, so he tends to handle more of those technical repairs, but I'm quite adept with a sewing machine, so I take care of the clothing repairs. It can take some time to switch your thinking, but it feels good to repair something and keep using it. In Chapter 15, I provide lots of other ways to reduce and reuse.

Recycling or composting waste

Recycling and composting are the two end-of-life scenarios for materials that have a positive outcome. Recycling is the process of collecting useable materials from discarded items and remanufacturing them into a new product. Composting also turns end-of-life materials into usable resources, namely fertilizer that's used to improve soils and grow more food. Both of these processes support a circular economy and keep materials in use.

As an individual, you can do many things to support recycling:

>> Educate yourself on recycling. Reading this book is a pretty good start.

>> Find a local composting service or set up composting at home (see Chapter 12 for more information).

>> Choose products that can be recycled or composted.

>> Buy recycled products.

Recovering the energy from waste

Once options for recycling and composting have been exhausted, the next alternative is to recover resources by converting the waste into energy. Waste can be converted to heat, electricity, or fuels that are used in many industries.

Waste to energy, when viewed as one part of the solution to the overall waste problem, can be a useful process, but it's generally inconsistent with a circular economy model and may compete with recycling for its feedstock. Recycling and keeping resources in use for as long as possible is preferable.

Sending waste to landfills

The final step in the waste hierarchy and the least desirable outcome is sending waste to a landfill. This is the smallest part of the pyramid in Figure 2-2 because our ultimate goal is to send as little waste as possible to landfills. Even well-managed landfills present a number of environmental problems and are a significant source of methane, a nasty greenhouse gas. Plus, when we send material to a landfill, we give up the opportunity to use it in a new product.

Currently, more than 50 percent of municipal solid waste is sent to landfills in most countries. A further 25 percent heads to recycling facilities for processing, and the remaining 25 percent is split between composting and incineration. However, if there are no local composting or incineration facilities, this last category may also be disposed of in landfills. That's a lot of material ending up in landfills! Clearly, we have a lot of work to do to improve these figures. Applying the waste hierarchy can help us produce less garbage overall and steer us toward more beneficial choices like reducing, reusing, and recycling. Keep reading this book, and I'll help you find out more.

Chapter **3**

Understanding the Problem with Waste

O ur throwaway culture — based on taking resources, making products, and then tossing those products away — pushes the planet's resources and health to their limits. Over the last century, we have mined, logged, trawled, drilled, leveled, and poisoned almost every inch of the Earth. And even though every item we own has contributed to this destruction, we don't always connect the two issues. Every item we own or use required resources and energy to be created and will require more resources to be disposed of. It's time we started considering the full impact.

Waste impacts our soils, air, rivers, and seas. But animals are affected in the most devastating ways. They can become entangled in or ingest waste, causing them to be injured or leading to their death. Plastic is one of the worst offenders, infiltrating every corner of the Earth from the deepest oceans to the highest mountains. It's even been found in the human body.

In this chapter, I explain how to look at waste differently by considering the full life cycle impacts of products. This will help you understand what is truly wasted when you throw something away. Plus, you get a good look at what's at stake if we don't recycle. The environmental cost of our waste is a depressing subject but one we must realize to understand the importance of reducing our waste. Reduce, reuse, and recycle isn't just a fun catchphrase; the future of our planet depends on it.

What a Waste

Have you ever stopped to think about what goes into making the objects and items we buy and use in our lives? Energy and resources are key inputs in the production of day-to-day products. Since the Industrial Revolution in the 1700s and 1800s, humans have been extracting resources and converting them into products. And it's not slowing down; the depletion of raw resources has increased exponentially, not only with the increase in population but with significant growth in consumption per person.

WARNING

In essence, we're taking valuable natural resources; extracting, processing, and manufacturing them with the help of energy and other resources like water; enjoying them for a brief time; and then discarding them. Meanwhile, we're negatively impacting the ecosystems of the Earth, putting stress on the plants and animals that share the planet with us. And then we're left with a huge pile of waste stretching to the moon and back that we can't work out what to do with.

In the following sections, I describe the life cycle of common materials, including the inputs and outputs required to create, use, and dispose of them. This is an important concept to understand when considering how materials degrade and the fact that there is no such thing as "away." I also explain where materials do end up when they aren't disposed of responsibly and the damaging effect they can have on our planet.

Looking at the life cycle of everyday materials

Most of us know that products are made in factories, but for these factories to get the materials, they must be extracted from the Earth and processed into usable material. Every step — design, extraction, manufacturing and production, transportation, retail, use, disposal, and recycling — has its own impacts. When you consider the effects of all of these steps, it's called *life cycle analysis*.

A life cycle approach to products is a holistic approach where you consider the environmental and social impacts of a product from its creation right through to its end of life. It helps you consider the impacts of every stage. You can get an idea of how this works in Figure 3-1. The conventional processes a product goes through based on a linear economy, described in more detail in this section, are depicted in the figure's center. Each one of these steps requires inputs of energy, water, and raw materials. Plus, each step has its own impacts, such as pollution or waste creation.

Here is a bit more detail on the steps of a typical linear process:

>> **Extraction of the raw material:** This includes mining, fossil fuel extraction, and logging of trees. Resource extraction is a highly intense process requiring a great deal of energy and equipment and can result in significant environmental impacts.

>> **Processing:** Raw resources are converted into materials that can be used in manufacturing, like converting fossil fuels into plastic. Depending on the process, a great deal of energy is consumed and waste created.

>> **Manufacturing and packaging:** Materials are modified to form products either by hand or machine using techniques like molding, machining, shaping, joining, sewing, and many more. These processes all require resources and energy.

>> **Transportation and storage:** Through each of these steps, materials and products must be sent back and forth to various parties, using up precious energy and emitting greenhouse gases.

>> **Purchase and use:** Next, the product starts its useful life. How long this life is can depend on many factors, and unfortunately it is often shortened by marketing pressure or built-in obsolescence.

>> **Disposal:** Finally, the product reaches its end-of-life (hopefully not prematurely). At this point, energy and resources are necessary to collect and transport the item to a recycling plant or a landfill. However, the end never really comes; there is no "away" (as you find out later in this chapter). The abandoned item might decompose slowly in a landfill, potentially releasing hazardous chemicals and greenhouse gases, or preferably it's sent to be recycled, where valuable materials are recovered.

When you recycle items, they go back into the middle of the cycle, skipping some of the intensive extraction and processing activities. This helps reduce the energy and resources necessary and reduces the negative impacts of these early activities. You can see in Figure 3-1 that when you reuse materials, you reduce the inputs and outputs even more significantly.

REMEMBER

To truly understand the importance of recycling, first we must appreciate the value of what we're actually throwing away.

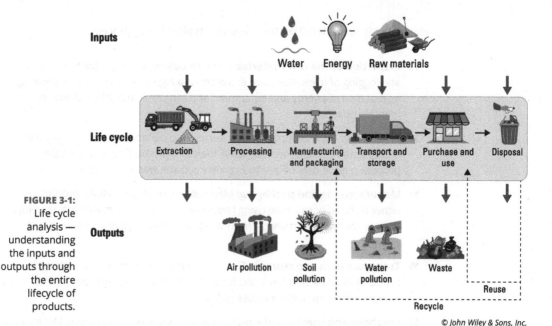

Inputs

Water Energy Raw materials

Life cycle

Extraction Processing Manufacturing and packaging Transport and storage Purchase and use Disposal

FIGURE 3-1: Life cycle analysis — understanding the inputs and outputs through the entire lifecycle of products.

Outputs

Air pollution Soil pollution Water pollution Waste

Reuse

Recycle

Taking until there's no more

Across the world, about 12 tons of resources are extracted for every person each year. These raw resources go into making all the products we consume. Whether it's a bottle of shampoo or our shiny new mobile phone, they all require resources. The bad news is the amount of resources we use annually continues to increase and is predicted to reach 18 tons per person by 2050.

The current linear economy, where we take these materials, make an item, use it, and discard it, is unsustainable. There is only one planet, and most of the resources it provides are finite. Even if those resources were to last longer than predicted, the price of continuously extracting resources until nothing is left is far too high. Not only does it leave nothing for future generations, but they will also be left with a polluted planet in crisis.

REMEMBER

The waste hierarchy in Chapter 2 shows us a better course. First, and most important, is to use less, and reduce our impact and our reliance on raw materials. Second is to keep using what we have already extracted, either by continuing to use products or by recovering the materials through recycling and reusing them.

CONNECTING RECYCLING AND THE CIRCULAR ECONOMY

You might have heard about a circular economy; it's become a fairly hot topic recently. The three main principles of a circular economy are to eliminate waste, keep products and materials in use as long as possible, and regenerate natural systems. So where does recycling fit into this?

Recycling is an important aspect of a circular economy, but it's only one part of the picture. A circular economy starts at the beginning and aims to completely design out waste and pollution. This is achieved by designing products that can be reused, repaired, and remanufactured so there's no need to recycle because they never reach their end of life. However, until we achieve this goal, recycling plays a crucial role in ensuring materials don't go to waste.

Recycling may be seen as a means of turning a linear economy into a circular economy, as demonstrated in the middle of the figure here. But recycling isn't enough on its own. To create a circular economy you must introduce reduce, reuse, and repair concepts, as demonstrated on the right-hand side of the figure. Recycling is simply one part of the bigger picture of a circular economy.

petovarga/Adobe Stock

Understanding how materials degrade

When exposed to the elements, every material breaks down over time, but how they do it and how long it takes can vary quite a bit. Here I take a look at the different ways materials break down:

>> **Organic matter:** Food scraps and yard waste decompose, meaning they're broken down into their original components by microorganisms. You might have heard it referred to it as *rotting*. How they decompose depends on the temperature, the amount of oxygen and water, and the sort of microorganisms present. For example, as temperatures rise, there can be more microorganisms, but over a specific temperature, they can't survive. Composting is a way to control this process and turn food and other organic waste into nutrient-rich material needed for soils.

>> **Plastics:** Unlike organic matter, plastics don't decompose. They break down through a process called *photodegradation*. As sunlight or UV rays hit the plastic, it breaks the bonds that hold the polymer's chains together. This causes the plastic to break into smaller and smaller pieces until they become microplastics or nano plastics, but more on that later. New research has discovered plastic-eating enzymes that might munch on our waste plastic. Discover more in Chapter 18.

>> **Metals:** Bacteria cannot consume metals; instead, metals corrode or rust when exposed to elements like oxygen, water, or other chemicals. The metal gradually deteriorates on the surface. This process can take from 30 years to 500 years. As metals corrode, they release toxic compounds like mercury, cadmium, or arsenic into landfills, which can escape from landfills and pollute the surrounding areas. For example, steel is coated in zinc, which is toxic to fish and can bioaccumulate, meaning it can build up over time, causing even more harm.

>> **Glass:** Although glass generally degrades into relatively safe materials, it can take thousands of years. What happens is that over time the surface of the glass absorbs moisture, and a process called *devitrification* occurs. This is where the outer layer crystallizes and breaks off into small flakes. You're pretty unlikely to see this happen to any of the glass you use daily; it's an extremely slow process that can take thousands of years.

>> **Paper and cardboard:** Paper is made from wood pulp and generally breaks down in a similar manner to organic compounds like food or yard waste. However, some paper is coated in plastic, like what you find in multilayer materials packaging like Tetra Pak cartons or frozen food boxes (see Chapter 10).

Knowing that there's no such thing as "away"

Sometimes you get a good feeling after putting an item into your bin: the feeling that you no longer need to worry about it. It's like there's an invisible boundary over your bin; once an item's in there, it's no longer your job to worry about it. Sure, you must remember to take the bin to the curb for pickup, but you no longer have any responsibility for what's inside. It's someone else's concern now.

We often use the term "throw it away," but have you ever wondered where "away" is? Well, the truth is there is no such place. Everything must go somewhere. Waste doesn't just disappear. It must be managed appropriately to ensure it doesn't threaten the environment and society. In the case of our waste, there are four options: it goes into the recycling process, to a landfill, or to a waste-to-energy facility, or it becomes litter in the environment. Each of these outcomes has consequences, some better than others.

REMEMBER

If we stop and think, "Where will my waste end up?" we can make better decisions at the bin and make sure our waste goes to the right place. Are we placing recycling in our recycling bin, or are we simply tossing everything in there so it can be taken to this place called "away"?

The Environmental Costs of Too Much Waste

The Earth cannot sustain the amount of trash we create. It's drowning in it! In Chapter 2, I point out that the average person generates around 3.5 pounds of trash daily. Multiply that globally, and we produce more than 2 billion tons of waste every year. So where does it all go, and what impact does it have?

Much of it ends up polluting the planet as litter. I'm sure you've heard that the ocean is full of plastic, but did you know that most plastic waste originates on land? Plastic and other litter can travel long distances from inland locations via waterways and storm drains. The final destination of most of the world's litter is the ocean. This pollution directly affects marine and land animals, who get stuck or tangled in it or, even worse, confuse it with food and ingest it.

The rest of our waste that isn't recycled ends up in open dumps, landfills, or incineration plants. Depending on how well these are managed, the environmental impacts can vary. Unsurprisingly, improper waste management contributes directly to many environmental issues, but even controlled sites have risks.

TRAVELING TRASH: PATHWAYS OF POLLUTION

You might wonder how a piece of litter dropped in the street in a big city can end up polluting the ocean. In fact, about 80 percent of marine litter comes from the land. Litter from sidewalks and streets is blown or washed into gutters, where it's carried into storm drains, most of which empty into streams or rivers. These waterways are gateways to the oceans. If you want to see how plastic litter travels from your hometown to the sea, take a look at The Ocean Cleanup's plastic tracker (www.theoceancleanup.com/plastic-tracker/).

Here's how litter can move from cities and parks and end up in the ocean.

1. Someone litters on the street, or a public bin is overflowing with trash, and the wind or rain picks it up and washes it away.

   Note: If you see a bin overflowing in a public place, don't just put your rubbish on top. Take your rubbish home with you and notify the local town or city authority that the bin is full.

2. Wind and rain wash the trash into a nearby sewer, creek, or river system, or onto the beach.

3. The trash travels through the sewer and into a waterway. Along the way, it can break up from exposure to the sun or impacts from wind and water.

4. Creeks flow into rivers, and rivers flow into the sea. The trash is carried through these waterways until it eventually reaches the oceans.

5. When litter reaches the ocean, it is carried around by ocean currents, is deposited on beaches, or finds its way to ocean garbage patches.

Everyone on the planet is responsible for avoiding ocean pollution. It doesn't matter how far away from the ocean you live. Own your trash! Be accountable for it, and If there's no safe place to discard it, always take it home with you.

In the following sections, I look into the main environmental impacts of too much trash.

Filling our oceans

Oceans are one of the most valuable natural resources on the planet. They control the weather, clean the air, help feed the world, support the livelihood of millions of people, and provide cultural and recreational benefits. They also provide a home to most species on Earth, from the largest animal, the blue whale, to microscopic organisms.

Yet more than 11 million metric tons of plastics pollute the ocean every year. That's about the same as two garbage trucks full of plastic every minute. To date, 200 million tons have already reached the sea. The issue is extremely urgent, given that plastic production isn't expected to diminish any time soon. We produce over 300 million tons of the stuff every year. It's no wonder it's predicted there will be more plastic in the ocean than fish by weight by 2050. Can you imagine? It's a horrifying thought, demonstrated by Figure 3-2.

Once the waste has reached the oceans, it gets picked up by currents and accumulates in certain spots. *Garbage patches* are a name for ocean areas where manmade litter and debris accumulate. In the past, they have been described as islands of trash, but they are actually vast areas where small pieces of plastic are intermingled with larger pieces like abandoned recreational and commercial fishing gear. The material does not just sit on the surface but can be found suspended deep into the ocean. Plus, it doesn't always stay in the same place; it can move with the currents and winds.

FIGURE 3-2:
Plastic waste floating in the ocean.

The plastic accumulates in these areas because of the rotating currents called *gyres*. The most well-known of the garbage patches is the Great Pacific Garbage Patch, located in the North Pacific gyre between Hawaii and California. But all of the gyres have plastic pollution floating around in them, including the Indian Ocean gyre, the South Pacific gyre, and the South and North Atlantic gyres.

The Great Pacific Garbage Patch is the world's largest accumulation of ocean plastic and is estimated to be twice the size of Texas. A total of 1.8 trillion plastic pieces are estimated to be floating around in it, approximately 80,000 tons. However, this estimate accounts only for the dense center of the patch. It's much bigger if you include the outer edges.

Endangering our wildlife

Whether it's a sea turtle with a plastic straw stuck in its nose, a bird with a belly full of plastic, or a seal choked by a plastic bag, images of wildlife harmed by pollution tear at the heartstrings. But when it comes to the effects our pollution has on animals, these are just the tip of the iceberg.

Thousands of species are impacted by plastic pollution. The list includes all species of marine turtles, more than half of whale species, and more than half of the total seabird species. And it's not just these large marine animals affected by our waste. Studies have found that many freshwater and land-based species also ingest plastic or become trapped. Organisms of every size and shape are getting entangled in or eating our trash. And to make matters worse, according to Oceana, most of these species are already teetering on the brink of extinction.

Pollution impacts wildlife in three main ways: getting stuck or tangled in waste, ingesting waste, or through secondary effects on ecosystems.

Getting stuck or tangled

Getting entangled or stuck in plastic and other debris can have devastating impacts, ultimately leading to an animal's death. Here are some examples of how it can affect them:

>> Many everyday items like packing straps, plastic bags, balloons, fishing nets, and lines can entangle animals. Examples of animals entangled in our plastic debris are presented in Figures 3-3 and 3-4. The result of entanglement can include the following:

- Often, the item can become so tightly coiled around an animal's neck or limb that it cuts the skin. Apart from the obvious pain, it can restrict the animal's breathing, limit its mobility, or result in the loss of a limb or even death.

- Loss of a limb or other restriction makes it hard for the animal to perform necessary tasks, like catching food or escaping predators.

- Entanglements can cause deformities as the animal grows, leading to lifelong difficulties.

- An animal may have a strap or fishing line caught around its mouth or throat, making it hard to eat.

>> Small animals can get their heads or limbs stuck in buckets, cans, or jars in their search for food. They can also become completely trapped inside and be unable to get out.

>> Debris, like broken glass jars or beverage cans, can injure animals.

(a)

FIGURE 3-3: Animals caught in our plastic waste. (a) A cockatoo with plastic pollution stuck around its neck. (b) A puffer fish caught in a plastic bag washed up on the beach.

(b)

Sue Martin/Shutterstock; mattjamesphotography/Shutterstock

FIGURE 3-4: Images of wildlife affected by waste. (a) A fur seal with a soda can caught on its bottom jaw. (b) Rescuers removing a plastic ring stuck around a seal's neck.

(a)

(b)

Ocean Conservation Namibia/www.ocnamibia.org/ last accessed February 21, 2023

REMEMBER

Please ensure you responsibly dispose of your leftover fishing line or other marine trash. And if a piece of trash can form a loop easily, cut it up before placing it in the bin. This helps protect animals if it somehow ends up in the environment.

Eating plastic

You think trying to identify all the different plastics is hard for us. Those bits of plastic can appear very similar to typical food for an animal. For example, sea turtles easily mistake clear plastic bags floating in the water for jellyfish, or a fish might gobble down tiny microplastics that resemble their regular food. Microplastics and microfibers are particularly easy for animals to ingest. You can find out more about these items later in this chapter.

TECHNICAL STUFF

Why do animals eat so much plastic? The answer might surprise you. Plastic not only looks like their typical food but can smell like it too. Pieces of plastic floating in the ocean are the perfect home for algae, small plants, and tiny animals. These mini worlds, in particular the algae, can release odors familiar to animals like birds and turtles, attracting them to the pieces of plastic.

SAVING SEALS FROM PLASTIC POLLUTION

Ocean Conservation Namibia was established in 2020 to help protect the 1.5 million Cape fur seals along the Namibia coastline. These seals are regularly exposed to marine debris and abandoned fishing gear, which can entangle them, cause significant injuries, and kill them. It's incredible to witness the team at Ocean Conservation Namibia chase down seals and rescue them from fishing lines, plastic bags, and other trash. Take a look at www.ocnamibia.org or on YouTube (www.youtube.com/c/ocean conservationnamibia).

Some of the issues caused by the ingestion of plastic include the following:

» An item causes a blockage, limiting an animal's ability to digest food.

» It can fill an animal's stomach and trick its body into thinking it's full, resulting in it starving to death.

» Once ingested, debris can cause internal injuries.

» Chemicals can leach from microplastics and be absorbed by the animal.

» Plastic can absorb pollutants from the surrounding water, which may be released when ingested.

Common items ingested by animals include plastic forks, straws, sandwich bags, polystyrene, children's toys, and bottle caps. In many cases, it takes only one piece of plastic to kill an animal. Fortunately, the green sea turtle rescued by Gumbo Limbo Coastal Stewards, in Figure 3-5a, survived despite having swallowed the plastic bags, balloons, and food wrappers shown in Figure 3-5b.

TIP

If you find an animal in distress, stay back and give it some space. Keep pets and other people away. Then call your local animal rescue center or local government.

WARNING

Soft plastics are fast becoming one of the biggest threats to animals. They're lightweight and easily carried by wind and rain into the environment. Be sure to dispose of them responsibly, either by recycling them (see Chapter 11) or by ensuring they don't become litter.

FIGURE 3-5: A juvenile green sea turtle (a) entangled in a fishing line was also found to have ingested large amounts of plastic bags, balloons, and food wrappers (b).

(a)

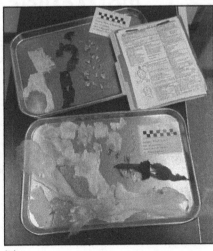
(b)

Gumbo Limbo Coastal Stewards/www.gumbolimbo.org/last accessed February 21, 2023

Examining effects on ecosystems

There are secondary effects resulting from plastic and other waste on ecosystems and the associated food chains. Here are some ways that ecosystems can suffer:

>> Many species impacted by ocean plastic play a crucial role in maintaining healthy ecosystems. Food chains or webs are delicate, complex relationships between species. These complicated webs are disrupted when one species' presence is reduced or removed completely.

>> Plastics are made with many chemicals that can leach into the environment. These chemicals can affect the local ecology and may even build up in certain areas.

>> Waste on the surface of water bodies can affect the conditions underneath, blocking sunlight from reaching algae or other organisms.

>> Ingested plastics can be passed through the food chain, affecting multiple species and ultimately impacting humans. This occurs when one animal eats another and ingests the plastic with it, a process called *biomagnification*. I describe this in more detail in the nearby sidebar.

WARNING

The full impacts of plastic and other pollution on the environment are not yet fully understood. And ultimately, changes in ecosystems may also end up having detrimental effects on humans.

BIOACCUMULATION VERSUS BIOMAGNIFICATION

Bioaccumulation is the buildup of chemicals in a living organism over time. For example, if a fish keeps eating the same toxic food, these toxins can build up over time and reach dangerous concentrations.

The process of *biomagnification* is when larger animals eat smaller animals that have ingested plastic or toxins, and these toxins are transferred to the larger animal.

The combined effects of bioaccumulation and biomagnification can lead to dangerous toxins being passed up the food chain. Some of these toxins might even be transmitted to humans.

Poisoning our soils

When we think of environmental pollution, we often consider the waterways and oceans, but many land areas are also affected by our waste. Pollutants reach soils by directly depositing waste in dumps and landfills, but they can also be transported by air, water, and wind. Here are some sources of soil pollution:

» Illegal dumping of waste or rubbish dumps is a source. In uncontrolled situations, waste can not only pollute the surrounding environment but is free to be transported throughout ecosystems.

» Old or mismanaged landfills are problems. Many older landfills and those in developing countries are constructed without strict standards. When the liquid produced by decomposing material in the landfill (leachate) isn't contained, it can escape into the surrounding groundwater and waterways. This material can be full of toxic compounds.

» Problems can occur in modern landfills. Even well-managed landfills can have issues. For example, liners may be compromised and leak, resulting in leachate escaping its confines and polluting the surrounding area.

» Litter is also a significant source of soil or land pollution. All sources of litter cause pollution through degradation, releasing chemicals, or breaking down into microplastics.

WARNING

Polluted soils can negatively impact local flora, fauna, and wildlife habitats. They can also affect agriculture in some regions and lead to the contamination of drinking water in nearby communities.

Polluting our air

Poor waste management can lead to air pollution and negatively impact nearby ecosystems, humans, and animals. This occurs when chemicals or particles that can cause harm are released into the air. Toxins may include carbon monoxide, nitrogen oxides, sulfur dioxide, and hydrocarbons. These emissions can contribute to acid rain, respiratory problems, and other health issues for humans and animals.

More often, air pollution occurs from the following activities:

» Uncontrolled burning of waste releases toxic compounds, like nitrogen oxides, sulfur dioxides, polychlorinated biphenyls, heavy metals, or dioxins, all of which can cause significant health issues.

About 40 percent of the world's waste is burned instead of recycled. Much of this occurs through uncontrolled burning in developing countries rather than in regulated incineration facilities. It might seem far away to us, but this waste often originates from developed nations. Find out more about the international trade in waste in Chapter 4.

>> Emissions come from landfills or open dumps. Despite controls applied to the operation of some modern landfills, they're not always sufficient to prevent emissions. In addition to greenhouse gases, landfills can emit other gases, including ammonia and hydrogen sulfide. This is the stuff that smells like rotten eggs. Although they make up less than 10 percent of the overall gas, exposure can cause health issues in nearby communities.

TIP

One great way to help reduce methane from landfills is to reduce the amount of food waste you put in your general garbage bin. You can find plenty of tips and tricks for reducing your food waste in Chapter 12.

REMEMBER

The problem is that air pollution isn't restricted to the location in which it occurs. There is only one atmosphere, so the entire planet suffers the consequences of air pollution no matter where it originates.

The Social Costs of Too Much Waste

In addition to the environmental and ecosystem-related issues caused by too much waste, there are numerous socioeconomic consequences. Some of the negative effects include the following:

>> The presence of trash may be offensive and unsightly and create safety issues like tripping hazards.

>> Litter and waste dumps can create breeding grounds for bacteria or other diseases that can impact humans. They can also attract pests like rodents or mosquitoes that help transfer these diseases to humans.

>> Pollution can result in negative impacts on tourism affecting the livelihoods of many in the community.

>> It costs money to manage waste and remove litter from the environment. In most cases, this cost is borne by local governments through tax dollars.

>> Land value near or around waste management facilities or dumps, especially mismanaged ones, can decrease.

>> Trash can impact fisheries by reducing fish populations or increasing maintenance due to trash tangled in boat propellers.

>> In addition to the unpleasant odors, landfill emissions can endanger nearby communities if they aren't properly regulated.

>> Waste management practices disproportionately affect low-income communities. Landfills, incineration plants, and recycling plants are more likely to be built in minority or low-income areas. Plus, many developed countries still export their waste to developing countries with lower environmental standards and minimal access to high-quality processing and waste management.

Our Plastic Planet

A seemingly endless stream of plastic items has invaded our lives and the planet we live on since the discovery of plastics. Since the outset, an estimated 8.3 billion tons of plastic has been produced globally. And every year, we generate another 400 million tons.

Today plastic is everywhere! It's in every corner of the planet, from the deepest depths of the oceans to the highest mountains. It's in the air we breathe, the water we drink, and the food we eat. And the biggest problem is it's not going away in a hurry. Plastics take hundreds if not thousands of years to break down, so most of it won't disappear in our or our children's lives.

With only 9 percent of plastic recycled across the globe, most of it ends up in landfills or incinerated, but a large quantity also pollutes the environment. It's estimated there will be more than 12 billion metric tons of plastic in landfills by 2050. Around the same time it's predicted that there will be more plastic than fish in the sea.

REMEMBER

The best solution is to stop plastic from becoming waste in the first place. Have you seen the waste hierarchy in Chapter 2? It describes the steps to help us reduce plastic — in order of priority, reduce, reuse, and recycle. Since 50 percent of the plastics we use are single-use or disposable, many of which pollute the environment, there's a good chance we can make a difference.

Seeing that plastic is here to stay

Plastic pollution has two main problems: It takes a very long time to degrade, and when it finally does, it breaks into smaller and smaller pieces called microplastics (see the next section). Because of this, almost every piece of plastic that was ever made is still with us. On average, plastic takes more than 400 years to degrade.

Here are some common plastic items and how long it's estimated they will take to fully degrade:

>> Plastic bag: 10 to 1,000 years

>> Styrofoam cup: 500 to 1,000,000 years

>> Plastic straw: 200 years

>> Plastic water bottle: 450 years

>> Plastic bottle cap: 500 years

>> Synthetic fabrics: more than 100 years

>> Beverage six-pack rings: 450 years

Homing in on microplastics

By now, you're aware of the plastic pollution problem, but did you know there's a much more serious issue that's not so easy to see with the eye? Hiding among the litter are tiny pieces of plastic called microplastics. They're so small that we can't see how prevalent they are in our ecosystems. But scientists have found them: deep in the ocean, in ice cores in Antarctica, high up in the mountains, in the air in London, and even in the human body.

Microplastics are plastics with a diameter of fewer than 5 millimeters (0.2 inches). Plastics don't break down so much as break up. So these tiny pieces of plastic are just small pieces of the same material. And their small size means they can be transported easily by wind, water, and waves.

There are two main types of microplastics:

>> **Primary microplastics:** These plastics are manufactured to be less than 5 millimeters in size and are released directly into the environment. Examples include microbeads (see the nearby sidebar), glitter, artificial sports turfs, or plastic nurdles (pellets) accidentally spilled during transportation.

Another primary source of microplastics isn't manufactured to be small but does originate from human use. These small plastic particles break off during use and enter the environment. The two key sources of this sort of microplastic are synthetic clothing and car tires, but they can be created from other sources like peeling paint.

>> **Secondary microplastics:** Secondary microplastics are the small particles created as water bottles or other plastic debris break down in the environment. Exposure to sunlight breaks the long polymer chains and causes the

plastic to split into smaller pieces. Single-use plastics (see the next section) are one of the primary sources of secondary microplastics. Over time, one plastic bottle can break up into more than 10,000 pieces of microplastic.

You can help reduce the risk of secondary microplastics by switching to reusables. Head to Chapter 15 to find some great swaps you can make.

TIP

The primary environmental concern of microplastics is ingestion by animals. These small pieces of plastic are easily mistaken for food and can cause serious damage, ultimately leading to death. Most of the 898 pieces of plastic found within a deceased one-month-old green sea turtle, shown in Figure 3-6, were microplastics.

FIGURE 3-6:
A total of 898 pieces of plastic, many of which were microplastics, were removed from this one-month-old turtle.

*Gumbo Limbo Coastal Stewards
/www.gumbolimbo.org/last accessed
February 21, 2023*

But the impacts aren't restricted to marine animals. Land animals are just as likely to be impacted, and the risk even extends to humans. These particles can be transferred from one animal to the next, making their way up the food chains, ultimately reaching the food we eat. The possible path microplastics take is shown in Figure 3-7.

FIGURE 3-7:
The path of
microplastics
from litter to our
plates.

Recent research has found microplastics in shellfish, table salt, bottled water, and even beer. Not all originate from pollution and marine litter, but they are all associated with plastic and how much we consume. Studies have already detected microplastics in the human body. In fact, it's possible that through the air we breathe, the water we drink, and the seafood we consume, we could be ingesting somewhere around 100,000 pieces of microplastics every year.

So how do these particles affect our health? The answer is we don't know yet. Research is still underway to understand how these particles affect human health, but the general feeling is that it's not very good.

REMEMBER

Reducing, reusing, and recycling help safeguard not just the environment but also our future and future generations. Throughout this book, I provide many tips and ideas for reducing your impact and recycling properly to keep plastics out of the environment.

WHAT ARE MICROBEADS?

Microbeads are solid plastic spheres with a diameter of less than 5 millimeters that are intentionally added to personal products like cosmetics, body products, or toothpaste to create an exfoliant or abrasive feel. A single tube can contain more than 300,000 tiny pieces of plastic. When you use these products, microbeads are washed down the drain into the wastewater treatment system and enter the environment.

If you discover a product has microbeads, the best thing to do is dispose of it in your regular garbage bin and recycle the container if possible. Beat the Microbead has created an app to help you check products for microbeads (www.beatthemicrobead.org). You can scan the ingredients of any product, and it will let you know if microbeads are present.

Surveying single-use plastics

A total of 40 percent of all the plastic used in packaging today is used in single-use packaging or products. Most of these items are used for a few moments and then tossed away with little regard for the resources and energy that went into making them. In fact, every day, the world uses about

>> 100 billion plastic bags

>> 500 million plastic straws

>> 1.3 billion plastic water bottles

>> 50 billion coffee cups

According to data from Ocean Conservancy, at least 8 out of the 10 most common items polluting our beaches are single-use plastics. This is shown in Figure 3-8, summarizing the latest data from the Ocean Conservancy. Many items could be recycled in curbside or specialist recycling, which is considerably better than letting them pollute the environment. For example, all beverage bottles and cans are recyclable.

ITEM	PLASTIC	SINGLE-USE	RECYCLABLE
1. Food wrappers (candy, chips, etc.)	✓	✓	Specialist
2. Cigarette butts	✓		✗
3. Beverage bottles	✓	✓	✓
4. Other trash (plastic pieces, clothing, metals)			✗
5. Bottle caps	✓	✓	Specialist
6. Grocery bags	✓	✓	Specialist
7. Beverage bottles (glass)		✓	✓
8. Beverage cans (metal)		✓	✓
9. Straws and stirrers	✓	✓	✗
10. Cups and plates	✓	✓	✗

FIGURE 3-8: Top ten list of litter based on cleanup data from Ocean Conservancy.

TIP

One of the easiest ways to stop single-use plastics from littering our beaches is to switch to reusables. With 80 percent of the items being single-use, this can have a big impact. You can find some great examples in Chapter 15.

STOPPING LITTER AT THE SOURCE

Here are some ways for you to keep litter out of waterways and, ultimately, the ocean:

- When you're out, take your rubbish home with you if you can. Don't use public bins if they're overflowing or when a strong wind is likely to blow the trash away.

- Don't be afraid to pick up other people's rubbish if you see it. It might be frustrating when others litter, but the most important thing is to remove the litter from the environment. *Note:* Please use caution and do not attempt to remove hazardous items like syringes or sharp objects unless you have the necessary tools. Syringes should be handled with tongs, placed in a container, and taken to a nearby hospital or other specialist site for disposal. They should never be handled with bare hands. If it is not safe, then leave it where it is and inform your local government of the location.

- Make sure your bins are secured at home when you put them out for pickup.

- Get yourself set up with reusable straws, bags, cutlery, and water bottles.

- If you smoke, take a mini ashtray, and don't drop your butts.

- Organize a beach or street cleanup.

- Recycle whenever you can and spread the message.

The Impact of Waste on Climate Change

Climate change refers to changes in the weather patterns and temperature of the Earth. These changes have been occurring naturally for millions of years, but in the last few centuries, we've seen an increase resulting from human activities. Much of this increase is due to rising levels of greenhouse gases in the atmosphere, the main culprits being carbon dioxide and methane.

The production of energy and heat is the main activity that releases greenhouse gases, but all activities that use energy contribute to their formation. Some emissions can be directly attributed to our waste management practices. In the following sections, I take a closer look at how waste contributes to climate change and how recycling can help mitigate it.

Accelerating climate with our leftovers

According to estimates, one-third of all food produced worldwide is wasted. It equates to over 1.3 billion tons of food wasted every year, including food that you, me, and all the restaurants, schools, and offices throw away daily and some food that never even made it to a store. Most of that food ends up in landfills where it rots away, releasing methane and carbon dioxide. It equates to about 8 percent of annual human-induced greenhouse gases, almost four times the emissions from the aviation industry. And those emissions just cover the last stages of food production; much more is released during cultivation, shipping, preparation, processing, and cold storage.

REMEMBER

Reducing food waste is one of the most important actions we can take to stop climate change. According to WRAP, a climate change nongovernmental organization (NGO), if every person in the United Kingdom stopped wasting food for just one day, it would have the same effect as planting half a million trees. Imagine the effect if the whole world stopped!

TIP

Luckily, reducing your food waste is relatively easy, and there are many things you can do. I provide lots of tips in Chapter 12.

Carelessly sending energy to landfills

I've probably repeated myself many times already, but I strongly believe one of the most important things to consider is the amount of energy and resources that go into the items we buy, use, and discard in our lives. Energy is required for every step in production, whether it's a mobile phone or a yogurt container. Energy is necessary to extract or grow raw resources, convert them into products, and transport them to you. If we are to significantly reduce our impact on the planet and slow the effects of climate change, we must consider the entire life cycle of the product. You can find out more about this topic earlier in this chapter.

REMEMBER

When you toss things into landfills without considering the potential future use, you essentially waste all the energy spent on their production. This is even more of an issue with single-use items, some of which are used for only a few moments before they are tossed in the bin.

Producing greenhouse gases

Landfills produce gas as bacteria break down organic matter during decomposition. How much gas is created depends on the type of waste and how old the landfill is, but on average, it's 50 percent carbon dioxide and 50 percent methane gas. There are a few other compounds, like nitrogen, oxygen, sulfides, and hydrogen, but their percentages are relatively low. Methane and carbon dioxide are both greenhouse gases that can trap heat in the atmosphere, warming the Earth.

Methane is particularly bad, and significant amounts are emitted from landfills due to the anaerobic conditions created when the waste is compacted and covered. Anaerobic means there's no oxygen available during the decomposition of organic matter. Landfills are the third largest source of methane emissions in the United States and many other countries.

Controls are applied in modern landfills to capture the methane and convert it into energy. However, thresholds determine when a landfill must implement these gas collection systems, so unfortunately, there's not always an obligation to do so. When systems aren't in place to capture the gas, it's often burned or flared to reduce safety risks, control odors, and lower environmental risks. Burning methane gives off carbon dioxide and water — a much better outcome than methane, but still a greenhouse gas.

Burning our waste

It's a great feeling to be rid of our waste for good. It can be a relief, like when you put an item in your bin and feel that you are no longer responsible for it. Incinerating waste feels a bit like this. In many cases, we send waste to be burnt, seemingly getting rid of the problem. The issue is that nothing ever really goes away. When waste burns, it transforms from a solid into a gas, leaving a small amount of toxic ash behind. Depending on the mix of waste, this gas can contain many compounds, some of which can be toxic.

When waste is burned in a high-quality waste-to-energy plant, the gases are captured, and toxic pollutants are removed before release. But they still release greenhouse gases. Compared to landfills, waste-to-energy has a lower impact. But it's estimated that more than half of the material incinerated could have been recycled or composted. I think the best approach is to follow the waste hierarchy (presented in Chapter 2) and minimize our use of landfill and incineration solutions as much as possible.

IN THIS CHAPTER

» Getting to know the different recycling services

» Exploring how curbside recycling works

» Introducing specialist recycling

» Understanding what happens to your waste

» Figuring out who pays for recycling

Chapter **4**

Making Sense of Recycling

R*ecycling* is the collection of valuable materials from waste so they can be turned into something useful again. Collecting and sorting materials so they are ready for reuse requires a lot of effort, and many people are responsible for making sure it happens. After collection, curbside recyclables go to a materials recovery facility, where they are sorted and cleaned to remove any contamination. Then they head off to a reprocessor for further treatment or, in some cases, go straight to a manufacturer.

Each material takes a slightly different path, and whether it makes it into a new product can depend on several elements. The two key factors are the level of contamination and the availability of markets. Many materials are successfully transformed into new goods or simply make their way back into manufacturing without us even realizing it. While some others don't make it because of too much contamination or a lack of demand for the material, hopefully this will improve in time.

In this chapter, you discover the difference between curbside recycling and specialist recycling. Then you take a look at what goes on behind the scenes. Like the majority of us, I'm sure you're curious about the fate of your recycling and whether it's actually recycled. I take you through what happens to your recycling and address some of the challenges the industry faces. Finally, I discuss who pays for recycling and what changes might come if we switch the responsibility to brands and manufacturers.

Figuring Out What It Means to Recycle

According to the *Oxford English Dictionary*, recycling is "the action or process of converting waste into reusable material." It's the process of taking unwanted materials that would otherwise be sent to landfills and turning them into materials that manufacturers can use to create new products.

Some common examples of recycling are

>> Collecting aluminum cans, washing them, melting them, and then using the material to make a new drink can

>> Separating a used plastic water bottle from other plastics so it can be washed, ground, melted, and then molded into a new plastic bottle

Recycling is the third level of the waste hierarchy (see Chapter 2), after the more essential actions of reducing and reusing. It guarantees that the materials are reused and kept in use, making it preferable to disposing of items in landfills or incinerating them.

There are two main methods of recycling: mechanical and chemical recycling.

>> Mechanical recycling is the most common method for treating recycled materials collected through curbside services and even many specialist recycling services. In this method, recyclable materials are processed without changing their chemical structure. For example, plastics are sorted, cleaned, ground, remelted, and reformed into products. This doesn't alter the basic structure of the material but simply cleans it and reuses it in a new product.

>> The other method for recycling is chemical or what is now often referred to as *advanced recycling*. This process applies only to plastics and uses chemicals to break them down into their original components. The final product may be used to create new plastic or products like fuel. There's a lot of interest in these techniques, but they are still under development. You can discover more in Chapter 18 about the future of recycling.

An effective recycling system can be achieved only through the cooperation and effort of many different groups. All of the following groups need to work together for recycling to be successful:

>> Brand designers and manufacturers who choose whether to use recyclable materials in their products and packaging

>> Consumers who choose whether to dispose of their waste responsibly

>> Local and federal governments who are responsible for ensuring that everyone has access to recycling services and implementing appropriate laws to support the system

>> Waste haulers, transfer stations, materials recovery facilities, and waste reprocessors whose job is collecting and processing your recycling

Discovering the Different Recycling Services

In this book, I refer to two primary types of services, curbside and specialist recycling. It's useful to understand the difference between your curbside service (if you're lucky enough to have one) and specialist recycling because items not accepted in your curbside service might be recyclable through a specialist service.

Curbside recycling is a waste collection service made available to homes to collect and process household packaging. It typically only includes packaging materials like paper and cardboard, plastics, glass, and metals, or some combination. However, what's accepted and how much separation the homeowner is responsible for depends on the local facilities. For example, in some areas, glass is not accepted; in others, plastic is either excluded or limited to one or two types.

Some locations don't have the convenience of a curbside pickup service at all. Instead, they must take their recyclables to a drop-off center or a transfer station. Generally, the rules are much the same, although users must separate materials into different bins instead of tossing them all in one or two bins as you do for curbside services.

Often curbside recycling is misunderstood as a service. It's not a catchall for everything you want to dispose of or recycle. It's a service provided by municipalities to collect and process most of the everyday packaging items that households use. That's why it's focused on the four primary materials — paper, glass, metal, and plastic — and usually only accepts packaging. Part 2 provides information on curbside recycling.

In contrast, specialist recycling services (covered in Part 3) are for any item or material that a company or government wants to collect. Collection points can range from your local transfer station to a drop-off location, mail-in address, or even a pickup service. There's a growing number of specialist recycling programs, and they accept all sorts of items like batteries, different varieties of electronic waste (e-waste), and packaging that can't be processed through the curbside system. As you would expect, availability depends heavily on your location.

In some cases, curbside recycling and what I refer to as specialist recycling overlap. If you're lucky to have additional materials collected at your curbside, such as soft plastics or food waste, that's fantastic. However, most of us need to supplement our curbside recycling by seeking specialist services. Keep reading for more information on curbside and specialist recycling.

Diving Deeper into Curbside Recycling

Recycling is essentially a reverse supply chain. Its purpose is to collect used materials from consumers and bring them together to be sorted, cleaned, and reprocessed into usable material. After all that, a market or manufacturer needs to be found who is willing to buy the material and use it in new products.

Although it can be a complicated system, in the following sections I take you through the main steps to help unravel the mystery.

Collecting curbside recycling

The first step in recycling is to collect materials that have reached the end of their life or are no longer useful. It's the step we're most connected with because the pickup takes place at the curb in front of our house (if you have a curbside service). What's collected depends entirely on your location and the services available in your area. In Chapter 5, I discuss the main reasons why curbside services differ from place to place.

Recyclables are usually picked up in large trucks. I loved when my neighbor's kids were young enough to come out and wave to the truck as it rolled along emptying bins in the morning. The driver must have enjoyed the attention because he always honked the horn. If you live in an apartment, you'll be less likely to experience this. Although trucks may drop by to empty the dumpsters in the parking lot or back of the building, you won't always see them. As I mention earlier, certain regions don't have access to curbside recycling services, so residents must take their recyclables to a recycling center or transfer station.

Distinguishing single-stream and multi-stream services

REMEMBER

Whether local curbside recycling services use single-stream, multi-stream, or something in between is one of the reasons recycling rules differ from one location to the next. The main difference between these two types of collection systems is how much separation the homeowner must do before pickup; see Figure 4-1. The collection types are

>> **Single-stream or comingled:** In single-stream or commingled waste streams, all the accepted recyclables are mixed together during the collection process and received at the facility in one batch. Garbage and recyclables are usually kept separate, though.

>> **Multi-stream:** In multi-stream collection, the homeowner must separate the recyclable waste into different categories before it's picked up. Categories for separation often include paper, glass, and plastic. In some locations, like the United Kingdom, there can be as many as eight or more bins for various materials.

Single-stream

Paper   Plastic   Cans

Multi-stream

© John Wiley & Sons, Inc.

FIGURE 4-1:
Single-stream versus multi-stream recycling.

Which method is better, single-stream or multi-stream, is frequently debated. Single-stream is cheaper and makes recycling much easier for you and me, but it requires more complex equipment to sort and separate the different materials. Multi-stream services result in much less contamination and a much better-quality product. However, it can be more expensive because of the logistics required to pick up all the different materials.

Many areas that have single-stream services are switching back to multi-stream to improve the quality of recyclables so there's a better chance of finding an end market. Given our current waste crisis, I believe making a little more effort is definitely worth it. The area where I live is about to introduce a separate bin for glass, something many places already have. I look forward to this change so I can do more to help reduce contamination.

Looking at the role of waste transfer stations

Waste transfer stations provide a temporary holding place for waste. From here, it's often sorted and transferred to larger trucks to be taken to an appropriate facility like a landfill, materials recovery facility, or waste-to-energy plant. These facilities are often located in remote areas outside or on the outskirts of cities. Running trucks back and forth from households directly to these facilities can be expensive and take a lot of time, so garbage trucks often drop off the waste at a transfer station. It can reduce the overall transport cost and associated environmental impacts.

Waste transfer stations can also double as drop-off locations for the general public. Some are even set up entirely for the public, where you can drop off your household waste. It's especially helpful if you don't have access to a curbside service. An excellent transfer station near my home provides different bins for many recyclables, including specialist items like e-waste, polystyrene, light globes, and even old paint.

The next stop from a waste transfer station is either a materials recovery facility (MRF), a composting facility, a waste-to-energy plant, or a landfill. In the next section, I take a look at what happens inside an MRF.

Going inside a material recycling facility

Once recyclables have been collected, they're sent to a sorting and processing facility. These facilities are referred to as materials recovery facilities, shortened to MRFs and pronounced "murf." At an MRF, recyclables are sorted and contaminants removed before they are processed and baled, ready to be purchased by an end user. From here, material that is too contaminated or has no end buyer may be sent to a landfill or waste-to-energy plant.

How the recyclable material is processed depends on several factors:

>> The sort of infrastructure the MRF has in place.

>> The type of waste that's collected in the area. For example, some areas might have more small businesses, which creates a different waste mix than areas that are more heavily residential.

>> What are the end markets for materials? An MRF may be better off sorting one material over another if there's a good end market for that material.

REMEMBER

MRFs vary significantly from one place to the next. Some are equipped with the latest technology, others use entirely manual labor, and some have a blend of the two. Both the type of equipment and its age can significantly influence how efficient and cost-effective an MRF is. This is one of the reasons why rules can vary so much (see Chapter 5).

Here I describe the typical process at an MRF, shown in Figure 4-2. This is where all the fun begins! Paper, metals, glass, and other items are sorted, and contamination is removed.

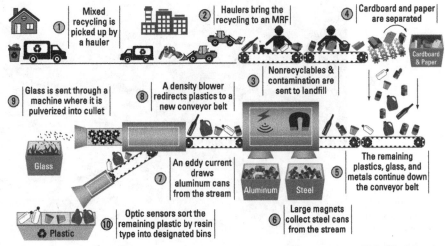

FIGURE 4-2:
The typical sorting process that takes place inside an MRF.

© John Wiley & Sons, Inc.

1. **Recycling is collected.**

   Single-stream or mixed recycling is picked up from your household and taken to an MRF.

2. **Material arrives at the MRF.**

Once the trucks have collected the waste, they drive to an MRF and dump their contents on the tipping floor. In between trucks, a front-end loader pushes the material onto a conveyor belt, and the sorting process begins.

3. **Presorting takes place.**

The first step in many MRFs is a presort. This is where workers hand-pick items from the conveyor belt that cannot be recycled, focusing on removing bulky objects or items that could cause safety issues down the line. The image in Figure 4-3 provides an example.

Workers at MRFs have a messy, dirty, and sometimes unsafe task. It's their job to pick out all the items that don't belong in a recycling bin. Some of the items these workers encounter are soft plastics, clothing, needles, moldy and smelly food waste, or worse: a dead animal, a dangerous battery, or even a loaded gun.

TIP

You can improve the working conditions for MRF hand-pickers by keeping contamination out of your curbside recycling bin.

FIGURE 4-3: Workers manually sorting waste at a material recovery facility.

DROPERDER/Shutterstock

4. **Screening takes place.**

Once the hand-pickers have removed most of the problematic contamination, the material moves along the conveyor belt to the sorting machines. The sorting of recycling material almost always starts with a vibrating or rotating screen that separates particles by size. An example of a rotating screen at work is shown in Figure 4-4. These machines have a screen with various-sized holes where objects can fall through. Flat pieces of cardboard will ride across, while cans or plastic bottles will fall through onto another conveyor belt to continue on their journey.

FIGURE 4-4:
A rotating screen is used at the material recovery facility to separate materials by size.

5. **Remaining materials move to the next stage.**

The remaining plastic, glass, and metal mix continues along the conveyor belt. Some MRFs use manual sorting in addition to the other equipment to remove contamination along the way.

6. **Magnets separate the steel.**

Extracting metals from the waste stream is important because there's usually a good market for them. The first step is to remove the ferrous or magnetic metals. Strong magnets placed above the conveyor belt attract ferrous metals like steel and pull them from the conveyor.

7. **An eddy current separates aluminum.**

An eddy current is used to separate nonferrous metals like aluminum cans from other waste materials. It uses strong magnetic fields generated by a spinning magnetic rotor, which propels the aluminum off the conveyor belt onto another one or into a container (see Chapter 9 for more details).

Once separated, the steel and aluminum metals follow a new path to remove any remaining contamination and prepare them for baling.

8. **A machine blows plastics on their way.**

A machine called a density blower uses a jet of air to send lighter materials like plastic onto another conveyor belt, leaving the heavier glass behind.

9. **Glass is processed.**

The remaining glass is put through a pulverizing machine to break it up into cullet, which is collected and sold to a glass processing facility.

10. **Plastic is sorted.**

Plastics must be sorted by polymer type to be of value. There are dozens of different plastics, and as I explain in Chapter 10, they are sometimes layered or mixed together, making them even more challenging to separate. Some facilities rely on manual sorting of plastics, while others have invested in optical sorting.

An optical sorter is used to help separate glass or plastics into different colors or types, making them more marketable. The optical sorter uses infrared light to identify materials by type, and a jet of air blows each item into the correct bin. Watching these machines and seeing how fast they can identify the different materials is fascinating. It's a pity there isn't one available for our bins at home!

REMEMBER

It's important to appreciate how challenging sorting recyclables can be. Following the rules of your local recycling facilities and sticking to the materials they accept helps make it more effective, creating a cleaner end product, and a greater chance it will be used in a new product.

After materials have been separated and cleaned of contamination, they are compacted and bound into a tightly packed bundle called a bale (see Figure 4-5). Glass, which cannot be baled, is usually crushed for transport to a processor. Plastic can be baled, but in some cases, the MRF may cut it into flakes for transport.

Processing and manufacturing bales

Bales can be sold to reprocessors or direct to a manufacturer. A *reprocessor* is a plant or facility that specializes in processing certain types of waste. For example, a plastics reprocessor may receive plastic waste from an MRF in the form of bales of milk bottles. They wash and shred the plastic, remove any remaining contamination, then melt it and turn it into pellets for resale to manufacturers. In some cases, reprocessors and manufacturing plants are combined at one location.

Everyday Recycler/everydayrecycler.com/last accessed February 21, 2023

FIGURE 4-5:
Bales of recycled metal cans and plastic bottles ready to be sent to a reprocessor or manufacturer.

If you want to know how the main recyclables like paper, glass, aluminum, and plastic are recycled and used in new products, you can find out in more detail in Chapters 6 through 9. Here are some typical examples to give you an idea of what happens next:

» **Plastic (see Chapter 6):** It's first sorted by type, such as polyethylene tereph-thalate (PET) or high-density polyethylene (HDPE), and then washed, ground, melted, and molded into new products. If the quality is good enough, these materials are turned back into the original products, like plastic bottles (refer to the nearby sidebar for some examples of success stories). If the quality is poor, they are more likely downcycled into products like fabrics and carpets or used as filler in roads.

» **Paper and cardboard (see Chapter 7):** Paper is often processed by the manufacturer either at the same facility or sorted at one facility and trans-ported to another. The paper or cardboard is shredded and mixed with water inside a large pulper to break down the bonds and remove impurities. This mixture is pressed and dried to form paper.

» **Glass (see Chapter 8):** Glass can be added directly back into the production process for new glass and blended with raw materials. For this process the glass must be separated by color, a process carried out at an MRF or a specialized facility. Glass may also be crushed into a sand and used in road base or to replace sand in construction activities.

>> **Aluminum (see Chapter 9):** Aluminum bales are sold to smelters, where contaminants are removed, and then the material is placed into a furnace to be melted. Recycling aluminum is a great success story. Most metals can be recycled infinitely without losing quality, and recycled aluminum can be back on the shelf as a new drink can within 60 days.

SUCCESS STORIES OF WHAT RECYCLED PLASTIC BECOMES

One of the best ways to gain trust in the system is to hear some success stories. So you know that most paper and cardboard get recycled and that aluminum cans can be back on the shelf in about 60 days, but what about plastic? Here are some inspiring examples of how companies are using recycled plastic to make new products:

- **Volution Group, in partnership with AO Recycling and Ultrapolymers,** is using plastic extracted from old fridges in the United Kingdom in their new ventilation products.

- **Aldi has partnered with Martogg and Trendpac** in Australia to help package their laundry and dishwashing liquids in 100 percent Australian recycled PET.

- **Preserve** makes toothbrushes, razors, and reusable tableware made from polypropylene (PP), collected from a network of suppliers across the United States.

- **Repreve** converts plastic bottles into recycled polyester (made from PET) fabrics used in hundreds of clothing and accessory brands worldwide.

- **MacRebur and the New York City Department of Transportation** installed the first plastic roads in New York City, incorporating a plastic additive made from waste into the asphalt.

- **Polywood** creates outdoor furniture from HDPE sourced from recycled milk jugs, detergent bottles, and shampoo bottles.

- **Happy Planet Toys** makes kids' toys and reusable plastic tableware from polypropylene milk bottles sourced in Australia.

- **Ultrapolymers** in the United Kingdom are recycling HDPE milk bottles into new milk bottles and putting them back on supermarket shelves.

- **Visy Industries and Coles** have created a water bottle made from 100 percent PET in Australia.

- **HP** has incorporated recycled plastics into a number of its products, including laptops and monitors.

- **Veolia** is supplying L'Oréal with recycled plastic derived from consumer packaging, in particular plastic bottles, for use in new cosmetic packaging.

- **LyondellBasell and Audi** announced they'll be installing plastic seatbelt buckle covers made from automotive plastic waste into the Q8 e-Tron.

These are just a few examples of our recycling making its way into new packaging or products. You can find many more examples on my website, `https://everyday recycler.com/`.

Exploring Specialist Recycling

Curbside is one of the most commonly recognized services for individuals; however, a growing number of drop-off centers and buy-back programs are available. These specialist recyclers provide great opportunities for hard-to-recycle items and are an important addition to curbside recycling.

Understanding what's different from curbside services

Specialist recycling services are offered by companies that specialize in recycling a particular type of material or product. These services range from battery and mattress recycling to e-waste (electronic waste) or even a local compost company. Some of these companies offer a pickup service, but mostly there will be a drop-off location or an address where you can post items. Some of the different types of services include

>> **Drop-off centers:** These are locations where consumers can bring their waste materials but that don't offer any financial incentive. An example of this would be the collection boxes provided in retail stores for batteries, mobile phones, or soft plastics.

>> **Buy-back centers:** Many locations have access to buy-back centers or refund programs. An example is a container deposit scheme, which is a service that collects mainly beverage containers and returns a deposit that was paid when the container was purchased.

>> **Transfer stations:** Many transfer stations provide different bins for the collection of items for specialist recycling like e-waste, polystyrene, or hazardous waste.

>> **Recycling centers:** Dedicated recycling centers may be available, like the roadside recycling centers in the United Kingdom, where bins are provided for all sorts of recyclables, including glass, clothing, shoes, or even books.

>> **Pickup services:** There are occasional services for specialist recycling that will pick up items from your home. For example, in Australia, you can book a pickup of old clothing and textiles, and they will pick it up from your door.

>> **Mail-in services:** You might also find a few mail-in services for items like mobile phones, batteries, and cosmetic packaging.

Depending on the recycled material, these services may be free or charge a fee, or you might even get a coupon or voucher.

Discovering specialist recycling options

There are many specialist recycling programs available for lots of different items. These programs will vary depending on where you live. In Part 3, I provide more details on several different specialist recycling services available today. Table 4-1 is a summary list to give you an idea of the types of things that can be recycled through these programs.

TABLE 4-1 **A Sampling of Specialist Recycling Services**

Soft plastics	Car tires
Plastic bags	Toner ink cartridges
E-waste or WEEE (electronic waste)	Polystyrene
Batteries	Crayons
Hazardous waste	Carpets
Mattresses	Fashion and textiles

TIP

Anytime you want to recycle something a bit different, try running an internet search simply by putting "how to recycle" before the word. You can also find some resources through recycling websites and apps that will tell you what is available in your local area (see Chapter 5). Don't be discouraged if you can't find a recycling service in your local area. The recycling industry is a dynamic and growing industry, with new services and facilities constantly popping up.

EXAMPLES OF SPECIALIST COLLECTION SERVICES

Whether or not you have curbside recycling, you can supplement your recycling by signing up for a special recycling service like the examples listed here. This will help give you the peace of mind that these materials are kept out of landfill and instead recycled.

- **Ridwell:** Based in Seattle with services available in many locations across the United States, Ridwell picks up hard-to-recycle items like batteries, light globes, soft plastics, clothes, and e-waste from your doorstep. They even have special collections for Halloween and Christmas. Jump on their website to see whether they're in your area or register your interest in your neighborhood. www.ridwell.com

- **TerraCycle:** You may have heard of TerraCycle; it has loads of recycling programs available for different items in many countries. Most can be mailed to them, but there are drop-off locations too. Many of the programs are paid for by the brands, so they are free to the public. You simply sign up and start collecting. Why not consider setting up a drop-off location if you run a retail or other business? www.terracycle.com

- **Recycle Smart:** Available in Sydney, Australia, Recycle Smart is set up to work alongside local town or city governments to divert hard-to-recycle items from landfills. Because of this relationship, the service is free to join, and you get up to two bags. You can pay a fee if you want to have more picked up. www.recyclesmart.com

- **Rabbit Recycling:** Available in Philadelphia, Pennsylvania, in the United States, Rabbit's service offers pickup of kitchenware, bathroom ware, batteries, light bulbs, clothing, soft plastics, electronics, and sports gear. They donate any items that can still be reused and separate the rest for upcycling or specialist recycling. www.rabbitrecycling.com

You can also find specialist recycling services through recycling websites and apps that will tell you what is available in your local area (see Chapter 5 for a list of websites and apps available). Plus, you can always check my website www.everydayrecycler.com for tips too.

Recognizing Why Some Things Aren't Recycled

You obediently separate plastic, check whether it can be recycled, give it a rinse, and happily place it in your recycling bin. In turn, you expect that it will be recycled and turned into a new product. Only then do you hear that much of our recycling doesn't get recycled but goes to a landfill or waste-to-energy plant instead. This is devastating and makes you wonder whether anything ever gets recycled. Has all your hard work sorting and checking rules been in vain?

The straight answer is no. It's not all in vain.

There are many different reasons why recyclables may not get recycled. Sure, some dishonest businesses deliberately break the law, but they are a minority. Many hardworking people in the waste industry are often as frustrated as you are to find they cannot send material to be recycled. They are continually looking for ways to improve by investing in new technologies and innovative materials.

REMEMBER

As I explain earlier, the recycling industry is a complex reverse supply chain with many different working parts. Sometimes it takes only one of these parts to break for the whole process to fall apart. There are many reasons why your waste may not get recycled after you put it in your recycling bin; in the following sections, I explain some of the most common.

Seeing that recycling contamination leads to landfills

Contamination is a major factor in why much of our recycling ends up in landfills instead of being used in new products. Depending on your location, contamination rates can range upward of 25 percent. That amounts to around a quarter of your recycling bin that may be filled with items that don't belong. Several variables affect the level of contamination, including

>> **Single-stream collection services:** Many recycling services are based on a single-stream collection, where homeowners toss all recyclables into one bin. Although this system makes it much easier for us to recycle, all that stuff rolling around in the trucks can lead to contamination between materials. Glass shards can embed in plastics or paper. Bottles and cans may get crushed, making it harder for the sorting machines to recognize them. As a result, many places are switching back to a multi-stream system, where the homeowner separates items into different bins before they're picked up, or

something in between. It can help reduce contamination and creates a cleaner recyclable material.

» **Wishcycling:** Many people continue to throw items in the recycling bin that don't belong there. Food waste, dirty diapers, batteries, e-waste, plastic bags, and clothes all create contamination that commonly leads to material being sent to landfills instead of being recycled. Our bad habits may even lead to recycling services being suspended or terminated for good.

Even materials that aren't as obvious can cause contamination. For example, recycling a drinking glass in your curbside bin may contaminate the recyclable glass and potentially send it to landfills.

REMEMBER

Avoid wishcycling and check what's accepted before you put it in the bin.

» **Communities must work together:** Unfortunately, even if you're a good recycler, what happens to your recyclables also depends on how good your neighbors are at recycling.

TIP

Share the message with your friends, family, and neighbors and let them know how important reducing contamination in their recycling bin is. Or better still, why not buy them a copy of this book?

Finding end markets for recycled material

For recycling to be viable, there needs to be demand for recycled products. Once processed, recyclables are bought and sold the same way as most raw materials. Prices are determined by supply and demand and can rise and fall depending on national and international markets.

The existence of an end market is one factor that influences whether your local curbside recycling collects certain items. Even if the recycling facility has the capability to collect, sort, and process a particular material, without an end market, it may not accept it. It's also a large factor in whether recyclable material, once collected, gets recycled or meets a different fate. If there's no end market, some companies may try to stockpile until one becomes available. However, in some countries, there are strict rules about stockpiling, which can lead to the waste going straight to a landfill instead.

REMEMBER

Raising the demand for recycled content is one way to address these problems. You can help make this happen by buying recycled products. Head to Chapter 16 to find out more.

Shipping recyclables abroad

From the early 1990s up until 2018, the developed world outsourced much of its recycling and sent low-quality waste to developing nations, particularly China, for treatment. It was an easy way to deal with poor-quality waste, given the relatively low costs and the few restrictions on contamination levels. This hindered local investment in recycling infrastructure for certain materials. Why would governments and the industry invest in infrastructure when there was a cost-effective solution available?

However, in 2018 China implemented its National Sword Policy and said "no more" to low-quality waste. Recyclers in the developed world found themselves in a bit of a quandary. A lot of waste started piling up as it no longer had a market. Efforts were made to find other markets, but not long after China's bans, many other nations, including India, Vietnam, Malaysia, and the Philippines, implemented their own bans or restrictions.

Despite these bans, many developed countries continue to send much of their low-grade waste to countries with insufficient infrastructure. A report by the BBC estimated that in 2020, about two-thirds of the United Kingdom's waste was sent overseas to countries such as Malaysia, Vietnam, Indonesia, and Turkey for recycling. For the United States, the story is not all that dissimilar. Many thousands of shipping containers filled with recyclables are still sent abroad to low-income countries. Unfortunately, it's often cheaper to export waste than to build infrastructure or send it to local landfill sites.

WARNING

Even if appropriate treatment facilities are available in developing countries, if those facilities have limited capacity, excess material may be illegally dumped or incinerated. For example, a large amount of plastic waste is burned to help reduce its volume. Environmental legislation is often insufficient to guarantee the correct treatment of waste and protection of surrounding communities and the environment.

A number of global initiatives aim to restrict the international trade of waste, particularly plastics. An amendment to the Basel Convention, an international agreement regulating the transportation of hazardous waste, was introduced in 2021 to address these problems. Signees can only send waste to other member countries and must obtain agreement from the receiving country beforehand. You can find out more about the Basel Convention in Chapter 13.

In addition to the Basel Convention, changes are being introduced across national and regional governments. Early in 2022, the European Union introduced strict measures on exporting plastic waste, banning shipments of unsorted plastic waste to non-OECD countries. (The OECD is the Organisation for Economic Co-operation and Development.) Similarly, Australia has regulated the export of waste-derived materials like scrap glass, plastic, and tires, restricting exports to material that is ready for use in products and doesn't require any further processing that could potentially cause harm to the environment or communities.

There is still much-needed work to be done to ensure all countries deal with their waste responsibly and don't pass the responsibility to countries that lack the capability to deal with it safely. United Nations members are discussing a plastics treaty to help cut the world's plastic pollution. This treaty will be finalized by 2024 and will hopefully address some of the issues associated with the plastic waste trade.

REMEMBER

What can you do to help? The cleaner waste streams are, the more likely it is that a recycler will find a local or at least responsible market. By keeping contamination low, following the rules, and breaking any wishcycling habits, you can help improve the quality of waste collected. Of course, minimizing how much waste you produce in the first place will help too. You can also use resources like the e-Stewards program (`https://e-stewards.org/find-a-recycler/`) to find trustworthy and accredited recyclers.

Calling out unscrupulous operators

Recycled material may be sent to a landfill or for incineration instead of being recycled simply because a company is questionable. It may even be sent overseas illegally; refer to the previous section for details. Just as in any industry, some dishonest operators take shortcuts and willingly engage in unlawful activity without regard for the potential impacts. These problems must be identified and brought to light to ensure the issues are addressed, but they generally make up a very small percentage of the industry.

REMEMBER

It's important not to let these issues dissuade you from recycling altogether. We should not let one bad egg tarnish the whole industry. The recycling sector is continually investing in new technologies to be able to recycle more materials and working with businesses and governments to help improve the recyclability of packaging.

Examining the Cost of Recycling

Most recycling services are paid for by governments, either as a direct service or via a contractor. However, in some areas, the only services available are via private companies. Either way, the costs are usually passed onto the homeowner through taxes or directly.

However, there's another way recycling can be funded that's been around for some time. Extended producer responsibility (EPR), also known as product stewardship, is where the producer pays for the disposal costs. If this system was to become more widespread, it might save governments a great deal of money and result in a more efficient and stable recycling system.

Knowing who's paying for recycling

It costs money to move material from your curbside or local drop-off center to facilities and process it so it's ready to be reused. It requires considerable investments for the establishment of infrastructure and collection systems. And just like any business, there are ongoing maintenance, operations, and capital investment expenses.

The collection of recyclables can be a public or private service. However, both require a consistent source of income to cover operational expenses for long-term sustainability. A fee is imposed on residents or other service users to achieve this. Most public curbside services are charged as a flat fee or included in an owner's property tax or utility bill. Most of us probably pay little attention to this fee; as a result, many mistakenly think recycling is a free service. Those who only have access to a private collection service may better understand what it costs.

In addition to the regular fees to residents, cities can recover costs by selling compost and recycled materials or by producing energy from waste. This earning potential may be passed on to the waste hauler or recycler through the contract, or profits from the sale of recyclables may be shared.

A well-run recycling business can often generate enough revenue to help pay for itself, but there are risks, including the following:

>> Contamination can cost recyclers millions. Recycling facilities can find themselves with large amounts of material that may not be of a high enough standard to find a buyer. Not only have they had to process it, but now they must dispose of it. Recyclers would always prefer to sell recyclable material than send it to a landfill, but sometimes it's just not possible.

Putting the wrong thing into your recycling bin leads to additional costs for recycling businesses to remove and dispose of it.

>> Changes in source material like new packaging or changes in consumer behavior related to recycling may have an impact. If more recycling material is suddenly generated or the source material changes, it can increase costs or require upgrades.

>> Changes in government legislation might require capital investment or more rigorous reporting.

>> Fluctuating prices and demand for recycled material make it hard to predict earnings for the period.

Using EPR to finance the future

Another way for governments to cover recycling costs is to implement taxes on companies instead of consumers. One such tax is extended producer responsibility (EPR), also called product stewardship or the polluter pays principal. The concept is where a brand or manufacturer of a product is responsible for the environmental impacts of the product's end-of-life. In other words, the producer covers the costs for collection and recycling instead of the government. It promises to improve recycling services and to encourage brands to rethink their packaging and redesign for recyclability.

One of the earliest examples of an EPR system is the Green Dot system in Europe. When packaging displays this symbol, it demonstrates that the brand has paid a fee to a qualified organization to fund the collection, sorting, and recycling of used packaging. More than 20 years after its inception, this program is currently in use across 29 countries. Examples of products with EPR programs that you may have access to include paint, batteries, carpets, mattresses, pharmaceuticals and sharps, and electronic waste.

In addition to specific programs, overarching legislation can also help ensure recycling is funded. For example, recently the state of Maine, in the United States, has implemented an EPR law that will come into effect in 2027. This law requires companies that make products in Maine to pay a fee based on the tonnage produced and how recyclable the packaging is. These fees will be used to reimburse local town and city governments for the cost of recycling. Many other states and countries are looking into establishing their own systems.

REMEMBER

The benefits of an EPR system include the following:

>> It can provide sufficient funds to ensure equal access to recycling services across communities.

>> It ensures product manufacturers and brands take responsibility for their packaging at the end of life.

>> EPR can also help to incentivize businesses to

• Design out waste.

- Redesign their products to be more recyclable.
- Reduce the environmental impacts of their products.

The EPR costs may be passed onto consumers at some point, but we generally pay for disposal through our taxes anyway. I think it would be good to understand this cost when making a purchase. Understanding the full life-cycle implications of the goods we buy is vital (see Chapter 3) and being able to evaluate a product based on a cost that includes disposal makes us much more informed consumers.

Looking into the economic benefits of recycling

REMEMBER

When recycling works, it can have a positive effect on the economy as well as the environment. Some of the benefits include the following:

>> **Decreasing government spending:** Sending waste to landfills tends to be more expensive than recycling. Governments can save money by avoiding the costs of landfilling and the need to establish new landfill sites.

>> **Preserving natural resources:** Recycling reduces the expense of mining and ensures these materials are available for the future. For countries that don't have significant natural resources, the cost of importing can be expensive. They may reduce their dependence on external supplies by establishing a secondary source through recycling.

>> **Creating jobs:** Recycling contributes to job creation by improving existing services and expanding them. But the benefits also extend outside of the industry to manufacturers and reprocessors. It's estimated that recycling creates nine times more jobs than sending waste directly to landfills or waste-to-energy plants.

>> **Stimulating local economies:** Recycling can improve local economies by keeping materials flowing throughout communities rather than wasting away in a landfill.

>> **Lowering the cost of manufacturing:** Recycling can potentially reduce manufacturing costs by introducing secondary materials that may be of a lower value. It may also assist in reducing energy use, as it does with the introduction of recycled metals like aluminum into the manufacturing process.

Pushing or pulling — it's a balance

A crucial step in the success of recycling is the use of materials in new products. I feel a bit like a broken record saying this again, but if we aren't buying back our recycling, how do we expect the process to succeed? There needs to be a demand for materials for there to be a market. That means there needs to be manufacturers that want to use the material in their products and consumers who want to buy that product.

The economics are driven by supply and demand, as for any business. A good way to understand your role is through the push-pull effect. In a typical push system, manufacturers or brands predict what products to produce and market those to the consumer. However, the opposite, a pull system, is where product production results from consumer demand. In other words, when there's demand for a product, manufacturers will make it.

The best result is when these two forces work together. Imagine you want to move an armchair. You can either push it or pull it; either way, it's hard work on your own. Yet it's considerably easier to shift if you have help, like someone pushing from one side and someone pulling from the other. This is the push-pull effect, illustrated in Figure 4-6.

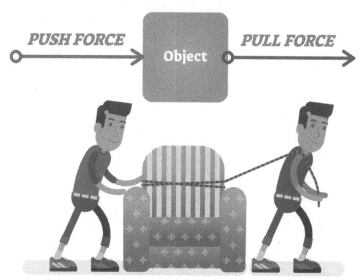

FIGURE 4-6: An illustration of the push-pull effect making the job easier when both forces are in play.

VectorMine/Adobe Stock

By applying these strategies to recycling, we can help ensure the demand or pull force for recycled products is equivalent to the push by manufacturers who are making recycled products. As consumers, we can help create the pull that the system needs to drive manufacturers to use recycled content.

This pulling effect doesn't have to come from consumers; it can also come from governments or companies. One way would be for them to mandate the use of recycled content in their own procurement policies. Another way to drive change is to legislate the use of recycling content. For example, in the European Union, the Single Use Plastics Directive requires that companies that make products from PET (Plastic #1) use at least 25 percent recycled PET. Legislation like this helps build a stable market for recycled PET. If you want to find out how you can play your part, head to Chapter 16.

2

Grasping Curbside Recycling

Master the basics of curbside recycling services by kicking bad habits and getting familiar with the tools available.

Figure out the many types of plastics and which ones belong in your recycling bin.

See what resources are needed to make paper and cardboard and how they are recycled.

Get the lowdown on glass recycling rules, why your area may not accept it, and what you can and can't recycle.

Discover how to identify different metals to recycle them more effectively.

Examine multilayer materials to appreciate their advantages while considering the difficulties they present for recycling.

IN THIS CHAPTER

» **Understanding why there are so many rules**

» **Revealing the many recycling symbols**

» **Unlearning bad recycling habits**

» **Keeping your bin free from contamination (and other standard rules)**

» **Seeking support when you need it**

Chapter **5**

Conquering the Basics of Curbside Recycling

We create an enormous amount of waste throughout our lives. And household waste continues to grow, driven by our desire for convenience and easy access to products. Fortunately, much of this material is recyclable. And if you're lucky to live in a country where curbside recycling is provided, much of it can be recycled through these services.

Curbside recycling services provide homeowners with a convenient way to dispose of much of the recyclable waste we create. It's designed primarily for collecting household packaging waste like paper, plastic, metals, and glass. This waste accounts for between 40 and 50 percent of the waste we generate, so that's a pretty handy service.

The rules for curbside recycling depend on the availability of local infrastructure and the policies implemented by local governments. Their effectiveness is also influenced by brands as they introduce new products, change packaging, adopt labeling standards, and make other changes to the products we buy. This is why the rules can often seem confusing and complex for homeowners like you and me.

But there's a way to cut through the confusion and make sense of your local curb-side recycling rules. In this chapter, I show you how to recognize and correct some bad habits you might have picked up. (Don't worry; you're not alone. I was just as guilty of some of these not that long ago.) Then I unravel why the rules for curbside recycling are so confusing and vary so much depending on where you live. After you master these rules and navigate what goes in and what stays out through the rest of Part 2, you'll be a superstar at recycling.

Uncovering Why Recycling Rules Vary So Much

One of the biggest frustrations for many of us is that recycling regulations vary from location to location. Some areas instruct you to place everything in a single bin, while others provide you with five containers and request that you sort the materials into each one. Some want you to put plastic bottles in your bin but keep your plastic yogurt tubs out, while others accept all your plastic containers no matter what plastic they're made from.

TECHNICAL STUFF

"Why can't the rules be the same for everyone?" I hear you ask. I've wondered the same thing myself. It would undoubtedly make things less complicated if the rules were the same everywhere. But unfortunately, it's not that simple. Each area has different circumstances to work with. There are regional differences in local infrastructure, rules and regulations, and the accessibility of end markets. Also, the types of materials recovered can differ from one place to another.

Here are some of the conditions that can change what services are provided where you live:

>> **Equipment at the plant or drop-off center:** The type of equipment installed in each facility differs. Recycling machines can require a significant amount of investment, so not all facilities can acquire and install the latest and greatest gear. Without these upgrades, your local facility may accept only certain types of material.

>> **Processing options available in your local area:** Many materials go through multiple steps in their recycling journey. They are sorted at a materials recycling facility (MRF) and then sold to other companies for further processing or manufacturing. The recyclables can be sold locally, interstate, or even internationally. Multiple factors affect the viability of this transaction:

- **Transport costs:** Facilities may be too far away to make it economical. For example, if there are no glass recycling plants near your local MRF, collecting and sorting glass from homeowners may be futile because it's too expensive to send it across the country.

- **Availability of a market:** The demand for the end product can also impact the demand for recycled materials. If no one is driving demand by buying recycled paper or glass products, even if facilities are available, the recycled materials may not have a market. In this case, the MRF may decide not to accept the material from homeowners. You can find out more about markets for recycled material in Chapter 4 and how you can help create a market for recycled products in Chapter 16.

And if no facilities are available, the material will have nowhere to go. It will need to be either stockpiled until a market can be found or sent to a landfill.

» **Differences in the community:** Access to recycling services can depend on the size and type of community. For example, smaller rural communities may not have the same access to curbside recycling as urban areas. Typically, these smaller communities will rely on recycling centers instead. Recycling services for apartments or condominiums also vary. Assuming recycling services are provided, they can differ from the local town or city rules because they may use a separate contractor.

» **Assorted waste streams:** Brands decide what materials to use in their packaging, but the waste haulers and recyclers are the ones that have to figure out how to collect, sort, and recycle it. Most consumers are unaware of how many different packaging materials exist, each with unique properties and a specific recycling process. This assortment of materials can be just as challenging for recycling facilities as it is for us and can lead to different rules in different locations.

» **Changes to policy:** Up until 2018, a large amount of recyclable material from developed countries was packed up in shipping containers and sent to China for processing. In 2018, China implemented a policy (the National Sword Policy) that heavily restricted the import of low-quality waste. Sadly, a lot of this waste started piling up as it had nowhere to go. In an effort to address this situation, many recycling services changed significantly and ceased accepting certain items or, in many cases, were completely discontinued. Fortunately, since then many governments and recycling industry members have worked hard to rectify the situation by investing in local infrastructure, addressing contamination, and finding other markets. Further changes are probably in store as the sector continues to improve.

RECYCLING CHALLENGES
IN APARTMENT LIVING

If you live in a unit, flat, apartment, or condominium, recycling can be very different from how it is at a single-family dwelling nearby. The services provided rely not only on where you are located but also on whether the complex management or landlord has implemented them. When services are available, they may consist of a communal recycling station managed by the complex or an external contractor. These are usually located in an outside area or sometimes in the basement. In multilevel complexes, you might have access to a waste chute or, in more modern buildings, multiple chutes with a dedicated recycling chute. This means that even when you shift from one complex to the next in the same area, the rules can change dramatically.

Whatever your circumstances are, most of the rules and recommendations I provide in this book apply. However, it's also important to familiarize yourself with the rules for your complex as they may differ somewhat from your local town or city rules. Contamination remains one of the biggest issues, where just one wrong item can result in entire batches of recycling going to a landfill or an incinerator.

Sadly, some places provide absolutely no recycling services. If this is the case for you, try talking to your complex manager or landlord; they may offer advice on nearby recycling services. And let them know you're interested in a recycling program as it might encourage them to set one up.

If you happen to live in a community that isn't interested in recycling, here are some tips for setting up your own recycling center in your apartment or flat:

- Look for a recycling center nearby and check what they accept. Otherwise, you'll need to search for specialist recycling options nearby. See the later section "Getting Help When You Need It" for some ideas on how to search.

- I recommend starting with a few materials with easily accessible drop-off locations like plastic or aluminum beverage cans or paper and cardboard.

- If you're fortunate enough to have plenty of space, you can set up an area with a few appropriately sized bins or tubs. If space is limited, you might need to be a bit creative.

- It's a good idea to consider how you will get the recyclables to the drop-off location. If you don't have a car, you might need to take a cab, public transportation, or a car through your local car-sharing network. Try encouraging your neighbors to recycle, and you might even be able to set up a car pool or schedule for drop-offs, sharing the load. Or you may be able to arrange for a specialist recycling collection service to organize a regular pickup from your complex.

Don't forget that it's always better to try to reduce first. Try running a waste audit (see Chapter 17), and then check out Chapter 15 for ideas on how reduce your waste. Refillables, like those for cleaning or personal products, can be a great way to reduce your plastic waste in an apartment.

Unscrambling Recycling Symbols

Recycling labels and symbols are supposed to help you determine whether an item is recyclable. But in many cases, they do precisely the opposite. Lack of legislation and the challenge of adhering to the different restrictions on what can and can't be recycled across different locations can be partly blamed for the issues. But brands are also responsible for informing their customers how to recycle their products and packaging correctly, and they don't always get this right.

WARNING

Some of the issues that make consistent labeling difficult include the following:

>> **Recycling rules differ from country to country.** Recycling rules differ between countries and even between states or towns in the same country. This makes labeling complex, particularly for global products that are sold internationally. The ease with which we can purchase a product online from any country complicates things. A brand may correctly label its product for one location, but it may be purchased by a consumer in a place where that product's packaging isn't accepted in curbside recycling.

>> **The universal recycling symbol is overused.** There are very few regulations on using the universal recycling symbol in labeling. Many brands use the recycling symbol even when an item isn't recyclable. Others use it to represent something other than recyclability, like recycled content.

Labels are an essential tool to help consumers navigate the complex world of packaging and recycling. In the following sections, I take you through some of the common symbols used and what they really mean. Then I show you the new and improved labels being promoted. These labels are designed to simplify recycling instructions for consumers, and I think they do a pretty good job.

Misunderstanding recycling labels

Common labels on packaging include the universal recycling symbol or "Mobius loop," or a variation of this called the "inverted Mobius loop." These symbols are overused and can't be trusted to provide conclusive information about whether an item can be recycled in your area. It's best to use other means of determining whether you can recycle an item, including the new labeling defined later in this chapter, the plastic identification labels (see Chapter 6), and of course, your local town or city recycling guide. Here I describe some of these ambiguous labels.

The universal recycling symbol or Mobius loop

The most common recycling symbol in the world is the Mobius loop. Gary Anderson created this universal recycling symbol for a competition held during the first Earth Day in 1970. The symbol is now recognized worldwide as a symbol that indicates recyclability. It consists of three arrows chasing each other in a triangle to form a closed loop, also called the chasing arrows symbol.

TIP

Today some creative license is taken with this logo so that it may appear differently in various locations. Some examples are shown in Figure 5-1, with different-sized arrows or even two arrows forming a circle instead of a triangle. Sometimes people even replace the arrows with bottles or other images.

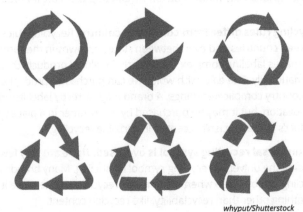

FIGURE 5-1:
Variations of the universal recycling symbol, the Mobius loop, or chasing arrows symbol.

whyput/Shutterstock

REMEMBER

Just because an item displays the Mobius loop for recycling doesn't mean it's recyclable in your local area. Always check with your local town or city. No world-wide standards are in place to enforce the use of the symbol, so a manufacturer can put this symbol on any item they like.

The inverted Mobius loop

When the Mobius loop is inverted as a white symbol in a black circle, it indicates the product is made from recycled materials. Often it's accompanied by text stating it's recycled and how much is sourced from recycled materials. Variations include a black Mobius loop with text underneath or inside the loop stating the recycled content. Figure 5-2 shows several examples of the recycled content symbol.

FIGURE 5-2:
The inverted Mobius symbol represents recycled content.

Recycled   **100% Recycled**   **50% Recycled**

© John Wiley & Sons, Inc.

REMEMBER

Although the symbol looks like a recycling symbol, it has nothing to do with whether the item is recyclable. This causes confusion, and many people easily mistake this symbol for the recycling symbol. For example, toilet paper packaging may display this symbol to indicate that it's made from recycled paper, but the toilet paper isn't recyclable.

The Tidyman symbol

The Tidyman symbol is designed to remind consumers to dispose of their waste responsibly, particularly when they are away from home. The 1969 symbol was introduced with the best of intentions, but today's more sophisticated packaging and recycling rules don't fit with the design's simplicity and don't give any indication of whether an item can be recycled. An example of the Tidyman symbol is shown in Figure 5-3.

FIGURE 5-3:
The Tidyman symbol.

best4u/Shutterstock

The Green Dot

Used primarily in the United Kingdom and European markets, the Green Dot symbol demonstrates that a brand or producer has contributed financially to offset the cost of recovering and recycling their packaging material. It's not so much overused, but it can be misinterpreted.

Introduced in the 1990s, the system is one of the earliest versions of extended producer responsibility (EPR), where brands are responsible for the costs associated with the entire product life cycle, including end-of-life. (I explain the concept of EPR in more detail in Chapter 4.) The funds are paid to a recognized organization established under the guidelines in the European Packaging and Packaging Waste Directive 94/62 and relevant national laws. Figure 5-4 gives an example of the Green Dot symbol.

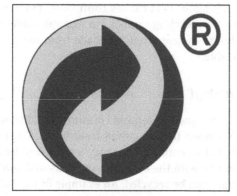

PRO Europe s.r.l./www.pro-e.org/
last accessed February 21, 2023

FIGURE 5-4:
The Green Dot
symbol.

REMEMBER

The Green Dot symbol shouldn't be confused with a recycling symbol. It has nothing to do with whether a particular item is recyclable. It simply indicates the brand has contributed financially to the cost of recycling, and strict rules are in place to ensure it isn't misused.

Plastic Resin Identification Codes

The Plastic Resin Codes, often called "plastic by numbers," are a coding system created to identify different types of plastics. The most widely used plastics are divided into seven groups. The resin codes help identify the type of plastic that an item or piece of packaging is made from, but they don't tell you whether the item is recyclable.

The image for the identification codes uses the Mobius loop symbol with a number 1 to 7 inside the chasing arrows; see Figure 5-5. As with the inverted Mobius symbol in Figure 5-2, this confuses people because they believe the presence of the Mobius loop means the item is recyclable. However, as you discover in Chapter 6, this isn't always the case.

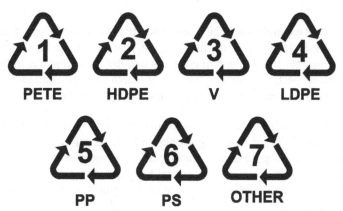

FIGURE 5-5:
The Plastic Resin
Identification
Codes.

REMEMBER

If you see a chasing arrows symbol with the numbers 1 to 7 inside, similar to Figure 5-5, it doesn't automatically mean the item is recyclable. It can help you figure out the kind of plastic the item is made from, but you'll still need to check your local rules.

The resin identification codes are not a perfect system but can be quite useful when you're trying to figure out whether you can recycle your plastic packaging. Many local governments and recycling services use the resin codes to indicate which plastics they do and don't accept. In Chapter 6, I provide more details on the resin codes and how you can use them to understand which plastics are recyclable in your local area.

Getting to know the new labeling

Most of the labels described earlier in this chapter don't offer much assistance to consumers like you and me in navigating the complex recycling rules. Fortunately, some very passionate and skilled groups are addressing this ambiguity in recycling labeling. Their solution is to provide on-pack labeling that is simple to understand and provides clear instructions on what to do with every part of the packaging. This last part is one of the important improvements. The new labels focus on the separate parts, giving clear instructions for each of the different packaging materials.

Consider a tub of yogurt as an example. It has various elements: a container, a plastic or aluminum seal, maybe a plastic lid for resealing, and sometimes even a cardboard sleeve to hold it all together. The recycling labels identify each of these separate components and communicate how to recycle them. In this yogurt example, there would be up to four labels on the packaging — one each for the tub, seal, lid, and sleeve.

Another example might be a cereal box that has a paperboard box and a soft plastic bag inside the box. In this example, there would be two labels on the packaging, one for the box and one for the bag. By indicating the instructions for each separate part, this labeling removes much of the confusion for consumers but also helps lower contamination rates. It's a win for everyone.

Another significant improvement introduced by these labels is that they consider the availability of recycling services as well as the material's recyclability. If an item isn't accepted in the majority of recycling services, it will be categorized as nonrecyclable. Even if the material is accepted in some locations, it may still be labeled as nonrecyclable if it's too challenging to recycle or if there are no viable end markets.

REMEMBER

These labels help you determine what can and can't go in your curbside recycling. However, the labels are based on what the majority of services collect and recycle, so they might not always be appropriate for your neighborhood. I recommend that you stay up to date with your local rules through your town or city government website.

In the following sections, I take a closer look at the three leading labels and how they work.

TIP

If your favorite brand isn't currently using the How2Recycle, OPRL, or ARL labels in the following sections, why not contact them and suggest they get on board?

The How2Recycle labeling

Found on product packaging in the United States and Canada, the How2Recycle labels aim to "get more materials in the recycling bin by taking the guesswork out of recycling." They also hope to improve our trust in recycling claims and increase the availability of recycling materials for use in new products.

The Sustainable Packaging Coalition identified a need for consistent labeling in 2012 and launched the How2Recycle labels in response. Brands must sign up for the program, but their packaging must undergo a recyclability assessment before they can use the labeling. This review helps them understand how their packaging performs and determines the appropriate logo. The How2Recycle team also provides recommendations for improving recyclability in the future. To date, over 2,600 brands have signed up.

The labels have four parts, as follows:

>> **Special instructions:** Tips are included on what to do before you place the item in your recycling bin. Some examples are "Rinse and Insert Lid," "Recycle If Clean & Dry," or "Remove Label Before Recycling."

>> **Recyclability icon:** A recycling symbol informs you whether the item can be recycled. There are four possible options:

- **Widely recycled:** Recycling of this material is available for the majority of Americans (60 percent) and Canadians (50 percent).

- **Sometimes recyclable:** The packaging is accepted in curbside recycling for between 20 percent and 60 percent of Americans or 20 percent and 50 percent of Canadians. It includes items commonly accepted but with significant challenges in processing or that struggle to find an end market.

- **Not yet recycled:** Recycling of the packaging is available for less than 20 percent of Americans, or it's very challenging.

- **Store drop-off:** This primarily refers to soft plastics like plastic bags and films that are recyclable at store drop-off locations.

>> **Packaging material:** Below the recycling symbol is a reference to the material — for example, paper, plastic, glass, or metal.

>> **Packaging component:** At the very bottom of the label is a description of the part or component. Examples include bottle, box, tray, bag, lid, or pouch. If the packaging has multiple parts, a label is provided for each one, like a glass jar and a lid.

Figure 5-6 provides some examples of these labels. To find out more, head to the How2Recycle website at www.how2recycle.info/labels.

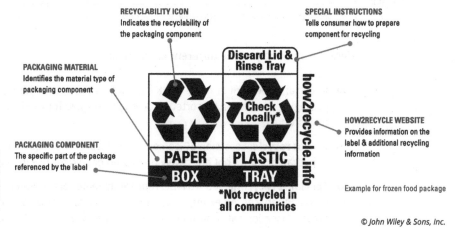

FIGURE 5-6:
Understanding the How2Recycle standardized labeling system.

© John Wiley & Sons, Inc.

The On-Pack Recycling Label (OPRL)

In the United Kingdom, you'll find the On-Pack Recycling Label (OPRL). The OPRL is a not-for-profit company dedicated to promoting recycling. Their labeling system delivers simple and consistent recycling instructions that can be applied across the UK. In addition to assisting consumers in navigating recycling, they aim to help reduce contamination, improve recycling rates, and encourage innovation in recycling. More than 400 brands, retailers, and charities currently use the labeling systems.

The simple "Recycle/Don't Recycle" labels provide clear advice so consumers can quickly determine whether the packaging is recyclable. Items are categorized into groups based on answers to questions like whether more than 75 percent of households have access to a service, whether recycling facilities process the material, and whether there's an end market. Examples are provided in Figure 5-7.

FIGURE 5-7: Examples of the On-Pack Recycling Label (OPRL).

Images thanks to the On-Pack Recycling Label (OPRL) — OPRL Ltd/www.oprl.org.uk./last accessed February 28, 2023

Here is a summary of the different categories:

>> **Recycle:** 75 percent or more of UK local authorities collect this type of packaging. Plus, it can be sorted, processed, and sold for use in a new product.

>> **Do not recycle:** Less than 50 percent of UK local authorities collect this type of packaging, or it's not effectively processed or sold for use in new products.

>> **Specialist recycling:** A third label represents materials accepted in specialist recycling services. An example is soft plastics like films and bags that have drop-off locations at supermarkets or, in some cases, are collected through curbside services.

A separate instruction is provided for each material type contained within the packaging with a short title to help you recognize which part it refers to, like bottle, sleeve, or box. There's also a brief instruction on recycling each piece, like "lid-on" or "rinse."

For more details about the labels, go to www.oprl.org.uk or www.recyclenow.com/how-to-recycle/understanding-recycling-symbols.

The Australasian Recycling Label (ARL)

The Australasian Recycling Label (ARL) was developed to address confusion over the recycling rules in Australia and New Zealand. It was developed in partnership with Planet Ark, PREP Design, and the Australian Packaging Covenant Organisation (APCO). The ultimate purpose of the labeling is to assist customers in finding simple recycling information while lowering contamination and improving overall recycling success.

The ARL also works closely with package designers and businesses through their Packaging Recyclability Evaluation Portal (PREP) to assess packaging and determine recyclability. All things are considered, including package size, weight, shape, inks and adhesive, and even the availability of collection services in different areas. A total of 150,000 PREP assessments were conducted by ARL program members in 2021.

The ARL specifies each component of packaging separately and indicates whether it can be placed in your curbside recycling bin, if there are special instructions on how to recycle it, or if it belongs in the general waste bin. Additionally, it offers simple guidelines on what actions consumers should take to properly recycle and minimize contamination.

The three sections of the labeling include

>> **Packaging component:** This section identifies the part of the item the instructions relate to, for example, box, sleeve, tray, or film.

>> **Recycling classification:** A symbol that indicates whether this specific part of the packaging is recyclable. There are three categories used in this section:

- **Recyclable:** This is the part that can be placed in your curbside recycling bin, identified by a solid or opaque recycling symbol.

- **Conditionally recyclable:** Denoted by the outline of a recycling symbol, this represents a part that requires special instructions to be followed, like scrunching aluminum foil into a ball before recycling it or taking soft plastics to a store drop-off.

- **Not recyclable:** A picture of a waste bin reveals the item is definitely not recyclable and goes in your general waste bin.

>> **Label instructions**. These are helpful instructions to aid you in the correct disposal. One example is "store drop-off," which refers to soft plastics that you can take back to the designated stores for recycling. Another example is "scrunch bottle and replace cap," helping to make sure your plastic cap gets recycled along with the bottle.

TIP

Figure 5-8 provides an example of the ARL logo. You can find out more about the ARL and the different instructions at `www.arl.org.au` or `www.recyclingnearyou.com.au/arl/`.

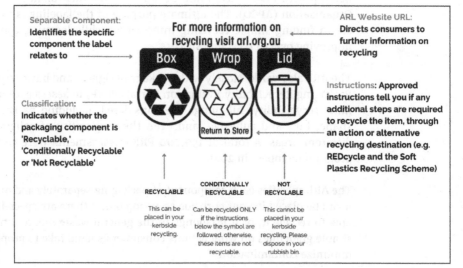

Images thanks to the Australian Packaging Covenant Organisation (APCO) — `www.apco.org.au`

FIGURE 5-8:
Understanding the Australasian Recycling Label (ARL).

Defining and recognizing greenwashing

We all want to reduce our impact, but navigating through all the labels and information can be frustrating and time-consuming. So we rely to some degree on the honesty of brands to tell us when products are good for the environment. We also rely on them telling us if a product or its packaging is recyclable or contains recycled content.

When a business or brand makes an untrue environmental claim for marketing reasons, this is known as "greenwashing." In the worst scenario, it's when a brand intentionally tries to trick customers into believing they are more environmentally friendly than they really are. Their objective is to raise their reputation or increase sales.

WARNING

Greenwashing is bad because it misleads people with good intentions into believing they're helping the environment when they may, in fact, be making the situation worse. It may be that they use a product more often because it appears to be more sustainable than it really is. Incorrect actions taken by customers due to greenwashing can cause more harm, such as placing an item in your recycling bin because the label states it's recyclable when it's not.

Here are some examples of greenwashing you might encounter:

>> Displaying recyclable, biodegradable, or compostable labels that aren't accurate for the product

>> Claiming their products have environmental benefits like saving energy when those claims are unsupported

>> Overstating the environmental benefits of their actions or products

>> Labels that use scientific language instead of plain language that everyone can understand

>> Using vague words or claims that don't actually tell you anything, like "eco-friendly," "sustainable," or "green"

>> Suggesting a product is made from recycled content when it's not

>> Claiming credit for environmental behaviors when those actions are required by law

>> The use of logos and endorsements that look like but are not linked to independent authorities

>> Lack of transparency (brands that don't display any information about their products, supply chain, policies, and ethics)

REMEMBER

It's important to realize that not all companies partake in greenwashing intentionally. Many companies genuinely want to do something good. Unfortunately, sometimes they might share information that turns out to be wrong, or they were misinformed themselves. Just like you and me, business owners can make mistakes or get confused by too much information.

I think the sign of a truly good brand is transparency. This is when a brand readily shares information and isn't afraid to own up to mistakes or misinformation. They openly admit to their errors, correct them, and apologize to their customers.

TIP

Always be kind if you approach a company to question the validity of its claims. You may not have the complete picture, so it's important to give them a chance to explain.

Breaking Free from Bad Habits

There's no doubt we're all very busy and short on time. I understand we don't have a lot of time available for recycling. But with less focus and no time to consider our actions, we can start to form bad habits.

Your efforts to protect the environment are absolutely worthwhile. And simply changing a few aspects of your thinking and actions will make a huge difference. In the following sections, I take a look at some of the most common habits and what you can do to break them.

Changing your view of curbside recycling

When considering curbside recycling, the most important thing to understand is the type of service offered. Curbside recycling is provided by local governments and the contractors they hire to collect and process common packaging waste generated by households. Depending on where you live, accepted packaging usually includes some combination of paper, metal, glass, and plastic.

REMEMBER

The curbside recycling system is not designed to handle every type of waste you produce as a household. It's primarily intended to cater to packaging materials only. Problems occur when we put the wrong items into our recycling bins. Food waste, textile and clothing waste, complex items like computers, or larger items like furniture don't belong in your curbside recycling bin.

Starting out by keeping it simple

REMEMBER

The easiest way to get to know the rules for curbside recycling is to start with what can go in and not focus on the list of items that can't. Curbside recycling is designed to collect packaging made from four main types of materials:

>> **Rigid plastic:** This includes rigid plastics only, such as milk bottles or shampoo bottles. Not all rigid plastics are accepted in every location. In Chapter 6, I explain in more detail how to check which plastics are accepted in your area.

>> **Paper and cardboard:** This includes office paper, school papers, magazines, catalogs, and newspapers. It also includes corrugated cardboard and paperboard boxes for shoes, tissues, or food items.

>> **Glass:** Including glass bottles and jars only. Note that glass rules vary significantly from place to place. Unfortunately, some curbside recycling services don't accept glass at all, but I discuss that in more detail in Chapter 8.

>> **Metal:** Cans, tins, and aluminum foil are accepted. Most other metal items will need to be disposed of at a metal scrapyard.

In Chapters 6 to 10, I describe recycling each of these materials in more detail. I help you understand why recycling them is important and list what's accepted and not accepted in most curbside services.

Preventing wishcycling

We've likely all been guilty of wishcycling at some point. You have an item to throw out, but you're unsure which bin to put it in. Is it recyclable? Or should it go to a landfill? You care about doing the right thing and don't want to send it to the wrong place. So, just in case, you place the item in your recycling bin, hoping that someone else will know whether it's recyclable. And if it isn't, hopefully they'll deal with it appropriately. This is what is referred to as *wishcycling*.

WARNING

Why is wishcycling so bad? The problem is that putting an item that can't be recycled in the curbside recycling bin can have some pretty dire consequences. Here are just a few examples of the problems it can cause:

>> It can contaminate the good recycling material, lowering the quality and reducing the potential of selling it to a manufacturer to make new products. In some cases, it can result in an entire batch of recycling being sent to a landfill.

>> Unrecyclable items can get stuck in the sorting and recycling machines, causing safety issues and costly shutdowns at recycling plants.

>> The extra costs from shutdowns and additional processing combined with an inferior product can impact the overall recycling profitability and, in the worst-case scenario, result in the cancellation of services.

You can avoid wishcycling by

>> Getting to know the recycling rules in your local area

>> Understanding what goes in and what stays out

>> Accepting that sometimes, unless there's a specialist recycling service, items must be placed in your general waste bin (see the next section)

Following one important guideline: When in doubt, leave it out

REMEMBER

One of the hardest things to acknowledge is that sometimes you're best off sending an item to landfill than contaminating all those good recyclables you've been collecting. If you've already read other chapters in Part 2 and checked what goes in and what stays out and still can't figure out whether an item is recyclable, it's okay to put it in the general trash.

TIP

When you discover an item that isn't recyclable, it's a good time to consider what alternatives are available. Why not start a "Landfill List"? We all do love a good list! Keep a notepad near your recycling bin; whenever you have to put something into the general waste bin because it can't be recycled, add it to your list. Review the list from time to time and see whether you can replace any of the items with recyclable or, better still, reusable items. You can go a step further and undertake a waste audit; discover how in Chapter 17.

Checking Out Common Rules

To help you get started with recycling, I want to explain some common rules and guidelines that apply no matter where you live. Keep the following sections in mind when you're recycling through your curbside service. Most of the same rules will apply if you drop off your waste at a waste transfer station or recycling center.

Separating items by material

A key part of recycling is sorting and organizing materials into different categories for processing. Methods for recycling the variety of waste created can be worlds apart. There are screens, eddy current separators, float tanks, and even things called hydrocyclones. This all sounds high-tech, but the important point is that each material requires a unique set of machinery designed to separate it from the overall mix and remove any contaminants.

REMEMBER

The more you can do to aid in sorting and organizing items into different types before they start their recycling journey, the more likely they'll find their proper path and avoid contaminating other materials. If an item or piece of packaging comprises more than one type of material and is easily pulled apart, then you should separate it. In particular, you need to separate it if one part is recyclable and the other isn't. This allows you to place the recyclable part in your curbside bin and dispose of the other part in the general waste bin or take it to a specialist recycler.

Here are some examples of different materials that you can separate easily:

>> Removing the cardboard sleeve from a pack of individual yogurt tubs.

>> Taking the soft plastic bag from inside a cardboard cereal box. In many places the bag can be recycled with a specialist soft plastic recycler (see Chapter 11).

>> Separating the metal or plastic lid from a glass jar. Rules around recycling lids can be quite confusing. Find out more about recycling lids in the respective chapters for plastic (Chapter 6) or metal (Chapter 9).

Curbside recycling rules vary from place to place, so the preceding examples may not apply in your area. For instance, in some locations, glass isn't accepted. Keep reading through Chapters 6 through 10 and use the worksheets provided to help figure out the rules that apply to you.

Keeping contamination low

Contamination in recycling is when the wrong material makes its way into the recycling process. It nearly always happens at the point when objects are placed in the recycling bin at home or a place of work. It's the result of confusion, wish-cycling (discussed earlier in this chapter), or unfortunately in some cases, people simply not caring.

The average contamination rate in the United States and United Kingdom is around 20 to 25 percent, meaning one in every four or five items doesn't belong in the recycling bin. Contamination is one of the biggest issues in recycling. The following sections explain how contamination occurs and what items should stay out of your recycling bin.

Understanding how contamination occurs

Contamination can happen when

>> The wrong materials are put into the recycling bin

>> The right item is put in the recycling bin, but it's not clean (find more detail on how clean recycling should be later in this chapter)

>> Items are placed in the recycling bin inside a plastic bag (note there are a few exceptions where residents are explicitly requested to place recyclables in plastic bags; see the next section)

Contamination can result in a whole batch of recyclables ending up in a landfill. The presence of contamination can reduce the quality and, therefore, the recoverable price of processed recycled materials. If the quality reduces too much, throwing all of the material in a landfill can be cheaper than removing the contaminants.

Nonrecyclable materials like plastic bags, clothing, and ropes can wrap around and get stuck in the shafts and axles of the sorting machines, forcing plant outages, endangering personnel, and costing the company time and money. Hazardous waste can lead to a similar outcome or, worse still, can result in explosions or fires inside the recycling trucks or at facilities. This is a particular concern when lithium-ion batteries are incorrectly discarded in recycling bins.

Other types of contaminants, like hazardous waste, food waste, and unclean recyclables in your curbside bin, create an unsafe and unpleasant workplace for recycling workers. Consider the job of the waste sorter, picking through people's waste everyday. Their job becomes much easier when recyclables are clean and restricted to acceptable items.

REMEMBER

You're the first line of defense in reducing contamination in recycling. Take a moment to consider whether an item is recyclable before you toss it in the bin.

Identifying items that don't belong

Although knowing what to recycle is as simple as getting familiar with the accepted four materials types, reviewing the list of items that definitely don't belong in your curbside recycling is helpful. Some of these items are recyclable, and even though they can't be recycled in your curbside recycling bin, there may be specialist recyclers. You can discover more about specialist recycling in Part 3.

REMEMBER

Here are the items that definitely don't belong in your curbside recycling bin. You can find a full list of items that don't belong in your curbside recycling bin by reviewing Chapters 6 through 10. You should always check the rules with your local town or city.

>> **No food waste:** Your leftover or out-of-date food doesn't belong in your curbside recycling bin. Uncover more about food waste and even how to start your own compost in Chapter 12.

>> **No tangling items:** Items that can easily get tangled in the machinery at recycling facilities are called *tanglers*. This includes ropes, garden hoses, cables, textiles, and clothing — basically anything that might wrap around machinery parts.

>> **No soft plastics:** Similar to cords and ropes, soft plastic packaging like plastic bags or plastic wrap can also get caught in machinery. Head to Chapter 11 to find out how to recycle your soft plastics.

>> **No dirty diapers:** Please do not put used diapers or nappy waste in your recycling container. They are unrecyclable and make working conditions for recycling center employees unpleasant.

>> **Pet poop bags:** Not too different from the icky factor of dirty diapers, pet poop bags, filled or not, don't belong in your recycling bin.

>> **Used tissues or paper towels:** Soiled and used paper towels or tissues cannot be recycled.

>> **E-waste or WEEE:** This includes old phones, computers, toasters, coffee machines, and basically anything with a battery or a plug-in cord. They don't belong in your recycling bin because they can contain hazardous materials. I explain more in Chapter 13.

>> **Batteries:** Batteries also contain hazardous materials, and certain types can even combust and cause fires. Recycle your batteries at a specialist location. You can find more information in Chapter 13.

>> **Light bulbs:** Even though they appear to be made from glass, bulbs contain many other materials, sometimes even toxic chemicals. Find out more on how to recycle them in Chapter 14.

>> **Household items:** Household items like home decor, toys, textiles, rugs, carpets, and appliances don't belong in your curbside bin.

>> **Outdoor items or items from your garage:** As with household items, most things in your garage can't go in your recycling bin. Some packaging is accepted, like cleaning bottles, plastic containers, or cardboard boxes, but be sure to check your local rules.

>> **Hazardous waste:** You'll need to carefully dispose of substances classified as hazardous waste like paint, fireworks, automotive fluids, herbicides, pesticides/bug spray, propane canisters, and gas cylinders. Check with your local town or city for a hazardous waste drop-off location.

>> **Biohazardous waste:** You can't recycle medical waste in your curbside recycling bin, including syringes, needles, and other medical or sanitary products.

>> **Construction or renovation materials:** Curbside recycling services can't process the waste generated from construction or renovation.

>> **Bioplastics, biodegradables, and compostable plastics:** None of these items can be recycled with standard plastics and so can't go in your curbside recycling bin. Find out more in Chapter 6.

Leaving items loose

Keep your recycling loose, and don't put it inside plastic bags unless explicitly requested in your local rules. For example, this is accepted in New York City, where some residents must put their recyclables in clear plastic bags.

WARNING

Plastic bags are the recycling industry's nemesis. They can shut down a recycling plant by getting tangled in the machines. Bags are also a problem because workers often have no idea what's inside them — a particular issue when they are black or solid-colored plastic bags. Opening the bags to find out what's in them is time-consuming and may even be considered too risky. What if, for instance, it was overflowing with soiled diapers? Due to these health and safety concerns, most plastic bags are never opened and are simply sent to landfills.

Knowing how much to clean

One of the most common questions asked about recycling is "How clean does it need to be?" It's important to keep your curbside recycling free from food residues because

>> Food or liquids can spill out and contaminate paper and cardboard.

>> Excess food residues can attract vermin.

>> Food residue can spoil and grow mold or bacteria, leading to unsafe conditions for the workers at recycling facilities.

While there should be no liquids or solid foods in your recyclables, a tiny quantity of food residue is typically acceptable. Give the objects a quick rinse; they don't need to be spotless. However, you may need to wash the container more thoroughly if it contains something like honey or mayonnaise. Here are some examples to help you understand how much is too much:

>> **Soft drink bottle or can:** Pour any remaining liquid out of the bottle.

>> **Mayonnaise in a glass jar:** Remove all remaining mayonnaise from the jar with a spoon. Rinse or soak the jar to dissolve any residue before washing it.

>> **Pizza box:** Use your best judgment. If your pizza box is covered in grease and cheese, then it's straight to the general waste bin, or you may be able to compost it. But if there are only a few spots, you can generally put it in your recycling bin.

TIP

Saving water is just as important as recycling, so don't use too much water when washing your recyclables. I recommend using your dishwashing water to clean your recycling to help save water. Another suggestion is to place them in the dishwasher when there's room.

Understanding that size does matter

Packaging materials should be a reasonable size to be recycled properly. This is mainly due to the machinery used at the recycling facilities. Small items tend to fall through the machinery and end up on the facility floor, where they get swept up and sent to a landfill.

A good rule of thumb is anything larger than a credit card can go into your recycling bin; otherwise, it must go in your general waste bin. Some items that can't be recycled due to their size include

>> Plastic bottle caps

>> Small pieces of paper

>> Soda can tabs

>> Beer bottle caps

>> Aluminum candy wrappers

TIP

You can collect small pieces of aluminum foil and roll them into a ball the size of a baseball or cricket ball and place it in your recycling bin.

The other end of the spectrum is when things are too big for the recycling facilities. Generally, the size of your bin will dictate what packaging will fit in, so if you have a large cardboard box, simply tear it up into reasonably sized pieces before placing it in your bin. Some locations will allow you to place items like this beside your bin for pickup, but you'll definitely want to check this before you do so. Otherwise, you can try your local recycling center.

Asking whether you should flatten items

The regulations regarding whether to flatten your recycling differ greatly from one region to the next. In some locations squashing or flattening aluminum cans or even plastic bottles is accepted and, in fact, encouraged. However, in other locations sorting facilities identify bottles or cans through their shape. If they're flattened, they can be missed by the machines and improperly sorted, possibly contaminating other waste streams like paper or ending up in landfills. Be sure to check your local rules.

Getting Help When You Need It

I hope I've helped you understand why it's important to contact your local government or check their online resources regarding the rules in your area. Take some time to become familiar with the rules and guidelines. I've created some easy worksheets in the rest of Part 2 so you can record your local rules in one place.

TIP

As I explain earlier in this chapter, rules can change from time to time, so I recommend checking at least every six months to see what's changed.

In Table 5-1, I list some websites that might help you find your local town or city recycling information, and in Table 5-2, I list currently available recycling apps for your phone.

TABLE 5-1 Websites to Help You Locate Your Local Town or City's Recycling Information

Location	Locator Website
United States	www.berecycled.org/how-to-recycle/
Canada	www.canada.ca/en/environment-climate-change/services/managing-reducing-waste/contact-information
United Kingdom	www.gov.uk/recycling-collections
Australia	www.recyclingnearyou.com.au/councils/

TABLE 5-2 Phone Apps to Help You Get Local Recycling Info

Location	App
United States	Recycle Coach
Canada	Recycle Coach
United Kingdom	Horizon
Australia	Recycle Mate

TIP

Many other recycling apps are available for different regions and countries. Head to the Google Play or iTunes App Stores and search for "recycle" to see what's available in your area.

IN THIS CHAPTER

» Getting to know what plastic is and the different types

» Grasping the importance of recycling plastic

» Exploring the different ways plastic is recycled

» Breaking down what can and can't be recycled in your curbside bin

» Finding ways to reduce the amount of plastic in your life

» Buying your recycled plastic back

Chapter **6**

Deciphering Curbside Plastic Recycling

O kay, we can all agree that plastics pose a serious threat to our environment. They pollute every corner of the planet, threaten wildlife, accumulate in landfills, and increase our dependency on fossil fuels. And somehow, even though we continue to generate more every year, the plastic recycling rate remains at a low of 9 percent globally.

Although painted as the number one enemy, plastic plays an integral role in our lives, and we must not forget the reason why we use it. An important example is how plastics can increase the shelf life of food, protecting it from bacteria and reducing food waste, a significant contributor to climate change.

Like it or loathe it, plastic is here to stay. Since a world without plastic is unlikely, we need to work harder to ensure we use plastic only when it's fit for purpose and designed for recyclability, and then make sure that it actually gets recycled. The problem is that recycling plastic is a challenging endeavor. Plastic comes in many different forms, each of which must be sorted from the others and recycled separately. Consumer recycling habits are crucial in this process.

In this chapter, I give you the tools to help you make sense of the everyday plastic packaging you might encounter. I start with how to distinguish between soft and hard plastics and explain why they're treated differently. Then I take you through identifying plastics using the resin codes. You find guidelines to help you discover which plastics are accepted where you live and how to apply this knowledge in your everyday recycling habits. Plus, I offer you some simple swaps you can make to reduce the amount of plastic waste you create.

Beginning with the Basics: What Is Plastic?

What, exactly, is plastic? It seems like something we should know, given how abundant it is! The dictionary definition of plastic is any material that can be shaped and molded when you apply heat or pressure. These characteristics are what drive our excessive use of plastic. In the following sections, you find out plastic's general traits as well as the resources and process used to make it and the different ways plastic degrades.

Plastic's typical traits

The molecular structure of plastics makes them suitable for a wide range of applications. Every type of plastic we create has a distinct appearance and texture. Some plastics are stretchy, some are brittle, while others are as tough as metal. They can be soft and flexible like a plastic bag or hard and rigid like a container. There are as many varieties of plastics as there are applications for their use. But luckily, there is only a small number that most of us interact with daily.

TECHNICAL STUFF

The building blocks of all plastics are molecules called monomers, which are joined together into long strings called polymers. A *monomer* is a molecule that can easily link to other identical molecules and form a long chain. This chain of monomers is what's referred to as a *polymer*. Monomers are mostly organic molecules containing elements like hydrocarbon, oxygen, nitrogen, sulfur, or chlorine.

These long polymer chains give plastic its properties. The characteristics depend on the type of monomer and how long the polymer chain is. Properties range from strength and durability to clarity, flexibility, and elasticity. What makes plastic so adaptable and useful to humans is the combination of each of these unique qualities.

The most common properties of plastics include the following:

>> **Lightweight:** All plastics are lightweight, particularly when compared to alternatives like glass or metal. Because of this, plastic is frequently used for packaging food. Think about the fuel savings between transporting a truckload of heavy-duty plastic bottles against a load of glass bottles.

>> **Strong and durable:** Another popular property of the different plastics is that they're very strong and can last a long time. They won't shatter when dropped and can handle some pretty rough treatment. The issue is that, as we now know, the durability of plastic has some serious adverse effects on the environment when it's not disposed of properly.

>> **Good chemical resistance:** Many plastics provide a protective barrier against chemicals. For this reason, plastic is commonly used to store nasty chemicals and cleaning goods. In food packaging, this chemical resistance prevents plastic from reacting with the foods it contains, a useful property. But not all plastics have this characteristic; some take on the smells and colors of food. You might have noticed this in your old Tupperware or other plastic containers.

TIP

To keep your plastic containers from becoming stained or taking on food smells in the kitchen, wash them as soon as possible. A tip to rid your containers of food smells is to store them with a pinch of salt inside. It helps absorb any residual odors. But don't forget to wipe the salt out before putting your lunch in it.

>> **Good at insulating:** Plastics don't allow electricity or heat to flow through them, making them excellent insulators. Some examples include these:

- Polystyrene or Styrofoam used in hot beverage cups means that heat won't transfer when you hold them.

- Styrofoam coolers keep the heat out and the cold in.

- Plastic is used to wrap electrical wires and cables to prevent other conductors, particularly people, from directly touching the live wires. Even without people nearby, it's vital to prevent fires or malfunctions that can result from bare wires. Polyvinyl chloride (plastic #3) is often used to cover electrical cables. (I describe the plastic numbering system and plastic #3 later in this chapter.)

>> **Versatile:** As I note earlier, the definition of plastic is a material that can be shaped and molded easily. It's one of the reasons plastics are so popular with designers and manufacturers. They mold plastics into many different shapes and sizes to create a large variety of products.

>> **Cheap to make:** Plastic is inexpensive to manufacture and mass-produce. You can see why plastic is the material of choice for many manufacturers when you combine this with the other attributes listed here.

Resources used to make plastic

Plastics can occur naturally or be synthetic. A good example of a naturally occurring plastic is cellulose, although most plastics you come across are made from fossil fuels. Making plastic requires a base material to create the polymer, but it also uses other natural resources. Here are the resources needed to make plastic:

>> **Base material:** Most plastics already in existence and being made today use nonrenewable fossil fuels as a base material. I'll refer to these as *conventional plastics* from here on. But many new plastics have been, and are still being, developed from renewable plant sources like corn, bamboo, or sugarcane.

TECHNICAL STUFF

Fossil fuels come in three forms: coal, natural gas, and petroleum (oil). They occur naturally in the Earth, formed from decomposing plant and animal remains buried for hundreds of millions of years. These substances contain many different hydrocarbon molecules, such as ethane, methane, and butane.

>> **Water:** Water is needed at all phases of plastic production, from oil and gas extraction and mining to polymer manufacture and product manufacturing. For example, it takes about 22 gallons (83 liters) of water to make just one pound of plastic.

>> **Energy:** It takes energy to do and make everything. So as expected, making plastic requires energy. Every step of the plastic journey, from raw material to the product sitting on our kitchen counters, consumes power. Energy is used not only during manufacturing and processing, but it's also necessary for moving raw materials and finished goods from one location to another.

>> **Chemical additives:** Chemicals may be added while forming plastics to generate distinctive properties for the end products. They might be added either for better marketing and design or to help protect the products they contain. There are hundreds of possible chemical additives used today. Examples include stabilizers to prevent the plastic from degrading in sunlight, plasticizers to increase flexibility, and dyes used to produce various hues.

RENEWABLE VERSUS NONRENEWABLE

Renewable resources are those that are capable of being replenished through natural processes. A good example is timber or plants that regrow easily.

Nonrenewable resources have a limited supply. Sooner or later, they will run out. Although technically, fossil fuels could reform, they're classified as nonrenewable resources because it would take hundreds of millions of years for that to happen.

How plastic is made

One of the reasons we find ourselves with a plastic problem today is because of the traditionally linear process of making plastic. In this process, raw materials go in, and waste comes out. And unfortunately, there's not too much consideration on where that waste goes. However, a far superior approach involves recycling waste and establishing a circular economy. (I go into more detail about this approach later in this chapter.)

Depending on the type of plastic and the desired end product, the process for making plastics can vary. Here are the common steps for making plastic in a linear economy (see Figure 6-1):

1. **Fossil fuel resources are extracted.**

   To make plastic, first we must find fossil fuel resources and extract them. This is a very energy-intensive exercise because many reserves are located deep in the Earth or beneath the ocean. Once discovered, fossil fuels are recovered either by drilling and pumping oil or gas from deposits or through surface or underground mining.

2. **The fossil fuel resources are refined.**

   Once extracted, the material is transported to a refinery, and high pressures and temperatures are used to break the hydrocarbon mixture into different products. You'll recognize some products, like petrol/gasoline and diesel fuel. This process also produces products like ethylene and propylene, referred to as monomers, which are the primary building blocks for most plastics.

3. **The monomers undergo polymerization.**

   The monomers are converted into polymers through a process called *polymerization*. During this process, the monomers are attached to each other to form the long polymer chains that make plastic. This stage involves manipulating polymers to produce the various forms of plastic we use daily. Chemicals are also added to develop specific properties and the look and feel of the end product.

4. **The plastic is pelletized.**

   The plastic is then melted and pushed through a small hole to form a long tube (like spaghetti). Once cool, it's cut into small pellets. These pellets, called *nurdles,* are ready for purchase by manufacturing companies.

5. **The plastic pellets are manufactured.**

   After being transported to a manufacturing plant, the pellets are melted and molded into various shapes and products. The product may undergo finishing touches such as joining, machining, or coating. The final results are evident in the multitude of plastic products at the supermarket and in our homes.

6. The plastic products are purchased and used.

Once plastic packaging is manufactured and the product is sealed inside, it's transported to the store, ready for you and me to purchase.

7. Consumers dispose of the plastic products.

Finally, the product or packaging reaches the end of its useful life and is discarded. At this point in a typical linear economy, the product or packaging would end up in landfills or, worse, pollute the environment. If we choose to recycle plastic packaging, we help create a circular economy for the material and ensure the materials are kept in use.

REMEMBER

It's good to consider this lengthy and complicated process when purchasing, using, and discarding plastic products. Often these products are cheap, but unfortunately, the price doesn't reflect the enormous effort and significant resources required to make them.

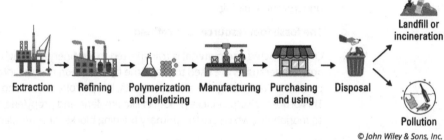

FIGURE 6-1:
The linear plastic-making process.

Extraction Refining Polymerization and pelletizing Manufacturing Purchasing and using Disposal

Landfill or incineration

Pollution

© John Wiley & Sons, Inc.

A different type: Plastic from plants

You might have heard the term "bioplastics," particularly more recently, as it has been growing in popularity as a replacement for conventional plastics made from fossil fuels. It's possible to make synthetic plastics from plant materials as well as fossil fuels, and these plastics are called bioplastics. The definition's focused on the materials used to make plastic instead of how it behaves at the end of its life (see the next section).

The defining condition for plastic to be a bioplastic is that the raw material used must be alive and renewable. A renewable source is capable of being replenished through natural processes. Typical examples of bioplastics include

>> **Starch-based plastic:** Corn or potato starch–derived plastics are among the most widely used bioplastics. You may come into contact with these

bioplastics in capsules produced by the pharmaceutical industry or in other packaging. They're becoming more popular today, as they're considered a replacement for petroleum-based plastic in flexible packaging.

>> **Cellulose-based bioplastics:** As well as being used for papermaking, cellulose extracted from plant materials and trees is used to make bioplastics. Applications include various types of packaging as well as molded products like sunglass frames.

>> **Protein-based bioplastics:** Derived from protein sources like wheat, soy, rice, or milk, protein-based bioplastics can be used in food packaging.

>> **Aliphatic-polyester bioplastics:** Made from sugar or cornstarch, a common example of aliphatic-polyester bioplastics is polylactic acid (or PLA). You'll find these bioplastics in many take-out containers, takeaway cups, plastic bottles, and utensils. They also have applications in the pharmaceutical and medical industries for implants and tissue engineering.

Bioplastics can be made from other materials like sawdust or composted food waste. Today bioplastics are becoming more popular with hopes of providing more sustainable alternatives to conventional plastics derived from fossil fuels.

WARNING

Just because bioplastic is made from plants and starts with "bio" doesn't mean it's biodegradable. Bioplastics can be biodegradable, nonbiodegradable, compostable, and in some cases, recyclable. The next section explains the differences between these terms.

Ways to degrade: Biodegradable, compostable, or just plain plastic

The plastic crisis is forcing many manufacturers to look for alternatives to conventional plastics, so biodegradable and compostable plastics appear everywhere and have been positioned as the "silver bullet to end plastic pollution." It's a good thing for the future of plastics. However, in the short term, it causes quite the confusion, not only in our homes but in waste processing too.

These categories aren't determined by the raw materials used to make the plastic but by how it degrades. For example, both conventional plastics made from fossil fuels and bioplastics made from renewable plant material can be classified as biodegradable.

In Chapter 3, I explain that all materials degrade, but only some biodegrade, and even fewer are compostable. Understanding the distinction between compostable and biodegradable plastics helps you make the right choice at the bin. The following list defines each type:

>> **Conventional plastic:** Made from fossil fuels, conventional plastics last for a very long time and degrade by breaking into smaller and smaller pieces called *microplastics.*

>> **Biodegradable plastic:** This breaks down in a defined period of time. When plastic is biodegradable, it doesn't mean it can be safely disposed of in the environment.

>> **Compostable plastic:** This decomposes within a short time, usually a few months, and leaves no toxins behind. There are two grades of compostable plastics: those that can be placed in a home compost, and those that require an industrial compost facility.

Not all compostable plastics are acceptable in home composting. Some items require certain conditions to decompose that are available only at industrial composting facilities. Check the label; if you're still unsure, try contacting the company that made the product to check with them.

Biodegradable and compostable products or packaging are not recyclable through your curbside recycling service but may be accepted in some curbside organics collections.

Understanding Why You Should Recycle Plastic

Since the 1950s, plastic manufacturing has nearly doubled, rising from 2 million tons to an astonishing 380 million tons annually. Despite this continued growth in plastic production, we still recycle less than 9 percent of it. Yes, you heard it right! The recycling rate worldwide is estimated at around 9 percent, and although some countries have made improvements, many are still far behind.

Plastic is strong, durable, lightweight, and resistant to chemicals. These qualities are great when we're using plastic products, but they're less advantageous once those products reach the end of their useful lives. Plastics can take hundreds of years to break down. As a result, almost every fragment of plastic produced is still in existence.

So, where does the remaining 91 percent that doesn't get recycled end up? Apart from a small amount that gets incinerated, it's either sitting in a landfill or polluting the environment. There is no question that plastic is wreaking havoc on our environment. It's polluting our rivers, lakes, and oceans; harming wildlife; and generating microplastics in every corner of the planet (see Chapter 3). Recycling your plastics won't solve every environmental issue, but it'll undoubtedly help minimize them.

>> **Minimizing microplastics:** When plastic does break down, it fragments into ever smaller pieces. Larger plastic items in the environment degrade in sunlight and water, speeding up the process. Once they're less than 5 millimeters in size, they're called *microplastics.*

Although there is still much to learn about how microplastics affect both the environment and individuals, recent research is concerning. Microplastics have been discovered in every nook and cranny of the planet. They're in the deepest oceans, the highest mountains, our soils, and our waterways. They've invaded every part of the planet and are likely making their way through the food chain to be ingested by us. Recycling plastic ensures that plastic stays in use and doesn't break down and infiltrate the environment.

>> **Protecting animals and the environment:** Every year about 11 million metric tons of plastic waste reaches the oceans. That's the equivalent of two garbage trucks of plastic dumped into the sea every minute. The hazard that plastic pollution presents to animals is among its worst effects. Animals are harmed by plastic pollution in two main ways:

- Sea life is killed or hurt when it becomes entangled in or imprisoned by plastic pollution.

- Fish, birds, and small animals eat microplastics or larger pieces, starving them and leaching toxins into their bodies.

If you knew that by placing your recycling into the correct bin, you could make the world a safer place for a turtle, a seabird, or even a small fish, would you do it? Of course, you would!

>> **Keeping plastic out of landfills:** Approximately 70 percent of waste plastic goes to landfills. The U.S. Environmental Protection Agency (EPA) reports that 27 million tons of plastic waste were sent to landfills in the United States in 2018. What a waste is all I can say! We could use all those materials to create new products and reduce our dependency on raw resources.

When landfills are mismanaged, plastics can blow around or get picked up by water and escape into the environment. Many plastics include chemicals, some of which are highly toxic. These chemicals can be absorbed by the soil and groundwater around the landfill, enter our waterways, and ultimately end up in the ocean.

TECHNICAL STUFF

Every ton of plastic recycled saves 7.4 cubic yards of landfill space.

>> **Reducing resource use:** After lowering our overall consumption, recycling plastic is the next best approach to lessen our reliance on fossil fuels. Replacing these raw materials with recycled plastic saves energy too. In fact, recycling one ton of plastic can save up to 16.3 barrels of oil and enough energy to power a house for almost seven months.

REMEMBER

A plastic bottle sent to a recycling facility is less likely to end up as pollution on the beach or at the bottom of the ocean. It also won't turn into microplastics and be eaten by a fish or turtle. We get the benefits of recycling, but more importantly, we help keep nature free and safe from our pollution.

Seeing How Plastic Is Recycled

Recycling plastics is a solution that helps us move away from the linear take-make-waste model for plastics toward a circular model. The most common method is mechanical recycling. Plastic can also be recycled using chemical processes that break it down into its original components. However, chemical recycling is an emerging technology that's not widely available (see Chapter 18), so I focus on mechanical recycling here.

Mechanical recycling involves cleaning, separating, and shredding the plastic to create a product that can be remelted and reused. This method is relatively simple but degrades the quality of plastics. The steps for mechanically recycling plastic are described here and illustrated in Figure 6-2:

1. **The consumer disposes of the plastic in a recycling bin.**

   When you place your plastic packaging in your recycling bin, you start the process and support a circular economy.

2. **The plastic is collected.**

   First, it's necessary to collect plastic waste from our residences and workplaces. For many of us, this is through curbside collection programs. However, other options are available for those without curbside collection services, such as recycling center drop-off locations, container deposit systems, and bottle banks. These services collect the plastic waste and take it to a materials recovery facility (MRF).

3. The collected plastic is sorted.

Many curbside recycling programs are based on single-stream collection. In this case, once received at the MRF, the plastic must be separated from the other recyclables like glass, paper, and metals. Explore more about how this process works in Chapter 4.

In addition to separating the plastics from other materials, they must be sorted into different plastic types and sometimes into various thicknesses and colors. Most facilities use automatic sorting machines; however, some still use manual sorters to help remove contaminants.

4. The plastic is washed.

The waste plastic is washed to remove any remaining contaminants like leftover food, grease, and other materials like labels and adhesives.

REMEMBER

You can help reduce contamination by looking up your local rules on what is and isn't accepted and keeping your recyclables clean and dry. I show you all the steps later in this chapter.

5. The plastic is shredded and pelletized.

After it's washed, the plastic is ground into small pieces. Further sorting and cleaning may take place at this step to ensure the highest quality. Finally, the plastic is melted and forced through a tiny hole, coming out the other side as long thin tubes. These are cut into small pellets, called *nurdles,* and sold to manufacturers for use in new products.

6. Recycled plastic products are manufactured.

High-quality recycled plastic may be used to make new products like plastic bottles. During manufacturing, recycled plastic is often mixed with new material to increase the quality. Material that isn't good enough for new bottles or containers is made into items like polyester car mats, clothing, or duvet stuffing.

7. The recycled plastic products are purchased and used.

The plastic product is delivered to the store and placed on the shelf, ready for you to buy and use. Once it reaches the end of its useful life, the process starts over again.

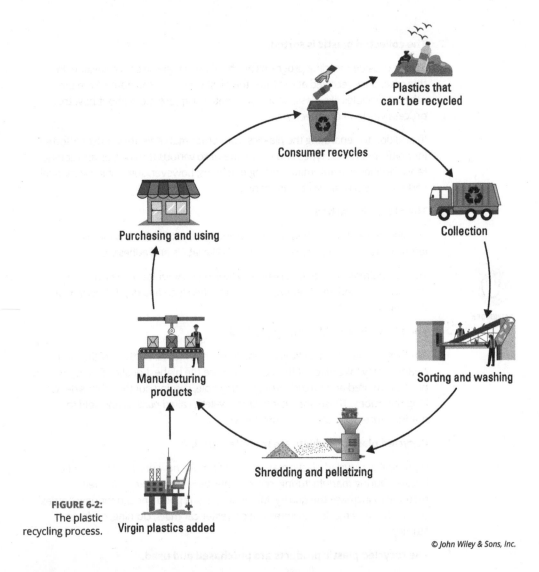

FIGURE 6-2:
The plastic
recycling process.

Plastics that
can't be recycled

Consumer recycles

Collection

Purchasing and using

Sorting and washing

Manufacturing
products

Shredding and pelletizing

Virgin plastics added

© John Wiley & Sons, Inc.

Figuring Out Why All Plastics
Can't Be Recycled

It's not just consumers who have a hard time with plastic recycling. The waste
industry faces many challenges when it comes to collecting and sorting plastics.
It's a complicated business with a huge variety of plastic packaging discarded
daily.

All plastics can technically be recycled, but whether they are actually recycled depends on the infrastructure, collecting methods, and accessibility to an end market. Plastic collection, sorting, and processing are pricey undertakings. Those expenses may never be recovered if there's no end market for the commodities.

REMEMBER

Each government area limits the type of plastic collected based on the infrastructure available for recycling and the potential of an end market. As a result, some areas accept only certain types of plastic, like plastic #1 and #2, through curbside programs. The more you and I can follow the rules and recycle only what is accepted, the easier the job will be for the waste processors. With any luck, things will change in the near future as demand grows for recycled content in new products.

TIP

Keep an eye out for specialist recyclers for hard-to-recycle plastics who might offer a pickup or drop-off location. For example, my local curbside recycling doesn't accept expanded polystyrene foam. However, I've found a recycling center that does take it. I collect my polystyrene for a few months, then head to the recycling center and drop it off.

Knowing What Plastic Items Can and Can't Be Recycled

With the vast range of plastics in our lives and no real guarantee they'll be labeled correctly, it's no doubt we are all confused. Here I try to break it down and help you make sense of the rules.

REMEMBER

Okay, so there are three fundamental questions that will help you identify plastic and decide whether it can be recycled in your curbside recycling. They are as follows:

>> **Is the plastic rigid or soft?** The first thing to appreciate is that plastic packaging comes in two forms, rigid and soft. Making this distinction is essential because the collection processes and recycling of rigid and soft plastics differ significantly.

>> **What's the plastic number?** The second step is to identify the type of plastic using the Resin Identification Codes. This code is handy for identifying everyday packaging and determining whether your local curbside recycling service accepts it.

>> **Is it accepted in my local area?** Finally, you must always check what is accepted by your local town or city. For example, some areas are not as focused on the plastic number but will describe the types of items you can put in.

These questions should help you recycle most of the plastic packaging you handle daily. The following sections provide more detailed information to help you work it out.

REMEMBER

There will be situations where you cannot find the answer to all of these questions. In this case, putting the packaging in the general waste bin is okay. I understand this can be hard to do. We all want to recycle as much as we can, but by keeping these unidentified pieces of plastic out of your recycling, you are helping to minimize contamination and increase the chances the other items will get recycled.

Recognizing rigid and soft plastics

So how do you work out whether a piece of plastic packaging is rigid or soft? Here's a short description and some quick tests to help you do this:

» **Rigid plastics:** Any plastic packaging item that's relatively inflexible and holds its shape when squeezed and pressed. It is molded into a form and does not give way or collapse easily. A great example is a shampoo bottle. It's firm and strong enough to stand up on its own, and when you squeeze it, it bounces back into shape. Rigid plastics might also be referred to as hard or firm plastics.

» **Soft plastics:** Made from thin and flexible plastic and may be referred to as flexible plastics or films. When you squeeze or crumple them, they scrunch up into a ball and don't always bounce back into shape. Examples include plastic bags, chip packets, pasta packets, plastic wrap, zip-top bags, freezer bags, soup pouches, and bubble wrap.

WARNING

Soft plastics don't belong in the majority of curbside recycling bins. The mechanical systems at recycling facilities are designed for hard materials, so soft items tend to get caught. They get wound up and stuck in the conveyor belts and other moving parts, leading to shutdowns. It can be unsafe for the facility staff to remove these hazards, a task which has to be done by hand, climbing up on the equipment and using a box cutter to remove them. Plus, there's the expense of shutting down the facility while the contamination is carefully removed.

TIP

Some curbside recycling services are starting to introduce soft plastic collection, but it's still safe to assume that soft plastics cannot go in your curbside unless you're instructed otherwise. The good news is you can recycle them through a specialist recycling service. It's relatively accessible because they have drop-off bins in many well-known stores. You can find out more about how to recycle your soft plastics in Chapter 11.

Using the plastic Resin Identification Codes

Identifying the type of plastic helps you be confident that you're putting the correct plastic into your curbside bin. The best way to differentiate between the most common types of plastics that you come across day to day is to use the Resin Identification Codes. You may already be familiar with this set of codes. It's also called the Polymer Identification Codes, plastic identification tool, or plastic by numbers.

TECHNICAL STUFF

The plastic Resin Identification Codes were created in the late 1980s by the U.S. Society of the Plastics Industry. Their purpose was to establish consistency and to help manufacturers and recycling facilities identify the various types of plastic. The Resin Identification Codes categorize plastics into seven groups. Groups one through six represent the most common plastics, at least those prevalent during the codes' development. Group seven was a catchall for any other plastics that didn't fit into the first six groups.

REMEMBER

Not all plastics are recyclable. Just because a product displays a Resin Identification Code doesn't mean that the product is recyclable or accepted by your curbside recycling service. The main problem is the chasing arrow symbol around the number, based on the Mobius loop symbol used to represent recycling. This leads many consumers to assume that any item with a resin code is recyclable, but unfortunately that's not the case. Some other issues with the Resin Identification Code include the following:

>> The resin code is voluntary, so not every plastic product will display it.

>> The codes don't distinguish between rigid and soft plastics. As I explain in the previous section, plastics are made into both rigid packaging and soft, flexible packaging. These have different collection and recycling processes.

TIP

New labeling has been developed that goes one step further in identifying the recyclable and nonrecyclable materials in packaging. I encourage you to look for these labels and use them to help determine what can and can't be recycled. In Chapter 5, I explain these new recycling labels and how to use them.

Now let's look at each of the seven types of plastics in more detail. In Table 6-1, I provide descriptions and examples of each and discuss whether they are recyclable.

Figure 6-3 condenses the information in Table 6-1 into an easy reference guide. Be sure to check the later sections on what goes in and what stays out, once you are familiar with the different plastics.

TABLE 6-1 **The Plastic Resin Identification Codes and Their Meanings**

Plastic Code	Description and recycling instructions
Plastic #1 PET	**Polyethylene terephthalate (PET or PETE):** One of the most widespread plastics you'll encounter is identified by the number 1 in the chasing arrows. It's lightweight but strong, providing an excellent protective barrier for liquids and foods. PET is used in both soft and rigid products. Many everyday items are made from PET. You'll be most familiar with plastic water bottles. Still, many other packaging items in your kitchen and bathroom, like shampoo and conditioner bottles, condiment bottles, and food containers, will be made from PET. You might not know that many of your clothes, household linens, and furnishings are also made with PET plastic. Plastic #1 is one of the most commonly accepted plastics in curbside recycling. If your local area accepts plastic, they'll likely take plastic #1, but only packaging items.
Plastic #2  HDPE	**High-density polyethylene (HDPE):** HDPE is stiff, strong, and durable and is recognized by the number 2 in the chasing arrows. It's often used for packaging because it has good chemical resistance, meaning it won't react with the foods stored inside. HDPE, which encompasses both soft and hard plastics, is frequently used in packaging and other items. Juice, milk, shampoos, conditioners, and other household cleaning supplies are packaged in plastic #2. Additionally, it's frequently used in soft plastics like bread bags, cereal box liners, and plastic supermarket bags. But you'll also find it used in other applications such as in kids' toys, outdoor furniture, and electrical insulation. Plastic #2 is the second most commonly accepted plastic in curbside recycling programs. Use the check sheet in Figure 6-4 to record whether your local area accepts plastic #2 packaging.
Plastic #3 PVC	**Polyvinyl chloride (PVC):** Although we've moved beyond the crazy styles of the '80s, PVC, or polyvinyl chloride, is used in many other objects. PVC is widely used because, as with many plastics, it's strong, lightweight, durable, resistant to chemicals, and inexpensive to make. Identified by the number 3 in the chasing arrows, you'll find PVC in construction materials like vinyl flooring, window frames, gutters, and plumbing pipes. It's also used in automobile parts, hospital supplies, sporting equipment like footballs, and some outdoor gear like raincoats and camping gear. Curbside recycling rarely accepts items made from plastic #3. So, try to avoid it altogether if you can.

Plastic Code	Description and recycling instructions
Plastic #4 **LDPE**	**Low-density polyethylene (LDPE):** Another durable, strong, and useful plastic LDPE is identified by the number 4 in the chasing arrows. It's frequently used in food and product packaging. In its rigid form, you might find it used to package condiments in the form of squeezable bottles. As a soft, flexible plastic, it's used in sandwich bags, frozen food bags, cling wrap, and grocery bags. Recycling of plastic #4 packaging materials has moderate acceptance throughout curbside recycling services.
Plastic #5 **PP**	**Polypropylene (PP):** Identified by the number 5 in the chasing arrows symbol, PP has similar properties to PET, HDPE, and LDPE in that it's strong, durable, lightweight, and doesn't react with chemicals. One of the most common packaging items made from PP is yogurt containers. It's also used in disposable cups, plates, straws, take-out containers, condiment bottles, plastic lids, and plant pots. In its flexible form, PP is used in diapers, rope, banknotes, and cereal box liners, to name a few. Plastic #5 packaging is recyclable and is accepted in many curbside programs.
Plastic #6 **PS**	**Polystyrene (PS):** This plastic is identified by the number 6 in the chasing arrows. Many polystyrene items aren't clearly labeled with this number, but they have quite unique characteristics that make them easy to identify. The most common kind of polystyrene is expanded polystyrene (EPS). It's also commonly referred to as Styrofoam, a trademarked polystyrene brand. You'll recognize it as the white foam blocks that look like a whole load of beanbag beans stuck together. EPS is pretty handy stuff, especially when it comes to protecting our purchases during transit. Packing peanuts, meat trays, egg cartons, disposable coffee cups, take-out containers (particularly the clamshell variety), and beer coolers are all made from EPS. Plastic #6 can also be found in rigid plastic products like cutlery, rulers, coat hangers, and some toys. Curbside recycling sometimes accepts plastic #6 in rigid packaging, but it's rarely accepted in its expanded form.

(continued)

TABLE 6-1 (continued)

Plastic Code	Description and recycling instructions
Plastic #7  OTHER	**Plastic #7 or all other plastics:** This group is a catchall for all types of plastics that don't fit into the six groups listed earlier. It includes plastics that have very different characteristics from each other and even includes bioplastics and biodegradable plastics. Some examples of plastics in this group include the following: • Polycarbonates (PC): Used in baby bottles, sports safety equipment, medical devices, automobile parts, and the housing for power tools. • Acrylonitrile butadiene styrene (ABS): The most notable item made from ABS is Lego bricks, but it's also found in other toys, computer keyboards, and power tool housing. • Acrylic: Also known as plexiglass, acrylic is used in many products ranging from aquariums, greenhouses, plexiglass windows, and furniture. • Polylactic acid (PLA): A biodegradable plastic made from cornstarch or sugar cane. Items made with PLA include take-out containers, takeaway cups, and utensils. • Nylon: Primarily recognized for its use as a fabric, it's also commonly used in ropes, threads, and car tires, and can be used in furniture. • Any other plastic you can think of that isn't listed in plastic #1 through #6; there are too many to list them all here. This group of plastics presents a challenge for recyclers who need to know exactly what a product is made of in order to process it at their plant. The more ambiguous it is, the higher the chance the recycler won't want to accept it. Some towns and cities now accept all rigid plastic packaging regardless of what sort of plastic it is. But unless you live in one of these areas, your plastic #7 packaging will most likely have to go in the general waste bin.

PET	HDPE	PVC	LDPE	PP	PS	OTHER
Polyethylene terephthalate	High density polyethylene	Polyvinyl chloride	Low density polyethylene	Polypropylene	Polystyrene	Other
Recyclable	Recyclable	Find a specialist recycler	Find a specialist recycler	Recyclable	Find a specialist recycler	Not easily recyclable

FIGURE 6-3: A quick guide to plastic resin codes and what can and cannot be recycled.

* Check with your local town or city government to confirm which plastics are accepted in your recycling bin or at a local specialist recycling drop-off point.

© John Wiley & Sons, Inc.

Often an item doesn't show a plastic resin code at all. In this case, you can check whether there is a recycling label on the packaging to help you (see Chapter 5 to get to know recycling labels). If there's no recycling logo, you can also check your local government website to see whether they've listed the specific product. If you cannot find any information to help you determine whether the item is recyclable, don't be afraid to place it in your general waste bin. It's better to send an item to a landfill than to contaminate other recyclables.

Asking about the local plastic rules

Recycling rules for plastic can vary significantly from place to place, but you can look for some common rules. Once you're familiar with these rules, you just need to understand what goes in and stays out, and before you know it, you'll be a pro recycler. Once you've read through these sections, try the handy checklist in Figure 6-4 later in this chapter to record your local rules.

Here are the typical rules that you might encounter in your local area:

>> **Does my local area accept soft plastics?** It's safe to assume that your local area doesn't accept soft plastic. However, keep an eye out when checking with your local government. A few places can now separate soft and hard plastics and may accept both. Some locations in Australia and Canada are trialing soft plastics in curbside recycling.

Recheck the rules in your local area every six months to keep abreast of changes and updates.

>> **What plastic resin codes does my local area accept?** The second most important rule to understand when recycling plastics is what types of plastic are accepted. There are two possible options:

- Your curbside service accepts all rigid plastics, no matter what resin code they are.

- Your curbside service accepts only specific plastic numbers — for example, only #1 or only #1 and #2.

It's important to know which plastics are accepted so you don't inadvertently contaminate your recycling. Just because there is a number with the chasing arrows symbol on the item doesn't mean it's accepted for recycling.

>> **Should I flatten my plastic bottles?** Some places require you to flatten your plastic bottles. There's no need to go overboard, but squashing your plastic bottles makes more room in your bin and in the collection trucks transporting them to a recycling facility.

» **Plastic caps on or off?** Plastic bottle caps are regularly.made from plastic #2, #4, or #5. As I note in Chapter 5, bottle caps are too small to be picked up by most recycling machinery. This is a problem, especially considering that bottle caps are one of the top 10 items found in beach cleanups. Many towns and cities now recommend that you place the cap back onto the bottle so it gets picked up in the recycling process. The lids are separated from the bottles once they reach the recycling plants.

WARNING

Check this rule with your local city or town because some locations still don't accept plastic bottle caps. In fact, some areas specifically request that you don't put bottle caps or tops back on bottles. The type of machinery set up at the facility will determine whether they accept caps on or off.

TIP

If this is the case, you can look for specialist recycling programs for plastic caps. A few examples are Green Tree Plastics, which runs a bottle-tops-to-bench-seats program for schoolchildren (www.greentreeplastics.com/abc-program/); milk bottle top recycling in the United Kingdom (www.ghsrecycling.co.uk/charity-scheme/); Lids4Kids in Australia (www.lids4kids.org.au); or you can find a local Precious Plastic business that might take them (https://community.preciousplastic.com/map).

» **Is black plastic accepted?** The problem with black plastic is you can't remove the pigment during recycling. When mixed with other colored plastics, black plastic can lower overall quality and affect the material's resale value. So recycling facilities prefer to keep black plastic out of recycling.

Meat trays, take-out coffee lids, plant pots, and several e-waste items often use black plastic. Fortunately, many businesses and supermarkets are replacing black plastic packaging with more recyclable clear and lighter-colored packaging.

Assume that black plastic isn't accepted in your curbside recycling unless you find out otherwise.

TIP

Garden items made from black plastic, like plant pots and seedling trays, can often be returned to garden centers for reuse or recycling.

REMEMBER

Try to keep contamination to a minimum. If you're unsure whether you can recycle an item, it's best to leave it out.

Following a few guidelines for plastic

Here are my top tips for recycling your plastic:

» **Only place packaging in your recycling bin.** Curbside recycling services are generally set up to accept only packaging materials like jars, bottles, and containers. Many other objects in our homes are made from plastic, but recycling centers cannot process them. Stick to recycling your plastic packaging, and you'll be on your way to becoming an expert recycler.

>> **Make sure everything is clean and dry.** Remove any foods and liquids from your plastic containers and rinse and dry them. This will prevent foods and liquids from contaminating other recyclables like paper and keeps your recycling sanitary during storage and transport. A quick rinse should be enough.

>> **Separate all parts that aren't plastic.** I mention in Chapter 5 that separating different types of materials is important whenever possible. If there are metal or glass parts to a plastic item, separate them before placing them in your curbside bin. See the respective chapters on glass, paper, metals, and multi-layer materials in Part 2 for more information on what can and can't be recycled.

TIP

Many plastic bottles for cleaning or personal care products are sold with pumps and spray tops. These items typically contain metal components, so most curbside recycling services don't accept them. You'll have to toss these items in your general waste bin. Try to avoid bottles with sprays or pumps whenever possible. If that's not possible, you can reuse the pumps or sprays on new bottles or look for refills. A few specialist recycling programs like TerraCycle (www.terracycle.com) will accept pumps and spray tops. Or better still, why not look into refill programs like Loop (www.exploreloop.com/shop/us), Neat (www.neatclean.com/), or Zero Co (www.zeroco.com.au/)?

>> **Leave labels on bottles.** Most labels get cleaned off during the recycling process, so there's no need to remove them. If you have time and can peel them off relatively easily, this will only help.

>> **Remove soft plastics where possible.** Some packaging items have a removable jacket of soft plastics with the product name and information printed on it. These are called shrink-sleeves and are usually used for marketing and information purposes. Some brands are now starting to include a perforated area on the sleeve, encouraging consumers to tear and remove them. Remove this jacket and recycle it with your soft plastics. See Chapter 11 for more information on recycling soft plastics.

Knowing what plastic goes in

Keep in mind while recycling your plastics that curbside recycling programs are intended only for packaging. Here I provide many examples of what goes in your recycling bin, but this isn't an exhaustive list. You'll come across other packaging items that aren't listed. After you've mastered the difference between rigid and soft plastics and can identify the resin codes, you're well equipped to figure out whether an item can or cannot go in your recycling bin.

Note the three key questions described earlier in this chapter: Is the plastic rigid or soft? What's the plastic number? And is it accepted in my local area?

Food or beverage plastic bottles and containers from your kitchen can typically go into the recycling bin. These containers and tubs, presented in Table 6-2, are typically made from plastics #1, #2, #4, or #5.

TABLE 6-2   **What Items Typically Go in Your Curbside Bin: Food and Beverage Plastic Containers**

Item	Examples of Items Accepted (Always Check Your Local Rules)
	Plastic bottles for • Soft drinks • Water • Juice • Milk
	Plastic containers for • Yogurt • Margarine • Spreads • Salad dressing or mayonnaise • Ice cream (plastic tubs only; see Chapter 10 for more information on paper-based ice cream containers)
	Squeezable plastic bottles including • Chutney containers • Mustard bottles • Tomato sauce bottles
	Plastic tubs, trays, and containers including • Clear plastic egg cartons • Clear plastic take-out containers

Nonfood plastic bottles, containers, and tubs from your kitchen, bathroom, or laundry can also go in. Examples are provided in Table 6-3. Similar to food packaging, they're frequently made from plastic #1, #2, #4, or #5, but may also be plastics #6 or #7.

TABLE 6-3

What Items Typically Go in Your Curbside Bin: Nonfood Plastic Bottles, Containers, and Tubs

Item	Examples of Items Accepted (Always Check Your Local Rules)
	Bottles for • Cleaning products • Shampoo and conditioners • Body wash • Cosmetics • Prescription medicine
	Tubs or containers for • Cleaning products • Cosmetics

TIP

If a bottle contains hazardous chemicals, it will need to be handled carefully and may not go in your curbside recycling bin; see Chapter 14.

Keeping some plastic items out

Table 6-4 is a list of the items that cannot be recycled in your curbside recycling bin. I recommend that you look for a specialist recycler wherever possible. You can find some great ideas in Part 3.

TABLE 6-4

What Plastic Items Stay Out of Your Curbside Bin

Item	Description of Items
	Plastic bags and soft plastics: • **Plastic bags:** You cannot put plastic bags in your curbside bin, either loose or to hold your recyclables, unless specifically directed to. Plastic bags can't be separated easily at most recycling facilities and get tangled in their machines. • **Other soft plastics:** Soft plastics like pasta packets, zip-top bags, bread bags, produce bags, and bubble wrap cannot go in your curbside recycling bin. You can recycle your soft plastics at drop-off locations in supermarkets and other stores in many countries. In Chapter 11, I reveal how to recycle your plastic bags and soft plastics.

(continued)

TABLE 6-4 *(continued)*

Item	Description of Items
	Plastic cups, cutlery, and plates:
	• **Coffee cups:** Coffee cups come in many different shapes and sizes. They're usually made from plastic-coated paper and can't be recycled through your curbside service, nor can the plastic lid.
	• **Plastic cutlery:** Plastic cutlery is too small for the sorting machines at recycling plants. It either falls through or gets stuck. Avoid plastic cutlery if you can, and buy your own reusable cutlery.
	• **Plastic cups and plastic plates:** They're made from a variety of plastics, but more often they're made from rigid polystyrene, plastic #6. They're also too lightweight for recycling machines to sort them. Most curbside services won't accept them, so plastic cups and plates usually go in your general waste bin.
	Many companies are replacing plastic coffee cups, plates, and cutlery with biodegradable or compostable options. Keep in mind that biodegradable and compostable plastics often cannot be recycled in curbside recycling bins either.
	Plastic straws: Commonly made from plastic #5, straws are too small and lightweight to be sorted and separated at the recycling plant. Say no to straws or buy a reusable one to carry with you.
	Clamshell take-out containers: These Styrofoam containers are generally white, foamlike, and made from plastic #6. They are rarely accepted in curbside recycling. These days many take-out containers are made from cardboard. But beware, the cardboard ones are often coated in plastic, so they don't absorb the food and therefore can't always be recycled with your paper.
	Polystyrene (Styrofoam) foam: It's safe to assume that items made from expanded polystyrene, like the white foam packaging from deliveries and packing peanuts, cannot be recycled in the majority of curbside recycling services. A few locations accept it, but it's best to search for a specialist recycler.
	Plastic toothbrushes: Toothbrushes don't belong in curbside recycling bins. Look for specialist recycling like the Colgate TerraCycle recycling program.
	Plastic toys: Most toys are made from more than one type of plastic or have metal and other parts. This makes them extremely difficult to recycle. Curbside recycling services can't handle them.
	Toys that are in good condition can be sold, donated to charity, or given away through a local Buy Nothing group.

Item	Description of Items
	Plastic coat hangers: They're usually made from plastic #6 and cannot be recycled in your curbside bin. Look for ways to reuse or avoid buying them and buy metal ones that are recyclable via a metal scrapyard.
	Polyester and nylon clothing: Most of our clothing is made of plastic, like polyester, produced from plastic #1. Even though they're plastic, recycling facilities cannot process them. In fact, they can be a dangerous contaminant and, like plastic bags, can get stuck in the sorting machines and cause plant shutdowns. If you want to find out what to do with your old clothes, head to Chapter 14.
	Plastic household goods: You might be wondering whether you can recycle some smaller plastic items from your kitchen or bathroom, like a plastic spatula or toilet brush. Unfortunately, you typically can't recycle these items in curbside bins.
	First, it's tough to work out what type of plastic they're made from. Many items don't display the Resin Identification Code. And second, they are commonly made from more than one plastic type or have metal parts. Try to use these items as long as possible, but once you're done with them, they must go in your general waste bin.
	Plastic face masks: A regular part of our lives now, plastic disposable face masks shouldn't be disposed of in your recycling bin. They belong in your general waste bin.
	Bioplastics, biodegradable and compostable plastics: Bioplastic made from plant materials cannot go in your curbside recycling bin. Neither can biodegradable plastic or compostable plastic. All three types can contaminate conventional plastics, so they belong in your general waste bin. If you're lucky enough to have access to a commercial composting service, they may accept your biodegradable and compostable plastics, but be sure to check with them. If you have a home compost, look out for items labeled as "home compostable"; you can find out more in Chapter 12.

Checking on a few unusual plastic items

In many situations, some locations accept an item, but other areas don't. I list a few examples in Table 6-5, and it's important that you check whether your local curbside service accepts the item.

TABLE 6-5

What Plastic Items to Check with Your Local City or Town

Item	Description of items
?	**Juice and milk cartons, Tetra Pak, or long-life cartons:** Food packaging like Tetra Paks and cartons could easily be confused with plastic because they usually have an outer coating of plastic. They are, in fact, made from multiple materials, including paper, plastic, and sometimes foil. For more information on what to do with multilayer packaging, head to Chapter 10.
?	**Plastic meat trays:** Recyclability depends on the type of plastic used for the meat tray. • White meat trays: Trays made from white plastic foam are usually made from plastic #6, polystyrene. Curbside recycling facilities usually cannot process this type of plastic. • Black foam trays: Black trays are rarely accepted by curbside recycling. The dark color makes it hard for sorting machines to detect them, increasing the risk of contamination with other recyclables. • Clear meat trays: Normally made from plastic #1, PET, which is accepted by most curbside programs. Curbside services usually accept these type of trays. This is a great example of how you can make a difference when shopping. Try to buy clear meat trays instead of black or white foam trays and it'll help reduce your impact. Discover more shopping ideas later in this chapter.
?	**Cookie or biscuit trays:** The plastic in biscuit trays is very thin and so might be confused for soft plastic. Sometimes they don't bounce back when scrunched. However, most soft plastic recyclers don't take them. These trays and other similar plastics like fruit punnets (baskets) are sometimes accepted in your curbside recycling bin, but it depends on your area, so you need to check.

Pulling it all together

In Figure 6-4, I provide a checklist to help you make sense of your plastic recycling and record all the rules that apply in your area.

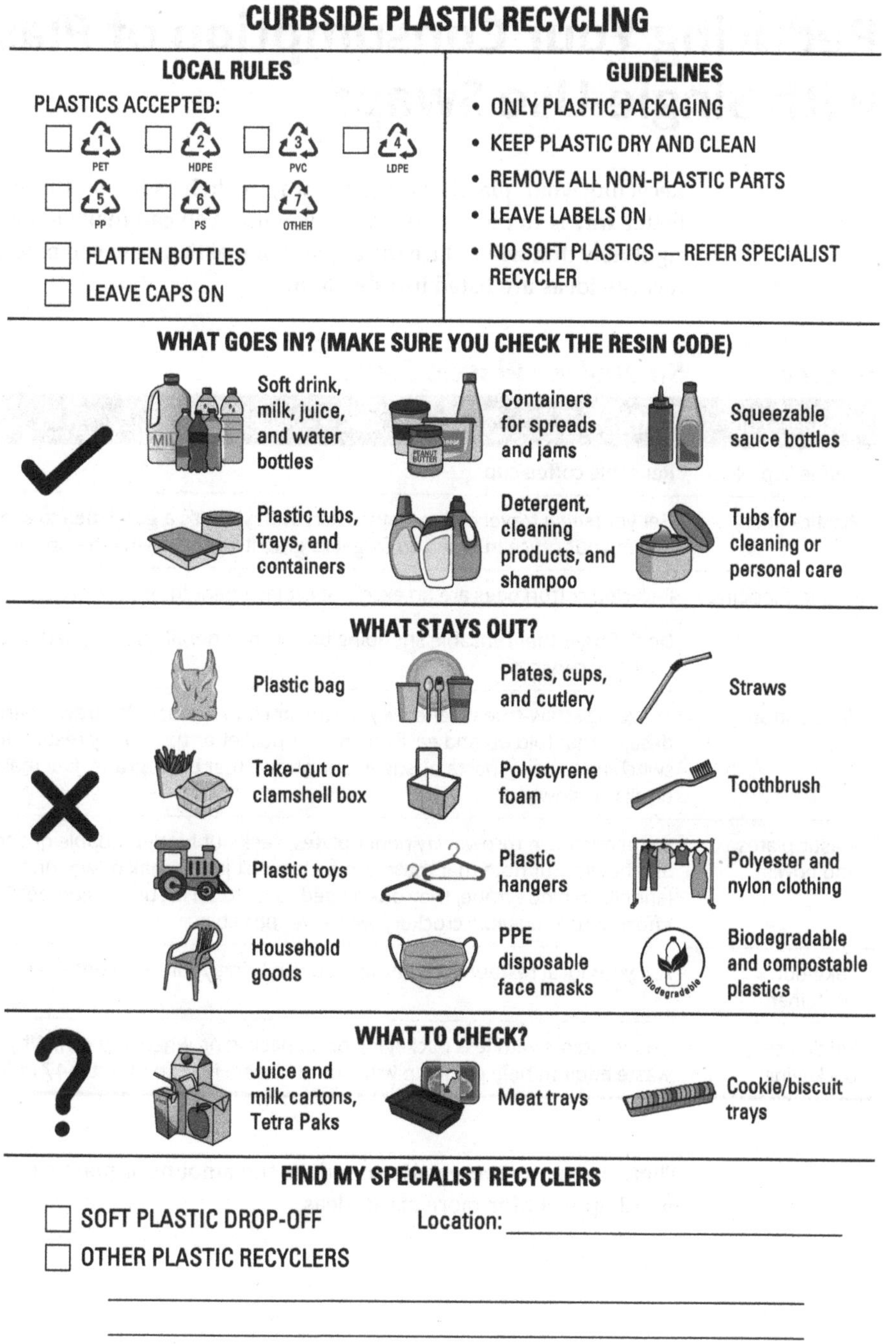

CURBSIDE PLASTIC RECYCLING

LOCAL RULES

PLASTICS ACCEPTED:

☐ ♲ 1 PET ☐ ♲ 2 HDPE ☐ ♲ 3 PVC ☐ ♲ 4 LDPE

☐ ♲ 5 PP ☐ ♲ 6 PS ☐ ♲ OTHER

☐ FLATTEN BOTTLES

☐ LEAVE CAPS ON

GUIDELINES

- ONLY PLASTIC PACKAGING
- KEEP PLASTIC DRY AND CLEAN
- REMOVE ALL NON-PLASTIC PARTS
- LEAVE LABELS ON
- NO SOFT PLASTICS — REFER SPECIALIST RECYCLER

WHAT GOES IN? (MAKE SURE YOU CHECK THE RESIN CODE)

✔

Soft drink, milk, juice, and water bottles

Containers for spreads and jams

Squeezable sauce bottles

Plastic tubs, trays, and containers

Detergent, cleaning products, and shampoo

Tubs for cleaning or personal care

WHAT STAYS OUT?

✘

Plastic bag

Plates, cups, and cutlery

Straws

Take-out or clamshell box

Polystyrene foam

Toothbrush

Plastic toys

Plastic hangers

Polyester and nylon clothing

Household goods

PPE disposable face masks

Biodegradable and compostable plastics

WHAT TO CHECK?

?

Juice and milk cartons, Tetra Paks

Meat trays

Cookie/biscuit trays

FIND MY SPECIALIST RECYCLERS

☐ SOFT PLASTIC DROP-OFF   Location: _____

☐ OTHER PLASTIC RECYCLERS

_____

_____

FIGURE 6-4: Plastic recycling worksheet.

© John Wiley & Sons, Inc.

Reducing Your Consumption of Plastic with Single-Use Swaps

Recycling your plastic is a great way to help address the plastic crisis, but a better way is to reduce how much you use. You can make many single-use swaps right now that will reduce the amount of plastic waste you produce right away. My favorite ideas are listed in Table 6-6.

TABLE 6-6   Single-Use Plastic Swaps

Replace This	With This
Coffee cup	Reusable coffee cup
Plastic cutlery	Get yourself a travel cutlery set to carry with you. It's a good idea to keep a set in the car and at your office in case you forget to grab it when leaving the house.
Plastic shopping bags	Recycled cotton bags are an excellent replacement for plastic bags. Don't forget that reusable shopping bags can generally be recycled through soft plastic recycling services.
Plastic straws	Try going straw-free whenever you can, or carry a reusable straw. There are some great designs that fold up and easily fit in your pocket or bag. Many restaurants and bars are switching to using pasta or sugarcane straws that biodegrade. Just make sure you don't drink too slowly!
Plastic plates and bowls	If you must use throwaway paper plates, seek out biodegradable or compostable plates and bowls. But note that these products won't just "break down" on their own or in a landfill. To biodegrade, they often need to go to an industrial composting facility. Make an effort to use reusable crockery whenever possible.
Take-out container	Ask your local restaurant whether you can bring your own container.
Single-use packaging	Choose items with less packaging or no packaging when you can. Why not complete a waste audit to help come up with some ideas? Head to Chapter 17 to find out how.

There are many more ways to reduce the amount of plastic you use. Try checking out Chapter 15 for more great ideas.

Making an Impact with Plastic Items at the Checkout

A vast number of recycled plastic products are available today. Two popular materials used in everyday consumer products are recycled PET and nylon, but many new products are using other plastics like polypropylene toys for kids. Here are some great examples of products you can buy today made from recycled plastic:

>> Clothing made from recycled polyester fabrics, including yoga and sportswear, outdoor gear such as raincoats, ski gear, swimwear, T-shirts, and even socks

>> Accessories like backpacks, luggage, shoes, sunglasses, jewelry, handbags, and phone cases

>> Reusable products, including drink bottles, shopping bags, and produce bags

>> Personal care products like toothbrushes and razors

>> Kids' toys

>> Indoor and outdoor furniture

>> Homewares and kitchenware

>> Dog and cat toys and beds

>> Flower pots, watering cans, and garden edging

>> Many rubbish and recycling bins, composters, and worm farms

TIP

If you would like to find more examples of recycled products, take a look at my recycled brand directory at www.everydayrecycler.com/directory. In Chapter 16, you discover why purchasing recycled goods is a crucial step in your recycling journey.

Chapter **7**

Mastering Paper and Cardboard Recycling

Despite living in an electronic age with many paperless options, we still use a considerable amount of paper. The average person uses six to seven trees' worth of paper every year, equivalent to about 610 pounds (277 kilograms) of paper. The good news is the majority of this paper gets recycled. In fact, paper and cardboard are one of the most widely recycled materials globally. Recycling rates vary from country to country, and many recycle over 60 percent. In the United Kingdom, it's reported to be as high as 80 percent.

That's a pretty good result, especially when compared to plastic recycling (covered in Chapter 6). So why should you keep reading this chapter if we're doing so well at recycling paper? Because there's still 20 to 40 percent not getting recycled, which can be up to millions of tons of paper ending up in landfills. More importantly, as paper degrades, it releases nasty greenhouse gases into the atmosphere.

On the flip side, recycling paper saves trees from being cut down and reduces energy and water consumption. I say we aim for a 100 percent recycling rate for paper and cardboard.

In this chapter, I explain all the resources that go into making paper and cardboard. Then I take you through the benefits of recycling it. Recycling paper and cardboard is straightforward when you break it down into what goes in and what stays out of your curbside bin. So I walk you through some simple rules and list the items you'll need to check with your local town or city. To help, I've even created a handy checklist for you to fill out and record your local rules. Finally, I give you some pointers on going paperless.

Beginning with the Basics: What Is Paper?

You know paper as the thin white sheets onto which we put information like writing or pictures. We use it for documents, reports, books, notepads, newspapers, magazines, and many other items around our homes. Paper stores our written words, allowing us to share information, record love notes, and keep track of our shopping lists.

Humans started writing things down more than 4,000 years ago, and it's played an essential role in human history, particularly in helping us record that history. Today paper is used for more than just record-keeping and recording information; it's a significant component in packaging products and many single-use items.

Paper is typically made from the fibers of cellulose from trees or plants. These fibers give plants their structure and, once separated, are extremely good at bonding with each other when they're dried. This is what forms a sheet of paper, but as you've possibly experienced, once it's wet again, it loses its structure pretty quickly. The following sections describe the resources and steps used to make paper as well as common paper types.

Looking at resources used to make paper

To make paper, you need a source of fiber, water, energy, and a few chemicals to help the process along. Here I take a closer look at the resources necessary to make paper:

>> **A source of cellulose fiber:** Most paper is made from trees, but you can also use plant materials like cotton, bamboo, flax, or hemp. The trees or plants

provide the necessary cellulose fibers required to create paper. (See the nearby sidebar for some fun facts on cellulose.)

>> **Water:** To extract cellulose fibers during papermaking, a great deal of water is required. In fact, without water, it wouldn't be possible to make paper. Fortunately, many paper manufacturers recycle and reuse their water throughout the process.

It takes 10 liters of water to make one single sheet of printer paper.

>> **Energy:** Papermaking is an energy-intensive process. It takes a lot of energy to harvest trees and transport them to the paper mill. Then there's the processing and extraction of cellulose, which also requires a lot of energy.

>> **Chemicals for pulping:** Chemicals are sometimes used in papermaking to break down lignin, the glue that holds the cellulose fibers together. Caustic soda and sodium sulfide are two common compounds used in this procedure.

>> **Chemical additives**: The addition of various chemicals can give paper different properties, like making it brighter or glossy. Paper is also commonly whitened using bleaches like chlorine and hypochlorite. Other additives are used to change the color, increase the paper's strength, or increase its resistance to moisture.

Making new paper

Even though we recycle a lot of paper, a lot of it still goes through a linear process in which the raw ingredients are collected, turned into paper, utilized, and finally thrown away in landfills. Later in this chapter, I go over a more appropriate method: circular rather than linear, reintroducing recycled paper and cardboard into the process.

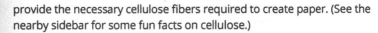

FOCUSING ON CELLULOSE FIBERS

Cellulose is the primary substance that helps plants remain still and upright. Without it, there would be nothing to hold the trees up. It's made up of hundreds of carbon, hydrogen, and oxygen atoms.

Cellulose is also an excellent example of a natural polymer. As I explain in Chapter 6, polymers are large natural or synthetic substances made up of much smaller repeating molecules that join together to form a larger structure. These natural polymers are not only used in paper but can be used to make textiles such as rayon, viscose, and modal.

First, let's go through the steps required to make paper. These steps are illustrated in Figure 7-1.

1. **Trees are logged and transported.**

   Trees are harvested from timber plantations, old-growth forests, or younger forests. They're then transported to a paper mill for processing.

2. **The harvested trees are debarked and chipped.**

   Since the bark of the trees doesn't contain cellulose, it's stripped off. Bark can also introduce contaminants, so removing it is essential. The logs are then chipped into small pieces to aid the pulping process, which is designed to help break down the lignin and extract the cellulose.

3. **The wood chips are pulped.**

   Pulping is designed to break down lignin, the glue that holds the cellulose together. This is facilitated with the help of heat and chemicals, helping to remove the lignin from the wood chips. The end result is a soggy mixture of cellulose, lignin, water, and chemicals called *pulp*.

4. **The pulp is pressed and dried.**

   Next, the pulp is put through a papermaking machine. The name sounds a little like something from a cartoon rather than the sophisticated machine that it is. First, the paper is spread out on a large mesh area to squeeze the water out and align the fibers in one direction. Then the water's pressed out, and the paper is dried as it goes through the rollers in the machine.

5. **The finishing process takes place.**

   The final step is to apply chemicals to improve the quality and durability of the paper and provide particular properties such as brightness, smoothness, or color. It's then cut into size depending on the desired end product.

6. **The finished paper is purchased and used.**

   The finished product can take on a variety of shapes and sizes, including food packaging, books, magazines, and printing paper.

7. **Consumers dispose of the paper.**

   The item gets discarded once we're finished using it. Of course, the bin you toss it into can change the path it takes from here, whether it's recycled or sent to a landfill.

MAKING ENERGY FROM TIMBER WASTE

The waste material from debarking the timber isn't good for papermaking, but it can be used as a biomass energy source. Biomass is a plant-based material that can be used as a fuel source to create heat and electricity. Paper mills capture the excess organic material and convert it into energy to help power the mills. Agricultural waste items like fruit or crops, manure, and even garbage are alternative examples of resources used to produce biomass energy. This process is also commonly used in landfills; they capture the methane gas generated by the decaying material and convert it into energy that can be introduced into the electricity grid.

FIGURE 7-1:
The linear papermaking process.

Logging   Debarking and   Pulping   Pressing and   Finishing   Purchasing   Disposal
chipping   drying   and using

Landfill or incineration

Pollution

© John Wiley & Sons, Inc.

Checking out common types of paper

We've created as many types of paper as there are uses. To meet the different needs, we've changed the basic recipe of paper to make all sorts of products. On a daily basis, you're likely to encounter many types of paper, and here I describe the most common ones:

» **Printing paper:** Also referred to as copy or office paper, this is the standard white general-purpose paper found in homes and offices. The good news is that brands that make printing paper use a large percentage of recycled content; many even use 100 percent.

» **Corrugated cardboard:** Cardboard is referred to as corrugated when it has three layers: two flat outer layers with a corrugated or wavy board in between. You can see this shape by looking at the end of a piece of corrugated cardboard. The middle layer provides strength and a cushion to safeguard the box's contents while the outer layers hold it together. Corrugated cardboard is often made with a high percentage of recycled content, because quality isn't as important.

>> **Paperboard:** Paperboard is simply a thick form of paper that's more than 0.012 inches (0.30 millimeters) in thickness. Examples of products made from paperboard include cereal boxes, shoeboxes, and gift boxes. In some cases, paperboard is coated in plastic; cartons for frozen food are a good example. You can find out more about these multilayer materials in Chapter 10.

>> **Newsprint:** Because news is constantly changing, newspapers are printed on thin, low-cost paper that isn't very durable. This type of paper is generally made from recycled paper and is actually referred to as *newsprint*.

>> **Tissue paper:** Tissue products are soft, thin, pliable, and absorbent paper products. The most common use of tissue paper is for sanitary products like facial tissues, napkins, paper towels, and toilet paper. Tissue papers can be made from recycled paper pulp. They must be highly absorbent and soft; no one wants a scratchy tissue when they're sick with the flu! Interestingly, they must also be quite strong. You might not want a scratchy tissue, but you also don't want a tissue that simply disintegrates in your hands when you blow your nose.

>> **Coated paper:** Coatings are applied to paper for various end uses. Here are some examples:

- **Waxed paper:** The paper is coated with paraffin wax to provide moisture resistance and nonstick properties.

- **Parchment or baking paper:** It has a thin coating of silicon to make it heat resistant for cooking purposes.

- **Paper cups:** These are often made from paper lined with a polyethylene plastic coating to prevent them from leaking or disintegrating when liquid is added.

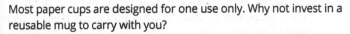

  Most paper cups are designed for one use only. Why not invest in a reusable mug to carry with you?

- **Photographic paper:** The paper used in photographs is coated with chemicals that help print the picture onto the paper. Luckily the popularity of digital cameras and home printing has meant this type of photographic paper isn't as popular today.

- **Receipt paper:** Although plain paper can be used, thermal paper is more frequently used. Thermal paper has a coating made of a substance that, when heated, changes color, making it possible to print receipts without using any ink. Because of the chemicals involved, receipt paper isn't recyclable.

Understanding Why You Should Recycle Paper

The raw materials used to make paper can be recycled and used to make new products up to seven times. However, if you throw that paper in the trash, it won't be recycled and instead will decompose over time, producing harmful greenhouse gases. The choice seems pretty straightforward. Recycling reduces the volume of raw materials needed, keeps resources in use, and saves energy, water, and trees from being cut down.

REMEMBER

Extending the life of paper by recycling has the following great benefits:

>> **Protecting forests:** Forests are a vital part of life on our planet. The many benefits of forests and woodlands include

- Releasing oxygen

- Providing a home and nourishment to many creatures

- Strengthening the ground and reducing erosion

- Increasing absorption of water into the soil

- Reducing air pollution and capturing carbon dioxide

- Cooling down our cities and homes by creating shade

- Bringing beauty into our lives

Harvesting trees is known to reduce the biodiversity in forests, something that can be challenging to recreate with replanting. It can also result in habitat loss, soil degradation and erosion, loss of nutrients, and increased invasive species. And unfortunately, the results of harvesting can stay with an area for a very long time. Recycling can reduce the need for raw resources and our reliance on logging these precious forests. In fact, recycling just one ton of paper can save seventeen trees from being cut down.

>> **Minimizing greenhouse gas emissions:** Recycling paper and cardboard can reduce greenhouse gas emissions and guard against climate change. At their end of life, if not disposed of correctly, paper products can contribute to climate change by emitting methane, a greenhouse gas. Methane is generated along with carbon dioxide when waste paper and cardboard decompose in landfills. Landfills are the United States' third-largest source of methane emissions into the atmosphere.

>> **Decreasing carbon dioxide:** Deforestation increases the volume of greenhouse gases in two ways. First, it releases carbon dioxide into the atmosphere, and second, it removes the ability of those trees to absorb carbon dioxide in the future.

>> **Reducing energy consumption:** The process of recycling paper saves energy when compared with making paper from virgin resources. Apart from the need to collect, sort, and clean the paper, you're also eliminating the energy-intensive processes of logging, debarking, and pulping the timber.

According to the U.S. Environmental Protection Agency (EPA), recycling one ton of paper will save enough energy to power the average American home for six months. That's a lot of power, especially considering that in 2018, 17 million tons of paper and paperboard were sent to landfills in the U.S. and 14 million tons in the United Kingdom. We're throwing energy away!

>> **Lowering water consumption:** You can't make paper without water. The water helps separate the cellulose fibers during the pulping process. Most people don't consider recycling paper as a means of conserving water or other resources. But according to the EPA, when you recycle one ton of paper, you can reduce the amount of water used by more than 50 percent, equivalent to around 7,000 gallons or 26,500 liters of water.

Seeing How Paper Is Recycled

Paper has been successfully recycled for centuries. As far back as 1031, the Japanese used the resources from discarded paper to make new paper. They were already embracing recycling and creating a circular economy. Even though the process used today is on a much bigger scale, it uses principles similar to the original paper recycling process.

Unfortunately, waste paper can go through this process only up to seven times. When paper and cardboard are recycled, they lose their quality because the cellulose fibers break down and become smaller and smaller. Sooner or later, they're too short to be used in new products. As a result, paper is effectively downcycled to lower-quality products. The following sections walk you through paper recycling steps and explain the importance of avoiding contaminants.

Exploring the steps of paper recycling

Recycling paper starts with the collection of discarded materials from consumers and businesses. These materials are sorted, separated, and sent to a processing plant, where they're made into new paper products. The process then starts over again, creating a circular economy. This process can be broken into the following steps and is also presented in Figure 7-2:

1. **Consumers dispose of used paper in their recycling bins.**

   The first step in this procedure is to put your dry, clean paper and cardboard waste in your recycling container.

2. **The discarded paper is collected.**

   Two critical factors affect the collection process: the type of paper and the degree of contamination. If certain types of paper make their way into recycling plants, they can cause problems. Later in this chapter, to help you get this right, I list what items are accepted and what should stay out of your recycling bin.

REMEMBER

   Many things can contaminate discarded paper, such as food scraps, grease, chemicals, and even broken glass. As a result, many collection services ask you to place your paper and cardboard waste in a separate bin or even tie it up in separate bundles. It lowers the risk of contamination and helps ensure your waste gets recycled. I explain the different ways contamination can occur in more detail in the next section.

3. **The collected paper is sorted and separated.**

   After your curbside recycling program has collected the paper, it's transported to a materials recovery facility (MRF). In a single-stream recycling system, paper and cardboard must be separated from other recyclables like plastic, metals, and glass. If you're lucky enough to have a multi-stream recycling system in your area, the paper is already separated and therefore much cleaner.

   Once sorted and baled, the paper is sent to a paper mill. Here further sorting may be undertaken to divide the paper into specific categories. As I note earlier, every time paper gets recycled, it loses quality, so to help maintain the different levels of quality, the facility sorts the paper into categories like corrugated cardboard, high-grade office paper, or newsprint.

4. **The paper is shredded and pulped.**

   The paper is then shredded and mixed with large amounts of water. This mix is loaded into a pulper and stirred to help break down the material.

5. **The pulp is cleaned.**

   Next, contaminants like ink, glue, and even staples are filtered out. It's important to remove these materials to ensure the quality of the pulp and therefore the end product.

TECHNICAL STUFF

   It's pretty fascinating how inks are removed. Air is blown into the pulp mixture, and the ink attaches to the air bubbles that form. As the bubbles rise to the top, they're removed along with the ink.

6. The pulp is pressed and dried.

Finally, the pulp mixture is processed into paper in a similar manner to virgin paper (see the earlier section "Making new paper"). In fact, virgin pulp is often mixed with recycled pulp to increase the quality of the end product. Final products can be made with 100 percent recycled pulp or may have different percentages of recycled content.

7. The new paper is purchased and used.

You, the consumer, purchase a product made from recycled paper or buy a food item packaged in recycled paperboard. Depending on what you decide at the bin, this could be the last step, and the paper goes off to a landfill, or you could start the process again by recycling your paper.

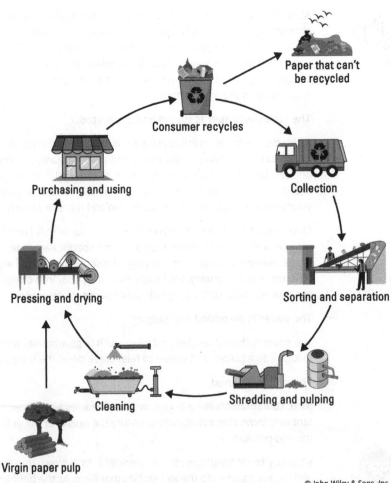

Paper that can't
be recycled

Consumer recycles

Collection

Purchasing and using

Sorting and separation

Pressing and drying

Cleaning

Shredding and pulping

FIGURE 7-2:
The paper
recycling process.

Virgin paper pulp

© John Wiley & Sons, Inc.

TIP

At the checkout, or before when possible, it's a good time to reflect on this process and consider if the product you're purchasing can be recycled.

Keeping paper free from contamination

REMEMBER

Paper must be kept free from contaminants because they can negatively impact the quality of the end product. They may even result in a whole recycling batch being sent to a landfill. Paper is at the greatest risk in single-stream collection systems, where it's exposed to many potential contaminants because it's mixed with other materials to be recycled like glass and plastic. The most common ways paper is contaminated include the following:

>> **Other types of paper:** Many types of paper are unrecyclable, and when mixed with regular paper recycling, it can cause problems. An example is waxed paper; it's coated with paraffin wax to resist moisture, which is great for use in our kitchens but makes it very hard to recycle. The problem is that you can't remove the waxy coating. And if it ends up at a recycling plant, it won't break down in the watery pulp because it's designed to resist water. This type of material can interfere with the quality of the whole batch of recycled paper. (Later in this chapter, I go through all the paper products that can and can't be recycled, so you'll have no trouble keeping contamination to a minimum.)

>> **Foods and liquids:** In Chapter 5, I discuss the importance of emptying containers before putting them in your recycling bin. This applies to all types, including plastic, metal, and glass containers. One of the critical reasons for removing liquids and foods from these containers is to protect paper waste. Beverages and foods can spill out and contaminate the paper in your recycling bin. If paper absorbs them, recycling becomes more difficult and sometimes impossible.

>> **Broken glass:** Small pieces of broken glass can embed themselves into paper and cardboard while collecting and sorting recycling waste. This is a particular problem in single-stream recycling, where multiple materials are tossed into the same bin. And this is one of the reasons why many local areas require you to separate your glass or, in some cases, don't collect it at all. You can find out about glass recycling in Chapter 8.

COMPOSTING YOUR PAPER INSTEAD

Did you know there's another way to dispose of your waste paper? You can compost it. Both paper and cardboard help to absorb excess moisture and circulate air through compost, factors that are essential for a successful compost.

It's important to get to know the different paper types and recognize which ones can and can't go in your compost. In general, you want to avoid paper that is heavily inked or that may be bleached, like many office papers, glossy magazines, and junk mail catalogs. You also want to avoid paper that has been coated or layered with plastics or metals.

Brown paper and corrugated cardboard are usually safe, but ensure you shred them beforehand. Newspaper is also commonly used for composting. The inks are often made from natural soy, so it's also relatively safe. However, be careful with overly white newspapers because they might be bleached.

To find out more about composting as a means to recycle your paper and your food waste, see Chapter 12.

Knowing What Paper Products Can and Can't Be Recycled

Recycling paper and paper products is easy once you get to know the rules. In the following sections, I take you through the standard rules for curbside paper recycling. Then I list the most common paper items you'll encounter and whether they can be recycled.

Asking about local paper rules

REMEMBER

Fortunately, the rules for paper and cardboard recycling are fairly consistent worldwide. There are just two things you need to check in your local area:

>> **Does your local curbside recycling program collect paper?** Most curbside programs will include paper; however, some may not collect it at all. Be sure to check that your local service collects paper and paper products. If you don't have access to curbside recycling, you might need to do some more checking like seeing what's accepted at your nearest recycling center or if your apartment complex has a paper and cardboard bin.

>> **Should you keep your paper separate?** Depending on whether your local service is single-stream or multi-stream, you might be required to separate your paper from your other recyclables. They may even provide a separate bin just for paper. As I explain earlier in this chapter, separating paper recycling from other recycling helps minimize the risk of the different types of contamination.

Following a few guidelines for paper

Here are my top tips for recycling your paper and cardboard:

>> **Keep paper and cardboard recyclables dry.** There are many reasons why wet paper should not be recycled, including these:

- The fibers of cardboard and paper can degrade if they get wet and then dry. It makes them less valuable and harder to recycle.

- Wet paper can get stuck in recycling facility sorting machines, causing costly shutdowns and maintenance costs.

- Wet paper poses a contamination risk for other recyclables.

- Wet materials weigh more, resulting in higher collection and transportation costs for waste material.

That's why it's essential to keep your paper and cardboard dry, and if they're wet, toss them in your general waste bin.

>> **Flatten cardboard boxes where possible.** Flat boxes are more easily sorted at the recycling facility, making them more likely to be sent in the right direction and not to a landfill.

TIP

>> **Ask whether the paper is too small.** If the piece of paper you want to recycle is smaller than a credit card, the machines will likely not pick it up. One way to ensure it gets captured is to place these small pieces inside a paper envelope.

>> **Ask whether the paper is too large.** If the cardboard box you want to recycle is too large to fit into your curbside recycling bin, tear or cut it up into reasonably sized pieces. Not only will it make it easier to fit the cardboard in your bin, but it will also help the cardboard progress through the sorting machines at the recycling facility.

>> **Ensure no food stains or contamination.** Paper or cardboard covered in grease or food can't be recycled and must be tossed into your general waste bin. Food contamination can be hard to clean from the recycled paper pulp mixture and can result in an inferior end product.

>> **Remove other potential contaminants.** Removing sticky tape or staples from paper or cardboard isn't essential; however, if there's an excessive amount, it's helpful if you remove it. I find some delivery boxes covered in so much tape that it's hard to believe there's any cardboard underneath.

TIP

In this situation, I try to remove as much tape as possible. It helps minimize the contaminants during processing and increases the likelihood that the paper will be recycled. It's only a few minutes for me but saves a lot of work at the other end.

>> **Ensure no paint or excessive dirt.** Paper or cardboard covered in paint or that is excessively dirty must go in the general trash bin. For reasons similar to food stains, the contaminants can be tough to remove and may render the whole batch of paper unrecyclable.

>> **Separate any plastic.** Remove any plastic wrapping from magazines, newspapers, or other paper items.

TIP

These definitely don't belong in the paper recycling process; however, you can recycle them with your soft plastics (see Chapter 11).

>> **Check whether the paper is layered with plastic.** Sometimes it can be difficult to work out if a piece of packaging is made from paper, plastic, or both. A lot of packaging uses a combination of materials like paper layered with very thin plastic sheets.

TIP

If it's shiny paper, then it's most likely layered with plastic. A test you can do is to grab the corner and try to tear it. If it tears like paper but has a shiny and smooth exterior, then it's likely a multilayer packaging made from paper and plastic. If it doesn't tear like paper, then it might be a soft plastic. You can recycle soft plastic through specialist recycling services. Chapter 11 explains everything you need to know about recycling your soft plastics, while Chapter 10 explains multilayer materials.

WARNING

Be careful not to unintentionally include plastic packaging, stickers, or paper-based cartons with plastic or metal layers when recycling your paper.

Knowing what paper goes in

In Table 7-1, I list all the paper products that are typically accepted in recycling bins. Be sure to check locally for anything you're unsure about.

TABLE 7-1

What Paper Items Go in Your Curbside Bin

Item	Description of items
	White or colored office paper: Used for printing, reports, and other communications in offices, office paper is usually white but is also available in various colors. It's made from a higher-quality fiber than newspapers or packaging, and recycling it to capture the materials and keep them in use is important.
	Cardboard boxes and packaging: Delivery boxes, shipping boxes, and Amazon boxes can all be recycled in your curbside bin. Flatten them before you recycle them and cut them into smaller pieces if they're enormous.
	Paperboard packaging: Boxes used to package cereals or other foods are recyclable. Simply flatten them and place them in your curbside bin. Remember to remove any plastic liners and recycle those separately with your soft plastics; I explain more in Chapter 11. If it's freezer packaging, see the later section "Checking on a few unusual paper items."
NEWS	**Newspapers:** Be sure to remove any plastic wrapping from newspapers before recycling them (see Chapter 11).
	Brown paper and paper bags: Be careful to recycle only brown paper. Waxed paper like baking paper, parchment paper, butcher paper, and deli paper are all coated with wax or silicone and can't be recycled. Paper bags should be okay as long as they are clean and dry.
	Cardboard egg cartons: Egg cartons are made from cardboard, clear plastic, or plastic polystyrene. Here I'm referring to the ones made from cardboard. How can you tell? The cardboard ones have a pulpy look to them, a bit like papier-mâché. If any eggs get broken, or the egg carton is wet or soiled, it goes in your general waste bin.
	Magazines, junk mail, and catalogs: Remove any plastic wrapping. Removing staples isn't necessary because they will be removed in the recycling process. Have you considered a digital copy of your favorite magazine? Or check whether you can opt out of getting marketing material sent to your home. It's a great way to reduce your paper consumption.
	Pizza boxes: There was a lot of media buzz about pizza boxes not being recyclable a while back. This was confusing for many people because they're made from cardboard, yet many said you couldn't recycle them. Well, you can rest assured your pizza boxes can be recycled; you simply need to apply common sense regarding any food contamination. In most cases a small grease stain is okay, but if it's covered in cheese or wet with oil, you must toss it in the general waste bin. You can recycle the lid separately by tearing it off. If you have a curbside compost service, they may take any wet and greasy cardboard.
	Product packaging like those for phones or computers: Many products come in paperboard or cardboard packaging. Remember to remove any parts that are not cardboard, like foam inserts or plastic bags, and then flatten the box before placing it in your recycling bin.

Keeping some paper items out

Figuring out what doesn't belong in your recycling bin is just as essential as knowing what goes in. Table 7-2 lists all the paper items that typically stay out of your curbside recycling bin.

TABLE 7-2   **What Paper Items Stay Out of Your Curbside Bin**

Item	Description of items
	Baking or parchment paper: Paper used for baking and other food-related activities such as baking paper, parchment paper, butcher paper, and deli paper is treated to make it greaseproof, waterproof, or even heatproof. For example, parchment paper is coated with silicon to give it heat resistance and to make it nonstick. Because of this treatment, these paper types can't be recycled. Reduce your use if you can or find alternatives like silicon baking sheets.
	Disposable paper cups: Paper or coffee cups are made from liquid paperboard, which is a mix of paper and plastic, making them difficult to recycle. These are virtually never accepted in your curbside recycling. Avoid them if you can, and carry your own reusable cup.
	Paper towels and napkins: Every time wood fibers are recycled, they get shorter and shorter. Sooner or later, they're too short to be used again. Although they don't belong in your curbside recycling bin, composting paper towels and napkins is a great way to dispose of them. You can find out more about composting in Chapter 12.
	Tissues: Similar to paper towels, tissue fibers are too short for recycling. However, the real reason is that nobody wants to recycle your snotty tissues. Keep used tissues out of your recycling bin. They definitely belong in your general waste bin. (Oh, but don't forget to recycle the cardboard box.)
	Receipt paper: Even though receipts are made from paper, they can't be recycled. This is because many of them are made from thermal paper, a type of paper coated with plastic to make printing easier. Although some receipts use plain paper, it's pretty hard to figure out which ones are which, especially at a recycling facility, so they all must go in your general waste bin.
	Photos: Although printed on paper, photographs have been treated with chemicals and can have a plastic coating. As a result, they're not recyclable, and placing them in your curbside recycling bin will contaminate the other paper recycling. If you no longer want to keep the memory, your old photos must go into the general waste bin.

Item	Description of items
	Gift wrapping paper: Even though we call it wrapping paper, many gift wraps don't have any paper in them at all. Only plain wrapping paper that tears like paper and has no embellishments like glitter or a glossy coating can be recycled. Most glossy and shiny paper-like plastic cellophane or metallic-look wrapping paper belongs in your general rubbish bin. Wrapping paper covered in tape, ribbons, bows, glitter, or other decorations also belongs in the trash. All of these materials can contaminate recycled paper.
	Stickers: Stickers cannot be recycled because they have an adhesive layer on them. In fact, many stickers have a plastic coating or are made completely from plastic.
	Paper plates: Paper plates come in many different shapes and sizes and are created from many different materials. Some are made from plain paper, while others have a wax or plastic coating that helps stop them from absorbing food. Most places don't accept paper plates because of the coating but also because they're often covered with food.

Checking on a few unusual paper items

Table 7-3 is a list of paper items that your local curbside recycling service may or may not accept. Rules can vary from place to place depending on the equipment available and end-market options at the recycling facility. In the next section, I provide a handy checklist you can use to record which items are accepted in your area.

REMEMBER

Look for your local town or city recycling information online or give them a call to check the rules. You can discover how to locate your local information and other helpful resources in Chapter 5.

TABLE 7-3 ### What Paper Items to Check with Your Local City or Town

Item	Description of items
	Juice and milk cartons, Tetra Paks, or long-life cartons: Two types of liquid cartons are found at the supermarket: those stored on the shelf and in the fridge. Both are made from multilayer materials, often paper and plastic but sometimes a layer of aluminum. Recycling multilayer materials can be tricky, so I have dedicated a whole chapter to them: Chapter 10.

(continued)

TABLE 7-3 *(continued)*

Item	Description of items
	Cardboard take-out boxes: Take-out boxes, even if made from cardboard, are often not accepted. The cardboard may be coated with wax or plastic and is often covered in food stains. However, check your local rules; some areas may accept dry, clean take-out containers.
	Frozen food boxes or cartons: Although mostly made from paper, frozen food boxes often have a layer of plastic. This layer helps protect the contents from moisture. If the inside surface is very shiny, then it's likely that the carton is coated in plastic. See Chapter 10 for more information on this type of box.
	Shredded paper: Acceptance for shredded paper depends on your location. In most areas, shredded paper is too small for the machinery at the recycling facility to collect and separate. The other problem is that cutting paper shortens the paper fibers and results in a low-quality recycled product. Check with your local city or town whether they accept it.
	Books: Many curbside recycling services accept books as mixed paper, but you'll need to check to be sure. For hardcover books, remove the dust jackets, binding, and cover because they may have plastic or other materials. You can usually leave the binding on paperback books. However, the best thing to do with a book is to pass it on or donate it to someone else to read.
	Mail and envelopes: Recycling envelopes can be tricky because there are so many different options. You can recycle plain paper envelopes or even envelopes with clear windows, but if they are lined with plastic or bubble wrap, they must go in your general waste bin. Recycling facilities cannot separate the plastic and paper.
	Manila folders and dividers: If made from paper, office products like manila folders can be recycled. But first, use the tear test to see whether they're actually made from plastic. If it doesn't tear like paper and is a bit stretchy, then it's most likely soft plastic (see Chapter 11). If it tears like paper but has a shiny and smooth exterior, then it's most likely a multilayer item (see Chapter 10). Neither of these can be recycled in your curbside bin.
	Greeting cards: If cards are made from plain paper, you can recycle them, but if they've got loads of glitter or other decorations, you'll have to put them in the trash. If your greeting card is one of those singing cards with a battery, make sure you remove the battery so it can be recycled separately. Batteries can be toxic if sent to a landfill. I explain more in Chapter 13.

Pulling it all together

The best way to make sense of all the rules is to record them in one place. The worksheet in Figure 7-3 is designed to help you check your area for what's accepted. You can refer to it whenever you need to refresh your memory.

REMEMBER

Keep this rule in mind: "If in doubt, leave it out!" If you're unable to find out whether you can recycle an item, it's okay to leave it out of your recycling bin and put it into your general waste bin.

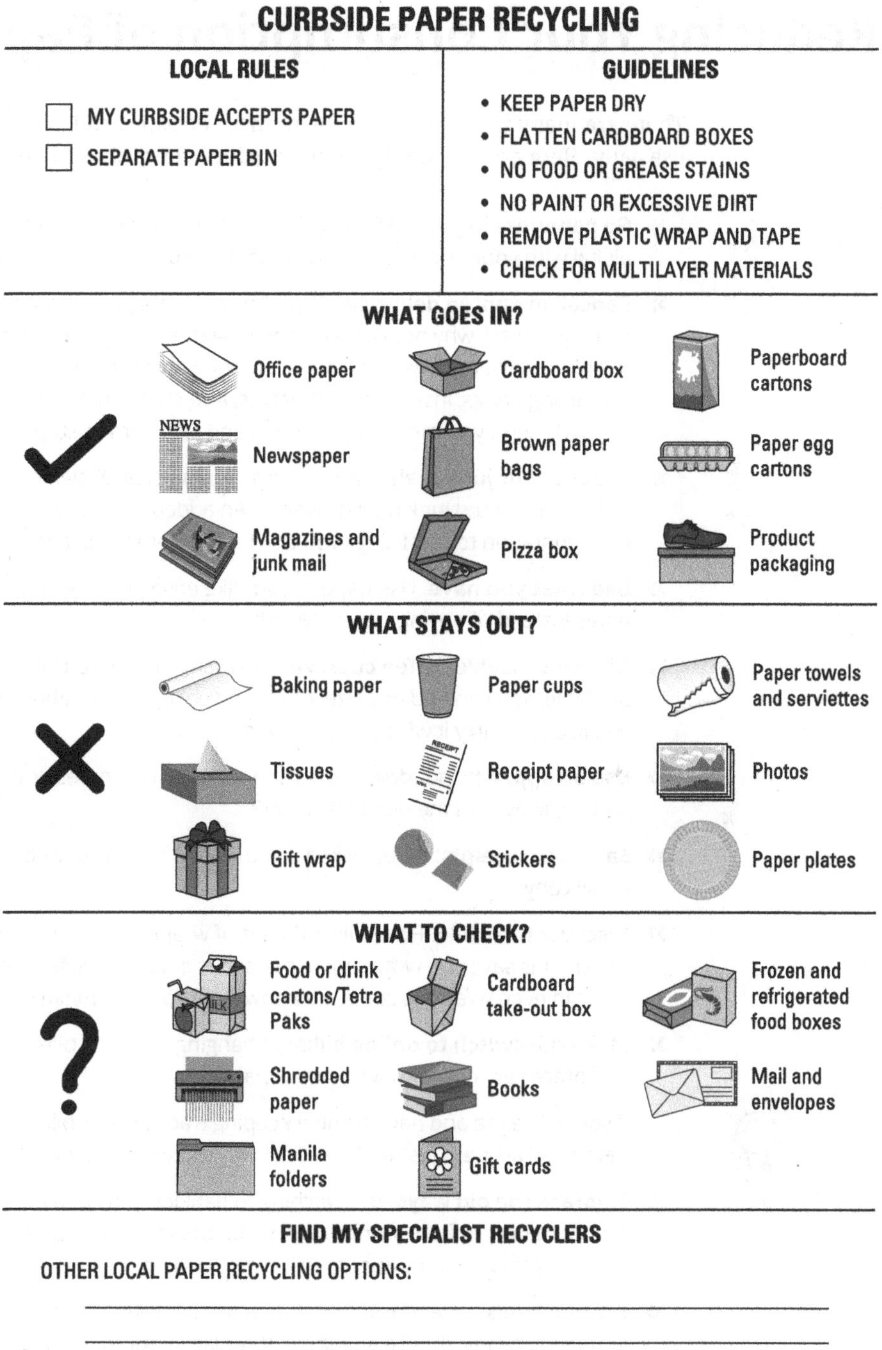

CURBSIDE PAPER RECYCLING

LOCAL RULES	GUIDELINES
☐ MY CURBSIDE ACCEPTS PAPER ☐ SEPARATE PAPER BIN	• KEEP PAPER DRY • FLATTEN CARDBOARD BOXES • NO FOOD OR GREASE STAINS • NO PAINT OR EXCESSIVE DIRT • REMOVE PLASTIC WRAP AND TAPE • CHECK FOR MULTILAYER MATERIALS

WHAT GOES IN?

✓	Office paper	Cardboard box	Paperboard cartons
	Newspaper	Brown paper bags	Paper egg cartons
	Magazines and junk mail	Pizza box	Product packaging

WHAT STAYS OUT?

✗	Baking paper	Paper cups	Paper towels and serviettes
	Tissues	Receipt paper	Photos
	Gift wrap	Stickers	Paper plates

WHAT TO CHECK?

?	Food or drink cartons/Tetra Paks	Cardboard take-out box	Frozen and refrigerated food boxes
	Shredded paper	Books	Mail and envelopes
	Manila folders	Gift cards	

FIND MY SPECIALIST RECYCLERS

OTHER LOCAL PAPER RECYCLING OPTIONS:

_____

_____

FIGURE 7-3: Use this worksheet to help understand what's accepted in your curbside recycling bin.

Reducing Your Consumption of Paper

There are many ways to reduce the number of paper and cardboard products you use daily. Here are my top tips to help reduce your impact and save trees:

>> **Go paperless in your office.** Make the change in your workplace and go digital with your documents and presentations.

>> **Cancel unwanted deliveries.** If you're getting magazines or newspapers you no longer read, why not cancel them altogether? Or you can look at switching to online delivery for your favorite content. You might also have some success contacting banks, insurance companies, and other organizations that regularly send you marketing material and ask them to stop doing so.

>> **Reduce your junk mail.** Place a "No junk mail please" sign on your mailbox to reduce unwanted junk mail deliveries. An added benefit is that you remove the temptation to buy things you don't need from the catalogs.

>> **Use what you have.** Use paper scraps like envelopes for shopping lists or notes instead of buying new notepads.

>> **Ditch disposable coffee cups.** With so many unique reusable coffee mugs available, you can find any size, color, and design you might want. Find one you like and carry it with you everywhere.

>> **Use an app.** Why not download a shopping list or a notes app on your phone and do away with the need for paper?

>> **Say no to receipts.** When asked if you want a receipt, say no or ask for an email copy.

>> **Discover furoshiki.** Furoshiki is the art of wrapping presents in fabric instead of paper. This saves on wrapping paper and is a way to reuse textiles and clothing. You can even wrap the gift in a tea towel or scarf and make it part of the present.

>> **Make the switch to online billing.** Changing to online bills for your home and office services will save a ton of paper.

TIP

If you're like me and have trouble keeping track of your bills, why not set up a new email address just for bills? That way, they won't get lost in your inbox.

>> **Embrace the old ways.** By switching to hankies and cloth napkins, you'll save a lot of materials from landfills and some cash too. You can even get reusable wipes to replace your paper towels in the kitchen.

>> **Try reusables.** Give reusable Teflon or silicon baking sheets a go. I switched to these recently; they're an excellent replacement for baking paper or parchment paper.

>> **Keep your eyes peeled.** Look for the Forest Stewardship Council (FSC) and other logos when purchasing new products. (See the next section for more information.)

>> **Make your own.** Try making your own recycled paper using old scraps of paper. It could be a fun thing to do with the kids.

>> **Reuse whenever possible.** You can reuse cardboard boxes for packing, storage, postage boxes, or even to make a fort for your kids to play in. If you've no use for them, try offering them to someone in the community through local internet groups.

>> **Donate your magazines.** See whether your local doctor or dentist office needs updated magazines for their waiting area.

>> **Join a library or book exchange.** Rather than buying new books every time you want to read something, why not find a community book exchange or join a library? I've rediscovered my local library recently and I am loving it; they stock lots of great *For Dummies* books too!

Making an Impact on Your Paper Use at the Checkout

There's a good chance you're already buying and using a reasonable amount of recycled paper. A lot of recycled paper is put back into the papermaking process and makes its way back into paper products. These recycled paper products cost and behave the same as products made directly from trees, so making the switch is easy and won't impact your day-to-day costs.

Here are some examples of recycled paper products you can start buying today:

>> **Office paper:** Choose paper that's 100 percent recycled so you will have the greatest impact.

>> **Recycled cardboard packaging:** Cardboard packaging regularly uses recycled content. It can be hard to know because they don't always declare it. I appreciate it when a company states that its packaging is recycled. That way, you know for sure.

TIP

If you cannot find any information on your favorite brand's packaging, don't be afraid to contact the company and ask them. You never know. They might even rethink their processes, knowing their customers are eager for change.

>> **Magazines and newspapers:** Many magazines or newspapers are already made with recycled paper. If you have a favorite magazine, why not check if they're already using recycled paper?

>> **Toilet paper and tissues:** You can find recycled toilet paper and tissues stocked in many supermarkets. If you can, avoid brands that produce bleached toilet paper, because this will also save chemicals and water.

>> **Paper towels and napkins:** Some great reusable alternatives for paper towels are available, but if you prefer to purchase single-use paper towels or napkins, look for ones made with recycled content.

>> **Greeting cards:** Keep an eye out for recycled greeting cards when buying gifts.

TIP

Buying certified timber products is a great way to become a more responsible consumer. You may have already come across various certifications that help distinguish between good and bad environmental practices in timber products. They support essential principles like land-use rights, community, and ecological impacts. Knowing these certifications will help you make the right choice the next time you purchase a product. There are three certifications to look out for:

>> **Forest Stewardship Council (FSC):** The Forest Stewardship Council (FSC) works with industries worldwide to minimize the negative impacts of forestry. Its mission is to promote companies that work to their set of principles and, in doing so, to help protect the world's forests for future generations. Their principles embrace legal compliance, land-use rights, indigenous people's rights, community, and environmental impacts, in addition to the protection of workers.

You can identify certified products by looking for the FSC logo. It's found on products ranging from tissues to furniture and even on paper packaging. Find out more about the FSC at www.fsc.org.

>> **Programme for the Endorsement of Forest Certification (PEFC):** Based in Switzerland, this nonprofit organization administers over two-thirds of the world's globally certified forested area. They provide certification in both sustainable forest management and chain of custody. Keep a look out for the PEFC label on products. When you see it, you can be sure they're a brand that supports forests. Check them out at www.pefc.org.

>> **Sustainable Forestry Initiative (SFI):** Based in North America, the SFI initiative is an independent nonprofit organization. They work closely with various groups to promote sustainable forests. They have several certifications, including forest management, the chain of custody, and certified sourcing, while providing plenty of fact sheets to help businesses make the right decisions. Take a look at their website so you're familiar with their logo, and keep an eye out for it when you are shopping. You can find them at www.forests.org.

IN THIS CHAPTER

» Defining what goes into glass

» Identifying reasons to recycle glass

» Getting to know the glass recycling process

» Working out what glass you can and can't recycle

» Decreasing your glass usage

» Making smart glass shopping decisions

Chapter **8**

Recognizing Recyclable Glass

G lass is infinitely recyclable, chemically inert, and relatively safe to use. These properties make it our preferred choice to store many of the consumables we use daily. But did you know not all glass is the same?

The bulk of glass products you may encounter daily, such as jars and bottles, are manufactured from standard or annealed glass and are easy to recycle. However, many glass objects around our homes, like drinking glasses, vases, windows, and mirrors, are made from different types of glass. To create these products, manufacturers modify the basic properties of glass and transform it into safer, more practical, or more attractive forms. However, by doing so, they make it much more challenging to recycle.

Understanding these different types of glass and applying this knowledge to your everyday recycling efforts helps improve recycling rates and minimize contamination. The rules are straightforward once you know them. In this chapter, you discover the basic rules for recycling your glass through a typical curbside recycling program. I explain the common rules and list the types of glass you typically can and can't recycle. Taking a glimpse at the glassmaking and recycling process is also a great way to understand some of the industry's challenges and how you can lend a hand.

Beginning with the Basics: What Is Glass?

Glass is a hard, solid, inorganic material made from natural resources. Humans have been using glass for thousands of years. We shape it and manipulate it into all types of products, using it to package our foods and beverages, in home decor, and as safe kitchenware for cooking. One of the most common ways we use glass is as windows that bring light and a glimpse of the outside world into our homes, offices, and cars.

Glass is used so widely because of its excellent properties. It's transparent, strong, heat resistant, and easily molded. Most importantly, glass is impervious to chemicals, meaning it doesn't react with food, which is why it's so popular for storing food and beverages. Add to that the ease of obtaining the raw ingredients and the fact that it is relatively cheap to make, and you can understand why glass is popular.

In the following sections, I explain the resources and processes used to make glass and look at the most common types of glass you encounter in your day-to-day life.

Resources used to make glass

Natural resources like energy, water, and minerals are required to make all of the products in our lives. Plus, finding, processing, and transporting all those materials requires energy. So let's take a look at the natural resources needed to make glass:

>> **Minerals:** The main ingredients in glass are silica, soda ash, and lime. You can make glass using only silica, but it becomes challenging to shape and mold it. Adding soda ash lowers the melting temperature, while lime helps stabilize the glass and make it stronger. All these materials occur as minerals in the earth's crust and must be extracted from deposits through mining processes.

Silica is a significant component of white sand — yes, the stuff at the beach. It's mined from quarries and riverbeds. Lime, or limestone, is collected through limestone mining. Soda ash is refined from trona deposits.

Trona is short for hydrated sodium bicarbonate. Phew! You can see why they shortened it. Trona is extracted through underground mining and transported to manufacturers worldwide. About half of the trona mined today is used to make glass, but it's also used in paper products, to make detergents, and in bicarbonate of soda, or baking soda, as it's commonly known. So, there's a good chance you have a box of trona in your cupboard.

>> **Energy:** Glassmaking is a very energy-intensive process that requires furnace temperatures in excess of 1,000 degrees Fahrenheit. Melting glass to these temperatures accounts for most of the energy used, but energy is also required to keep the glass molten during the molding and shaping processes. Plus, energy is also consumed when transporting the ingredients and the final product.

>> **Chemicals:** Many different chemicals are added to glass during manufacturing to create specific properties or characteristics. For example, adding boric oxide increases glass's temperature resistance, making it useful for cookware so it can go in a hot oven.

Taking, making, and wasting glass

To make glass, you first need to find and extract the minerals and other ingredients, then they all get mixed together and melted at a high temperature. The glass is then cooled and shaped into a bottle or jar. The method can vary depending on whether you're making a sheet of glass or a glass bottle.

The problem with this process is that it's linear and follows the take-make-waste life cycle. The issue with this antiquated economic system is the amount of energy and raw materials it requires to function and the amount of waste it generates. Later in this chapter, I show you a much better system designed around a circular economy where the waste is recycled and reused over and over again.

But first, here is a closer look at the steps for making glass bottles and jars, illustrated in Figure 8-1:

1. **The raw materials are mined and processed.**

    The first step is to find and extract all of the raw materials required to make the product — in this case, glass. As described in the preceding section, this requires sand, lime, and soda ash. Once all the raw ingredients are mined and processed, ready for use, they're transported to a manufacturing plant.

2. **The ingredients are mixed and melted.**

    The ingredients — silica, soda ash, and limestone — are melted at temperatures exceeding 1,000 degrees Fahrenheit. Once the glass mix has melted, chemicals are added to create the chosen properties. For example, adding iron or chromium oxide makes green glass for beer bottles.

3. **The molten glass is shaped and cooled.**

   Molten glass is poured into a blow mold, and then air is blown into the mold, forcing the glass to fill the mold and create the desired shape. Next, the glass is cooled. Altering the cooling method of glass can create more robust and heat-resistant glass. Annealing is the most common and involves heating and cooling the glass slowly to remove internal stresses and strengthen the glass.

   After molding and cooling, the glass is inspected by automated machines to identify bubbles and other stresses that can cause safety issues when in use.

4. **The glass products are filled, capped, and packaged.**

   Once the glass jars have been shipped to the product manufacturer, they are filled with the product, capped, and then packaged for transportation to retail stores.

5. **The glass products are purchased and used.**

   Once the glass packaging, with its product sealed inside, reaches the store, this is where you and I come in. We buy the product and take it home filled with our chosen sauce or favorite drink, ready to be consumed. When we've emptied the jar or bottle of its contents, we throw it out. Depending on our access to services and bin choice, it either gets recycled, goes to a landfill, gets incinerated, or pollutes our environment.

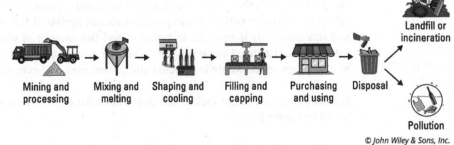

FIGURE 8-1:
The linear glassmaking process.

Mining and processing   Mixing and melting   Shaping and cooling   Filling and capping   Purchasing and using   Disposal   Landfill or incineration   Pollution

© John Wiley & Sons, Inc.

Common types of glass

Through the use of chemical additives or by altering the glassmaking process, you can create many different types of glass. Listing every kind of glass available would require a book of its own, so in the following list, I describe the types of glass you're likely to encounter regularly:

>> **Annealed glass:** Annealed glass, also referred to as *standard glass,* is made using the basic recipe for glass without any additional chemicals, heat treating, or coatings. The glass is cooled slowly, resulting in a stronger glass that's less likely to crack or shatter. Even with this added strength, annealed glass still breaks into long, jagged shards. Most of the glass jars and bottles you handle everyday are made using annealed or standard glass.

>> **Heat-strengthened glass:** To make heat-strengthened glass, annealed glass is reheated and cooled more quickly. This makes the glass twice as strong. Although it's more likely to hold together than untreated, it'll still fragment when broken. Typical uses include glass windows or mirrors.

>> **Tempered or toughened glass:** Tempered glass, often referred to as *safety glass,* is made through extreme heating and rapid cooling of the glass. This makes the glass up to five times stronger than annealed glass. Tempered glass breaks into small pieces, making it safer than untreated glass. Tempered glass is used in the automotive industry, shower screens, and freezer-safe containers.

>> **Lead glass:** Adding lead oxide to the recipe gives the glass a more brilliant appearance and makes it easier to shape or cut. However, it becomes softer and therefore can scratch or break very easily. Lead glass is known for its use in leadlight windows, but it's also found in thermometers, TV parts, and crystal glassware.

>> **Borosilicate glass:** The addition of boric oxide increases the glass's temperature resistance and overall durability. Everyday items made from borosilicate glass are light bulbs and lab glassware, but Pyrex or Corning Ware are perhaps the best-known examples.

>> **Laminated glass:** Laminated glass is made by bonding two or more sheets of annealed, heat-strengthened glass or tempered glass with a vinyl or PVC plastic layer. The vinyl layer holds the glass together when it breaks rather than shattering. Laminated glass is used extensively in the automotive industry and housing products.

Understanding Why You Should Recycle Glass

The durability of glass makes it one of our favorite packaging materials. However, it also means that when it's sent to a landfill, it'll be around for a very long time. Glass takes thousands of years to decompose. That's a very long time, but the good news is that it won't leach chemicals or break down into harmful materials.

In fact, waste management companies often use crushed glass as an inert cover in landfills to help contain odors and prevent unwanted pests.

Even though glass has few negative impacts, leaving it sitting in a landfill is a bit of a waste, especially when it's so easily recycled. And sadly, there's plenty of it going to landfills.

In 2020 the U.S. Environmental Protection Agency (EPA) reported through their "Advancing Sustainable Materials Management" report that only 32 percent of glass bottles and jars were recycled in the United States. Turn that around and it translates into 68 percent of glass bottles and jars ending in landfills. It's not so different in other countries either. According to the Department of Agriculture, Water, and the Environment, Australians recycled only 59 percent of their glass in 2018–19. This is firm evidence that we can do things better.

Glass recycling saves energy, reduces greenhouse gas emissions, and helps protect our environment. Plus, glass is infinitely recyclable, so keeping it from landfill is a no-brainer. Here are some great reasons to recycle your glass:

>> **Keeping resources in use:** Recycling glass keeps materials that have already been extracted in use and reduces our reliance on new or virgin resources. Plus, glass can be recycled over and over again without losing quality, so it's definitely worth keeping it in use.

>> **Recycling resources to reduce environmental impacts:** Recycling glass and using the recycled materials to make new products helps reduce our reliance on raw resources like silica, lime, and soda ash and minimize our impacts on the planet. Mining the raw materials needed for glassmaking can interfere with natural drainage and groundwater and threaten biodiversity. Reducing our reliance on these raw materials and the associated mining practices will minimize these adverse effects.

As I note in the earlier section "Resources used to make glass," glass is made primarily from silica sand. These sands can be extracted from land quarries and riverbeds but may also be collected from marine or coastal areas. Extraction processes for mining sands have many environmental and social impacts, including the following:

- Loss of ecosystems and threats to biodiversity by destroying habitats along riverbeds and coastlines

- Alteration and interference with natural drainage and groundwater

- Degradation and land erosion because there's less protection from floods and storms

- Loss of topsoil resulting from vegetation removal in the mining process

- Social impacts such as loss of tourism and effects on local industries

These are just the effects of silica mining. Lime and soda ash must also be sourced, and each of these materials comes with its own environmental impact.

>> **Saving precious space in landfills:** Glass takes up to one million years to break down. Its inert properties mean it's unlikely to damage the environment, but it can build up. Filling landfills with recyclable glass means we'll require larger landfills and more resources to handle the materials that wind up there.

According to the EPA, 7.6 million tons of glass bottles and jars are sent to landfills in the United States annually. If all that wasted glass was recycled, it would save more than three football stadiums of raw materials and the precious energy and water used to make products.

>> **Decreasing greenhouse gas emissions:** Making glass is an energy-intensive process that releases greenhouse gases. Furnace temperatures required to melt the raw ingredients exceed 1,000 degrees Fahrenheit. Plus, when these raw materials are heated to make glass, they release carbon dioxide as a by-product. Carbon dioxide is a key contributor to climate change.

Using recycled glass minimizes these emissions. It also cuts energy use because recycled glass melts at a lower temperature than raw materials. This means less energy is needed when recycled glass is used.

You can make a big difference when you recycle your glass:

- Recycling one glass jar can save enough electricity to light an 11-watt compact fluorescent light (CFL) bulb for 20 hours.

- Using six tons of recycled glass in place of raw materials avoids the release of one ton of carbon dioxide.

Seeing How Glass Is Recycled

Glass recycling starts with collecting used or discarded glass via curbside and other collection services. Collection through curbside recycling can be via a single-stream recycling system or a multi-stream system:

>> If your local recycling is via a single-stream process, your glass goes in the same bin as your paper, metal, and plastic recycling.

>> If your area uses a multi-stream system, you should be provided with a specific bin for collecting your glass.

There are other variations; it all depends on where you live and the types of infrastructure available at your local facilities. The following sections further explain the steps for recycling glass.

WARNING

Many locations don't accept glass in your curbside recycling at all. Always check your local rules before placing glass in your mixed recycling bin. You can read through the later section "Asking about local rules" and use the worksheet in Figure 8-3 to help you navigate the different rules.

The steps of glass recycling

REMEMBER

A fantastic example of the circular economy in action is recycling glass and using it to create new glass jars and bottles. Before waste glass can be used in a new product, quite a few steps are required after the glass is delivered to a recycling facility. These steps are described here in detail and shown in Figure 8-2:

1. **The consumer recycles glass.**

   When you place your glass packaging in your recycling bin, take it to a bottle bank, or drop it off at a container deposit depot, you take the initial step in starting this process.

2. **The glass is collected and moved to a processing facility.**

   Glass is collected through curbside recycling, bottle banks, container deposit schemes, or other drop-off locations. The glass is then taken to a material recovery facility for further processing.

3. **The glass is separated from other materials.**

   If collected through curbside services that use a single-stream collection method, the glass must be separated from all other recyclables like paper, plastic, and metal.

   Large non-glass materials are also removed from the glass at this stage — things like jar lids or any item that isn't made from glass. Depending on the facility, a variety of techniques may be used, such as manual sorting, the use of magnets to remove metals, or the use of dryers to remove labels.

4. **The glass is sorted by color.**

   Glass is sorted into different colors to obtain the highest-quality recycling material. The regular colors are clear, green, and brown. You cannot change the color of glass during the recycling process, so it's best to sort the different colors first. (Check out the nearby sidebar "Using light to sort glass" for details on an interesting sorting process.)

5. The glass is crushed and cleaned.

The glass is then broken up into smaller pieces, which is referred to as *glass cullet.* Remaining contaminants, including ceramics, bottle tops, or any metal parts, are removed with magnet separators or optical sorting machines.

6. New glass is made.

The cullet is combined with raw ingredients in a furnace to create new glass bottles. These are delivered to a manufacturer, filled, and put back on the store shelves.

7. The new glass is purchased and used.

The glass product is delivered to the store and placed on the shelf, ready for you to buy and use. Once emptied, the glass is disposed of in the recycling bin, and the procedure is repeated.

The preceding steps describe the process for recycling glass so it can be used to make new glass containers. However, glass can also be recycled and used in fiberglass or simply crushed and used in construction material like concrete, roads, or simply as backfill.

Why some curbside services don't collect glass

Many people become frustrated when their curbside service doesn't accept glass. They see this as a sign that the recycling industry is broken or failing. However, this isn't the case at all. In fact, it's a sign that the recycling industry is working hard to maximize the quality of recyclables and to increase the probability that materials are used to make new products.

USING LIGHT TO SORT GLASS

Optical sorting machines are used to sort glass and remove contaminants. Using a bright light, these machines can easily identify glass from other materials like ceramics or plastics. When light is shone on the materials, some is absorbed, and some is reflected. Cameras record the reflected light waves. Like a fingerprint, each material has a different pattern of light waves and is identified.

When an item that isn't glass is detected, it will trigger a blast of air at the spot on the conveyor belt where the material is. The air propels the material off the conveyor belt and into a different bin. The different colors of glass each have their own distinct pattern of light waves, so optical sorters can also be configured to sort them.

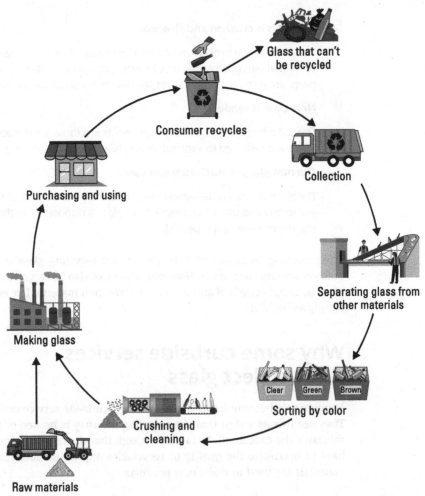

Glass that can't
be recycled

Consumer recycles

Collection

Separating glass from
other materials

Clear   Green   Brown

Sorting by color

Crushing and
cleaning

Raw materials

Making glass

Purchasing and using

FIGURE 8-2:
The glass
recycling process.

© *John Wiley & Sons, Inc.*

Depending on where you live, there are several reasons your local curbside service doesn't accept glass. Here are some of the most common reasons:

>> **Glass as a contaminant:** In single-stream recycling, glass is mixed with paper, plastic, and metal by the homeowner and separated at the facility. The problem is, as glass breaks up into smaller pieces, it can become lodged in the paper and plastic waste. This lowers the value of the recycled paper or plastic material or, worse, renders it no longer recyclable and results in it being sent to a landfill. Many services try to resolve this issue by refusing to accept glass.

Another way to solve this problem is to switch to multi-stream recycling. Multi-stream collection is where the homeowner separates different materials into different bins: plastic in the plastic bin and glass in the glass bin. This helps keep the broken glass away from the other recyclables and improves the quality.

>> **Availability of an end market:** Recycling services may not accept glass because of poor economics. The viability of glass recycling can be determined by the value of recycled glass cullet and the availability of a nearby market. Glass is heavy and expensive to transport, especially when the nearest facility is very far away. Combine these high costs with the low payout for recycled glass, and it can be challenging to cover your expenses, let alone make a profit.

TIP

If you live in an area where glass isn't accepted, you may have other options like a bottle bank or a container deposit scheme. You can find out more about these in the later section "Looking at Specialist Glass Recycling."

The trouble with different glass colors

People are drawn to colored glass, but the blue, green, and brown hues aren't just for good looks. Created by adding chemicals into the basic glass mixture, the colors protect the contents of the glass from exposure to sunlight. In particular, green and brown glass is used for this purpose.

The most common colored glass types include

>> **Clear glass:** This is made from the basic glass formula of silica, soda ash, and limestone.

>> **Brown glass:** Carbon, iron, or sulfur is added to the molten glass.

>> **Green glass:** Copper or chromium is added to the molten glass.

The problem is that glass retains its original color during and after recycling. You can't change the color, so you're stuck with the original color or a mix of colors. As a result, color is critical in determining the market value for recycled glass cullet. Clear glass usually has the highest value and is most likely to be made into new products. Green and brown glass values vary largely on location. For example, areas that have established wine regions might favor green glass.

To solve the issue, many locations require you to separate and sort your glass recycling by color before it's collected. In other areas, recycling facilities use optical sorting machines to identify and separate the glass by color (see the earlier sidebar "Using light to sort glass"); therefore, the homeowner is off the hook.

REMEMBER

To understand which rules apply, you must check with your local town or city government.

Knowing What Glass Items Can and Can't Be Recycled

There are a number of rules for recycling glass that vary depending on where you live. Figuring out how to recycle glass in your local area is as simple as checking these rules and then checking the types of glass that go in and stay out.

REMEMBER

Not all glass is recyclable in curbside recycling services. Knowing the different types of glass and which ones you can recycle helps keep contamination to a minimum and increases the likelihood your recyclables will be made into something new.

Asking about local glass rules

Curbside recycling rules for glass vary widely from location to location, so it can get a little confusing. I suggest you begin by reading through this section to help understand the different rules.

TIP

Next, you need to do a little homework to find the rules that apply in your local area. You can find most of the answers on your town or city's website or by contacting them directly. If you live in an apartment complex, you also need to check your building rules. To help with this exercise, I provide a worksheet that you can fill out in the later section "Pulling it all together."

REMEMBER

Here are the rules you will want to check before you start recycling glass in your curbside service:

>> **Does my curbside recycling service accept glass?** As discussed earlier in this chapter, there are many reasons why your recycling service may not accept glass. The most important thing for you to check is whether your service takes glass. If it doesn't, don't worry; there are other possible ways you can recycle your glass. The upcoming section on specialist glass recycling outlines these alternatives.

>> **Do I have a separate bin for glass?** When glass is mixed with other recyclables, it can cause many issues, the worst of which is when they have to send all the recyclables to a landfill. As a result, many services require you to

separate your glass into a different bin. Check if your local area has separate bins for glass.

>> **Does my service collect only particular colors?** A few locations accept only specific colors of glass. Clear, green, and brown glass bottles and jars are usually acceptable. Colors like blue may not be accepted in some locations. And the occasional local area requests that you recycle only clear jars and bottles. Look out for these rules and note down what your area accepts.

>> **Do I need to sort glass by color?** Recycling different colored glass together can lower the value of the recycled material. As a result, some locations require you to sort your glass by color to increase the value. Check if your area requires different colors to be sorted.

REMEMBER

Don't be afraid to ask questions. It's in everyone's best interest that you understand your local recycling rules and keep contamination to a minimum.

Following a few guidelines for glass

To recycle glass in your curbside bin, follow these guidelines:

>> **Place only glass packaging in your recycling bin.** Curbside recycling is designed to collect and process glass packaging. Even though made from glass, other household items like vases, kitchenware, and drinking glasses are rarely accepted. Stick to containers like jars and bottles, and your local recycling provider will be very happy.

Note: A small number of curbside recycling programs accept glass items other than jars and bottles and turn them into sand for use in construction. But unless this is explicitly requested in your local rules, put only bottles and jars in your curbside recycling bin.

>> **Remove all food residue.** Although glass gets cleaned during the recycling process, it becomes problematic when there's excess food. Liquids or foods can spill out and contaminate paper or other recyclables. Besides, it makes sense to minimize smells, mold, and the risk of attracting flies or vermin. Nobody wants a smelly, fly-ridden bin around their home.

TIP

If a quick rinse isn't enough to remove sticky food from glass jars, I place them in my dishwasher along with my regular dishes. It makes cleaning a lot easier and saves water too.

>> **Remove parts that are not glass.** Lids on glass jars or bottles are made from metal, plastic, or in some cases, a mix of materials. Many areas require you to separate the lid from the glass jar or bottle, recycle it separately, or place it in the trash if it's not recyclable. Other places may ask you to leave the lid on the jars.

See Chapter 6 to uncover what to do with your plastic lids and Chapter 9 for where to recycle lids made from metals.

>> **Leave labels on jars or bottles.** If labels on jars or bottles can be removed easily, feel free to take them off, but there's no need. They'll be removed during the recycling process.

WARNING

>> **Don't break glass; leave it intact.** The majority of curbside recycling services doesn't accept broken glass. Some people find this confusing because glass generally breaks during collection and sorting. The problem is broken glass can become a safety issue for workers who collect your bins. Plus, intact bottles and jars are much easier to sort and handle. Broken glass continues to break up into smaller and smaller pieces, and it can become too small for the machinery to sort or even pick up. These smaller pieces of glass are also more likely to become embedded in other recyclables like paper, causing contamination and possibly getting sent to landfills.

Knowing what glass items go in

Curbside recycling is designed to collect and recycle glass packaging for food and beverages, including glass jars and bottles. These glass objects are made from annealed glass, and there are many benefits to recycling them. Table 8-1 identifies the recyclable items accepted in the majority of curbside services.

TABLE 8-1 ### What Glass Items Go in Your Curbside Bin

Item	Description of Items
	Glass bottles including • Soft drinks bottles • Juice bottles • Wine and beer bottles • Sauce bottles
	Glass jars and containers for food storage: • Glass jam jars • Condiment jars like those for pickles

REMEMBER

If you're unsure if an item belongs in your curbside recycling and you cannot find any information about it, then it's okay to put it in the general trash can. It's best to avoid putting it in the recycling bin, hoping it'll get recycled. We call this wishcycling!

Keeping some glass items out

Other than disposable glass packaging and storage items, most glass objects in your home aren't recyclable through curbside recycling services. They're usually made from a type of glass that's been altered through heat or chemicals. Altering glass can increase its melting point, which can cause issues if it's mixed with standard recyclable annealed glass. Table 8-2 provides a list of the glass items that don't belong in the majority of curbside recycling bins.

TIP

Many of these objects can still have life in them. Donating or selling them is a great way to keep them in use and save them from landfills.

TABLE 8-2   **What Glass Items Stay Out of Your Curbside Bin**

Item	Instructions and Tips
	Drinking glasses: It's nearly impossible to determine what kind of glass is used in the various drinking glasses in our homes. This means the risk of contamination is extremely high, and in most areas, they don't go in your curbside recycling bin. • Regular drinking glasses • Wine, champagne, and cocktail glasses • Beer glasses • Shot glasses
	Decorative glass: It's very hard to recycle ornamental or decorative glass decor pieces like vases, candleholders, or stained-glass decor. It's difficult to know what sort of glass was used to make them. Plus, they can be coated with paint or other materials, making them difficult to recycle and more likely to cause contamination. They should be placed in your general waste bin.
	Kitchenware and tableware glass: Kitchenware like glass pitchers, bowls, glass cooking pots, and other bowls and plates are rarely accepted in curbside recycling bins. Place them in your general waste bin.
	Heatproof containers such as Pyrex or Corning Ware: Ovenproof baking dishes and other glass baking products use glass that's been heat treated. This treatment makes them safe to use in your oven but means they won't melt in most glass furnaces and will lead to contamination. Keep them out of your curbside recycling bin.
	Ceramics, china, and porcelain: Ceramic or china crockery may seem similar in texture to glass, but they're made from clay. Ceramics or china will break up like glass when placed in your curbside recycling bin and cause contamination throughout the process. It can lead to a whole batch of glass being sent to landfills.

(continued)

TABLE 8-2 *(continued)*

Item	Instructions and Tips
	Light bulbs and tubes: Although made with glass, light bulbs and tubes contain many other materials that aren't recyclable in your curbside bin. They also don't belong in the general waste bin as some materials can be hazardous. The good news is that many specialist recycling programs are available. See Chapter 14.
	Glass mirrors: The glass is coated with a layer of aluminum or silver to make a mirror reflect. This coating makes mirror glass tricky to recycle. There are many different ways to reuse mirrors, like donating them or replacing the frames and giving them a new life.
	Window glass: Windows are made from many different glass types, including annealed, heat-strengthened, tempered, or laminated (covered earlier in this chapter). Even if you could work out which type of glass it is, most curbside recycling facilities aren't set up to handle window glass. Look for a construction recycling yard, or talk to your builder about what options there might be for your old windows.
	Glass syringes and other medical or lab instruments: Medical-related instruments and equipment made from glass aren't recyclable in your curbside recycling. With such a high risk of disease transmission, they must be treated as hazardous waste. See Chapter 14 for more information on disposing of hazardous waste safely.

Checking on a few unusual glass items

Table 8-3 lists a few items worth checking before you toss them into your recycling bin. Some localities accept them, and some don't.

Pulling it all together

The best way to make sense of all the rules is to condense them into one place. I've created a worksheet to help you pull it all together. Plus, it's something you can refer to when you need to refresh your understanding or if you move to a new location and need to recheck the rules. You can find the glass recycling worksheet in Figure 8-3.

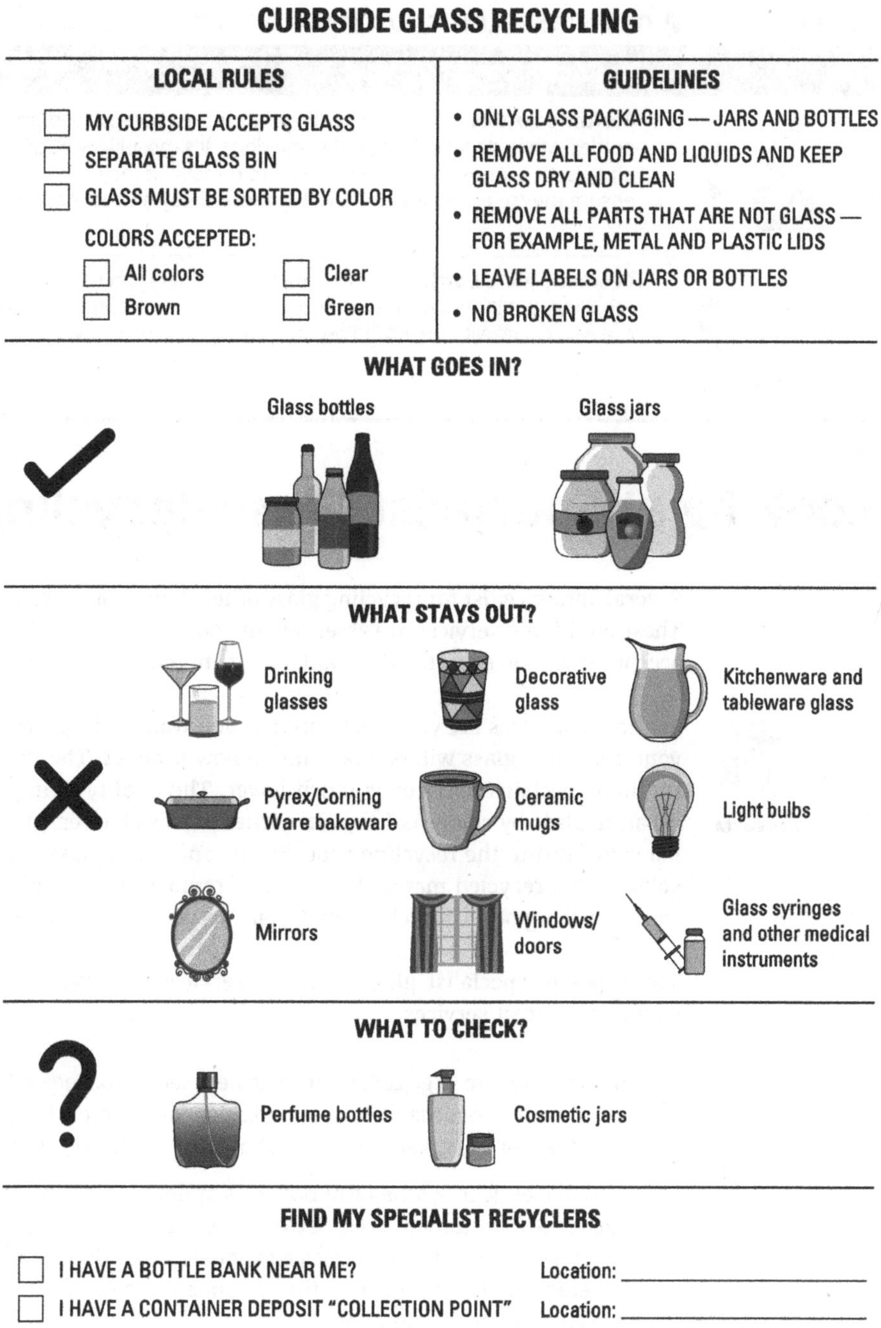

CURBSIDE GLASS RECYCLING

LOCAL RULES

☐ MY CURBSIDE ACCEPTS GLASS

☐ SEPARATE GLASS BIN

☐ GLASS MUST BE SORTED BY COLOR

COLORS ACCEPTED:

☐ All colors   ☐ Clear

☐ Brown   ☐ Green

GUIDELINES

• ONLY GLASS PACKAGING — JARS AND BOTTLES

• REMOVE ALL FOOD AND LIQUIDS AND KEEP GLASS DRY AND CLEAN

• REMOVE ALL PARTS THAT ARE NOT GLASS — FOR EXAMPLE, METAL AND PLASTIC LIDS

• LEAVE LABELS ON JARS OR BOTTLES

• NO BROKEN GLASS

WHAT GOES IN?

Glass bottles   Glass jars

WHAT STAYS OUT?

Drinking glasses   Decorative glass   Kitchenware and tableware glass

Pyrex/Corning Ware bakeware   Ceramic mugs   Light bulbs

Mirrors   Windows/doors   Glass syringes and other medical instruments

WHAT TO CHECK?

Perfume bottles   Cosmetic jars

FIND MY SPECIALIST RECYCLERS

☐ I HAVE A BOTTLE BANK NEAR ME?   Location: _____

☐ I HAVE A CONTAINER DEPOSIT "COLLECTION POINT"   Location: _____

FIGURE 8-3: Use this worksheet to summarize the glass recycling rules for your location.

TABLE 8-3 **What Glass Items to Check with Your Local City or Town**

Item	Instructions and Tips
	Perfume bottles: It's worth checking if your area accepts perfume or aftershave bottles. Many do take them, but some don't. It's most likely because of the metal and plastic pumps that can be difficult to remove. If they are accepted in your area, ensure they're empty and remove the metal spray and lid if possible.
	Cosmetic glass bottles: Many cosmetic containers can be recycled in your curbside recycling. But it's important to check because some locations don't accept them. You can also check with the brand because many have their own recycling programs.

Looking at Specialist Glass Recycling

Several options exist for recycling glass other than your curbside recycling service. These additional services are essential for those whose curbside collection doesn't accept glass; however, they're available to anyone.

REMEMBER

Specialist services are your best option if you want to improve the likelihood that your discarded glass will be made into a new product. The risk of contamination through specialist services is much lower. The quality is improved because you separate glass by color. As I explain earlier in this chapter, glass retains its original color during the recycling process, so separating glass will help improve the value of the recycled material. Plus, they remove the risk of glass breaking and contaminating other recyclable materials, as occurs in multi-stream recycling.

Two types of specialist glass recycling services are available: bottle banks and container deposit services.

>> Bottle banks are large collection containers set up conveniently for the local community to deposit their glass packaging for recycling. Check with your local town or city government if you have one of these in your neighborhood.

>> A container deposit scheme or bottle bill offers a few pennies back to you in exchange for returning a recyclable bottle. In places where container deposit schemes are established, a small additional cost is added when purchasing a beverage bottle. This money is then refunded when you return the bottle or recycle it at a specific location.

The majority of the rules for specialist recyclers are similar to curbside recycling, except that they only accept beverage containers like glass, plastic bottles, and aluminum cans.

Reducing Your Consumption of Glass

TIP

There are lots of ways you can reduce how much glass you use every day. The following list provides just a few ideas to get you thinking. I provide many more ways to reduce your impact in Chapter 15.

>> Cooking your own foods helps reduce the amount of new packaging you buy.

>> Buying things in bulk helps reduce overall packaging and other impacts like energy use and transportation. It often also has the added benefit of reducing costs.

>> Refillables are a great way to reduce your overall packaging. Beauty care products are a great example; many brands make refillable supplies for your powders or foundations.

>> Glass objects in good shape can be given away to friends or family or donated to a charity store. A great way to gift your old glass items to others is by joining a local Buy Nothing group on Facebook, or you may have other local community sharing groups.

>> You can reuse glass jars, bottles, and other containers in many different ways around the home. Here are some of my favorites:

- Store your homemade foods. It's a great way to keep your food fresher for longer and avoid food waste.

- Store excess foods using glass jars you already have instead of buying more plastic storage.

- Store herbs or spices in the cupboard.

- Store your office's pens, tacks, paper clips, or other items.

- Organize and store your toiletries such as cotton balls.

- Make your own candles using old glass jars.

- Use as a vase or to serve water at the table.

If you're interested, you can find loads more DIY ideas on Pinterest and YouTube.

Making an Impact with Glass Items at the Checkout

TIP

You can create the biggest impact when you make decisions at the checkout before purchasing. Try considering these things the next time you're out shopping:

>> When buying products at the supermarket, choose clear glass packaging instead of colored glass. Clear glass is made from the basic ingredients — sand, limestone, and soda ash — and has no chemicals added for color. You can't remove color once it's been added to glass, even through recycling. Because of this, market rates for clear glass are often much higher, and it's more likely to make its way into a new product.

>> Buy good quality. It might seem more expensive initially, but buying good-quality glass items for your home will save you money in the long run and reduce material wastage.

>> If you're looking for new items like drinking or wine glasses, why not seek out companies that use recycled glass? Better still, why not buy secondhand ones?

>> When renovating your home, try asking your builder or supplier if they have countertops or tiles made with recycled glass that you can choose.

>> When buying products from brands you use regularly, ask them whether they use recycled glass in their packaging. You might be pleasantly surprised, and if not, you may get them thinking about making a change.

High-quality recycled glass will almost always make its way back into the manufacturing process, where it's mixed with raw materials and made into a new glass container. This closed-loop process is called *bottle-to-bottle recycling*. With any luck, you're already buying recycled glass at the supermarket.

If the recycled glass is too contaminated for new bottles or there's no nearby manufacturing, it may be used in construction materials such as concrete or backfill (see the nearby sidebar for more information). In addition to construction-related products, many local artists use recycled glass to make attractive jewelry or unique decor. Buying local helps to support your community as well as the recycling industry.

So the great news is that your recycled glass can be used in many different products. You can help realize a successful glass recycling industry by recycling right and keeping an eye out for recycled glass products.

TURNING GLASS BACK TO SAND

In addition to markets that use recycled glass to make new glass bottles or jars and other products, there is a growing market for recycled glass sand. The benefits are that, depending on the end product, the material often doesn't need to be sorted by type or color, and it can include hard-to-recycle items like Pyrex, drinking glasses, crockery, window glass, and other household glass items.

The sand is used in many different ways, including the following:

- Road base: This foundation for roads can save overusing costly asphalt and provide strength and stability.

- Drainage and pipe backfill: Recycled glass sand is helpful for backfilling areas or can replace gravel for landscaping.

- Sea-bed backfill: Glass sands can be used to backfill seabed erosion areas or to create artificial reef structures.

- Landfill covers: Crushed glass may be used as a cover at landfills to control odors and prevent vermin.

- Glassphalt: Crushed glass can be used in place of sand to make asphalt for road construction.

- Construction materials: Recycled glass can be used in concrete, bricks, tiles, and other construction materials.

- Abrasives for sandblasting: Recycled glass can replace raw sand.

Not only does sand recycling make use of glass that wouldn't typically have an end market, but it also replaces raw resources that would generally be consumed. As the demand for recycled glass sand grows, items commonly not accepted in curbside recycling may become more readily accepted. Keep an eye out for changes in what glass your local town or city government accepts.

IN THIS CHAPTER

» Recognizing different metals and how they're made

» Appreciating the benefits of metal recycling

» Checking out the metal recycling process

» Exploring what metals you can and can't recycle

» Looking at ways you can reduce your impact

Chapter **9**

Identifying Metals and Where to Recycle Them

O ne of the most successful recycling stories is that of metals. They're easy to recycle, they can be recycled repeatedly without any loss in quality, and there's an excellent market for the material. In fact, you might already be using recycled metals and not even know it.

And it doesn't end there! The benefits of recycling your metals extend much further than simply reusing the material. Most importantly, we reduce our reliance on virgin resources by recycling metals. That means less energy-intensive mining impacting our natural environment. This translates to less energy use, fewer harmful chemicals, and fewer holes in the Earth. It also means that fewer valuable materials are wasting away in landfills. Recycling metals is a win-win every way you look at it.

In this chapter, I describe the various types of metals and the effort involved in extracting them and converting them into products. I give you the necessary information to recycle metals in your curbside bin successfully, providing you an understanding of which metals can go in and which ones can't. I also give you some options for recycling your metals through specialist recyclers.

Beginning with the Basics: What Are Metals?

TECHNICAL STUFF

Metals have played a significant role in human history. We've even had eras of history named after them, like the Bronze or Iron Ages. Hunters and gatherers harnessed metal's strength to make tools as far back as 5000 BCE. One of the most significant advancements in human civilization was learning how to extract these elements from the Earth and transform them into a variety of useful items. Since then, humans have found many ways to harness the benefits of metals, expand their applications, and even discover new metals.

Metals are identified as materials that are solid, shiny, and opaque. They're also known for being good electrical conductors, allowing an electric charge to flow through them. Metals most commonly found in the home are aluminum, copper, iron, gold, silver, nickel, and zinc. Some are used in their native forms, like gold and silver, while others get mixed together to create alloys with enhanced properties, like bronze or stainless steel. Perhaps confusingly, metal alloys are commonly just referred to as metals.

Common household objects containing metals include pots and pans, cutlery, drink cans, food tins, and household electrical equipment and appliances. As well as being found in many everyday items, metals are critical to many industries. Where would the aviation, automobile, and other transportation industries be without steel and aluminum? Metals have helped humans fly through the air, dive deep beneath the ocean, and build skyscrapers up to the clouds.

In the following sections, I explain how metals are made and different types of metals you may encounter.

Resources used to make metals

Although metal is found naturally in the Earth's crust, resources are needed to remove it and turn it into the goods we are familiar with. The following list looks at the resources required to complete this transformation:

>> **Ore:** A naturally occurring material containing valuable minerals. One of the most well-known examples of ore is bauxite, a material that's mined to produce aluminum. Ores are located in the Earth's crust and must be extracted and processed to release the minerals or metals inside. (See the nearby sidebar "Defining minerals, rocks, and ore" for more about different mining terms.)

>> **Energy:** Mining is a highly energy-intensive industry. All of the processes required to get metal from the ground and put it into a product in our home or workplace use a large amount of energy.

>> **Chemicals:** The various refining methods used to remove metals from ores are not only energy intensive but involve many chemicals. These chemicals can be toxic and must be handled carefully. For example, cyanide separates gold from its ore, but it's a highly toxic substance that can kill humans. Although many countries closely regulate or ban the use of cyanide, accidents can happen. The less we need to rely on processes requiring such dangerous chemicals, the better.

>> **Water:** Mining uses water primarily for mineral extraction, processing, and dust suppression. Mines acquire water from various sources depending on what is available. Sources can include groundwater, rivers, or nearby lakes. The amount of water used depends on what sort of mineral is being extracted and the type of mining operation. Large-scale mines can use more than 60,000 cubic meters or 16 million gallons of water daily. Managing water is an important environmental issue for mines today, and many work hard to reduce their water use through recycling and improved management.

DEFINING MINERALS, ROCKS, AND ORE

There are many terms used in mining that can get a little confusing. Here I explain these terms, so they make more sense:

- **Mineral:** A naturally occurring crystalline solid made from an inorganic compound or element. Minerals can be pure metals like gold and silver or nonmetallic compounds like quartz or calcite.

- **Rock:** A rock is a substance that's made up of more than one mineral. Some examples you might recognize are granite, sandstone, and limestone.

- **Ore:** Ore is a type of rock that contains valuable minerals. A good example is bauxite ore, a clayey rock that contains aluminum.

- **Metal:** Metals are elements, meaning they cannot be broken down further. Metals are generally identified as solid, shiny, and opaque materials. Examples are gold, copper, aluminum, and silver.

How metals are made

Metals occur naturally in the Earth's crust, but most require some effort to convert them into a useful form. Processing ore into metals starts with exploration and ends with the disposal of the material. In a take-make-waste linear model, these materials are sent to a landfill at the end of their life.

Here are the steps for processing metals, illustrated in Figure 9-1. As you follow the steps, consider all the resources, energy, and effort wasted when this material is simply tossed into a landfill.

1. **Geologists explore for ore.**

   First, we must find the ore. Tremendous effort goes into locating ore bodies below the surface of the Earth well before even one piece of rock is removed. Geologists review as much data as possible, but once they've found a likely ore body, they must test their theory. They drill holes, take samples, and run geotechnical analyses to confirm the location and size of the ore body. Both energy and resources are used to execute these tasks.

2. **The ore is excavated.**

   The next stage after an ore body has been established is to excavate the ore from the ground for processing. The two main methods used to remove ore are open-pit mining (quarries) and underground mining:

   - In open-pit mining, also known as surface mining, the ore is removed directly from the Earth's surface. Miners essentially excavate a large hole in the ground to retrieve the ore. Open-pit mining is the most common method for extracting ore, but it's successful only when ore deposits are close to the surface.
   - Underground mining is used to extract much deeper deposits. Shafts and tunnels are excavated, often through solid rock, to access the ore and transport it to the surface.

3. **The ore is crushed and milled.**

   The ore must be separated from any rocks or other elements that were dug up during the excavation. The ore goes through multiple crushing and milling machines to break it into smaller pieces and then grind them into fine particles ready for processing. Equipment like feeders, jaw crushers, ball mills, and roll crushers invoke images straight out of a science fiction novel.

4. **Metals are extracted from the ore.**

   The remaining raw materials must now be separated from the metals. Three methods are commonly used to extract metals from ore: heating, chemical processing, or electrolysis. For instance, electrolysis is used to extract aluminum from its ore, whereas substantially more complex chemical procedures are needed to separate rare earth metals. Once extracted, the metal may go through additional steps to refine it further and remove impurities.

TECHNICAL STUFF

Electrolysis is a technique used to remove impurities from metals. It works by passing an electric current through the molten metal using two rods, an anode, and a cathode. This creates a chemical reaction that leads to the pure mineral depositing onto one of the rods, where it can be easily collected while leaving contaminants behind.

5. **The metals are manufactured.**

   The metal is sent to a factory, where it's transformed into products. There are many ways to fabricate metal into an end product. They involve processes like casting, cutting, forging, extrusion, machining, stamping, and welding, just to name a few.

   Many metal products that we use are made from metal alloys. As I explain earlier in this chapter, this is where more than one metal or some combination of metals and nonmetal materials are mixed to make a product with enhanced properties. Stainless steel is a well-known example used in many everyday products.

6. **The metals are distributed and purchased.**

   Metals and alloys make their way into consumer goods, structural materials, and vehicles. Metal packaged products make their way to supermarket shelves, where you and I can purchase them.

7. **Consumers dispose of the metals.**

   In the case of products packaged using metals, like aluminum soda cans or steel food cans, once we've emptied them of their contents, we throw them out. Depending on your access to services and bin choice, they'll either get recycled, go to a landfill or an incineration plant, or end up polluting our environment.

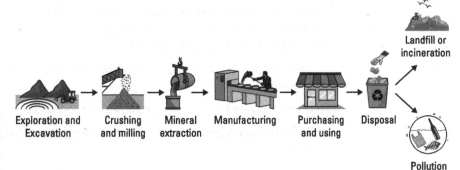

FIGURE 9-1:
The linear steps for extracting and processing metals from ore.

© John Wiley & Sons, Inc.

WHERE DO YOUR METALS COME FROM?

Rich mineral deposits don't occur in every country, so once the ore has been processed, it may be transported from the country of origin to a producing country. China and Australia lead the way in aluminum mining, but China, India, and Russia are the top producers of aluminum. The countries that mine the most iron ore are China, Brazil, and Australia, whereas China and the European Union have the highest steel production. The countries with the largest mines aren't necessarily the top producers; some nations may export ore while others export processed metals.

It's still possible that the aluminum or steel in your soda or soup can is mined or produced locally, as there are many smaller producing countries, but it's important to keep in perspective just how far the materials that you use every day may have traveled.

Common types of metals and metal alloys

REMEMBER

There are two categories of metals and alloys: ferrous and nonferrous.

>> **Ferrous metals:** They contain iron and are known for their strength and durability. The most common example of ferrous metal is steel.

>> **Nonferrous metals:** They don't contain iron, so they have different properties from ferrous metals. They're more flexible and have more resistance to rust and corrosion. Examples of nonferrous metals include aluminum, brass, bronze, silver, copper, lead, and gold.

Some of the most common metals you will encounter daily include

>> **Aluminum:** Without aluminum's incredible strength and very low weight, jet planes would never have gotten off the ground. Not only does it have a high strength-to-weight ratio, but it's also particularly rust resistant. The most recognizable items made from aluminum are beverage cans and aluminum foil. But our lives are filled with aluminum products. Here are just a few items that often include this versatile material:

- Electronic products like laptops, tablets, smartphones, TVs, and sound equipment

- Homewares like furniture, picture frames, and appliances

- Kitchen products, including pots and pans, baking dishes, cutlery, and utensils

- Sporting goods like bicycles, ski bindings and poles, and mountain-climbing equipment

- Construction materials like aluminum window frames

» **Steel:** Undoubtedly the most common metal, steel is an alloy made from carbon and iron. Adding carbon makes it stronger. Many products use steel, from refrigerators and washing machines to building structures, railways, cars, trains, and planes. Steel is also very important in storing food in cans.

» **Stainless steel:** Stainless steel is an alloy made from iron, carbon, chromium, and possibly small amounts of other metals. The chromium helps create a barrier against corrosion. You likely have a lot of stainless steel around your home, like pots and pans, toasters, microwaves, ovens, mixing bowls, cutlery, and other utensils.

» **Carbon steel:** By adding more carbon to the steel alloy mix, you end up with carbon steel. The result is even harder and stronger than regular steel. Carbon steel's main application is in construction, but you can also find it in gears, cables, and airplanes.

» **Wrought iron:** This form of iron has been heated and worked into shape with tools. Products include balcony railings, doors, furniture, and other decorative pieces.

» **Copper:** A metal with a long history, copper is mainly known for being an excellent conductor of heat and electricity and very resistant to corrosion. Copper is also malleable and ductile, which means it can be hammered into shape or easily made into wires. Another handy feature is copper's antibacterial properties. Copper is one of the very few metals that can kill microorganisms on its surface. We use copper in electronics, water pipes, kitchenware, jewelry, tools, and electrical devices.

» **Bronze:** A copper alloy containing tin, bronze is most notably known for the "Bronze Age." It's a hard metal with good corrosion resistance and electrical conductivity. Today iron and iron alloys have replaced many of the products once made from bronze. Despite this, bronze is still widely used for certain engine parts, ship propellers, musical instruments (like bells and gongs), and decorative homeware items like door knobs and handles.

» **Brass:** Although brass didn't get a prehistoric period named after it as bronze did, it's known to have existed since 300 BCE. It's an alloy of copper and zinc and is popular not only for its functional properties but also because of its attractive golden color. Typical uses are furniture, musical instruments, and many industrial applications like plumbing, ammunition and gears, and hinges.

Understanding Why You Should Recycle Metals

A good way to appreciate the impacts of metals and their production is to consider the long path from raw material to the tin cans in your cupboard. There's excavation, crushing, separation, manufacturing, and then transportation to the store and to your house. It's a lot of energy and resources for a small steel can that you've just emptied and are about to toss into the recycling bin. At least I hope that's what you're going to do. Not only do all those steps use a lot of energy and resources, but they also pose significant risks to the environment.

One of the best things about metals is that they can be infinitely recycled. Metals never lose their quality or degrade in the recycling process and can be used over and over again. In fact, metals like aluminum can be recycled and back on the supermarket shelf within as little as 60 days.

REMEMBER

Metal recycling is one of the most valuable things you can do, and luckily, it's pretty straightforward. Yet globally, more than half of the aluminum cans purchased yearly are tossed in the trash or pollute the environment. Aluminum cans can take hundreds of years to break down, so they will sit there for a long time. Meanwhile, we continue to use virgin materials to make new cans. It's a terrible waste for such a useful and easily recycled resource to languish in landfills.

In the following sections, I take you through the many other advantages of recycling your metals.

Preserving natural resources

Everything we consume requires resources. We'll eventually run out if we keep using virgin resources for every product we make and use. Either that or the Earth will be so full of holes from us mining the stuff, it'll look like Swiss cheese.

Despite our concerns over climate change and the environment, demand for materials like aluminum and steel continues to grow. And the problem is intensifying as developing countries build their economies. Recycled metals can help offset this growth in demand and reduce our reliance on raw materials. Appreciating the value of an object and ensuring it continues on its circular journey through recycling to a new product helps minimize the impacts.

Decreasing carbon emissions

Mining and processing metals are extremely energy-hungry activities. Mining uses almost 10 percent of the world's overall energy consumption and results in considerable carbon dioxide (CO_2) emissions. According to McKinsey, the production of metals, in particular steel and aluminum, contributes about 4.2 gigatons of CO_2 equivalent emissions.

The source of energy use and associated emissions in mining include the following:

>> There's a heavy dependency on fossil fuels in the form of diesel used in heavy machinery.

>> Due to the remoteness of mining activity, diesel generators are frequently used to generate electricity on-site.

>> Significant energy input is necessary for metal refining and ore processing.

>> Most mineral deposits are situated in remote locations and require significant energy for transportation, not to mention the shipping and other transportation required for international usage.

REMEMBER

Using recycled materials can offset this energy significantly. Recycling metals uses less energy and produces less carbon dioxide than virgin metal production. In fact, recycled steel uses more than 60 percent less energy than producing steel from iron ore. Recycling just one aluminum can saves enough power to run your TV for three hours. You're wasting significant energy along with the materials if you toss your metal cans in the general trash.

Preserving the environment

WARNING

Mining is destructive to the natural environment in many ways. Thankfully, many regulations and laws are in place that protect the environment and communities from the impacts of mining. However, it's difficult to remove all of the risks. Here are just a few of the ways mining impacts the environment:

>> Surface mining can leave large open pits — so large they can be very difficult to rehabilitate. Plus, soil removal related to the establishment of mines and associated site facilities can harm the environment and have a detrimental effect on the local fauna and flora.

>> If not appropriately managed, mining can have a devastating impact on groundwater and local waterways. Wastewater from mining processes can contaminate surrounding groundwater or waterways. In the worst case, the water is polluted with toxic chemicals like arsenic or mercury.

>> Underground mining can affect groundwater. Mining operations require significant amounts of water, which often come from nearby groundwater sources. Some underground mines may even pump groundwater away from a site to operate the mine without flooding. Removing groundwater can lower water levels in streams, rivers, and lakes and impact soil conditions, biodiversity, and local communities.

>> Mining can expose sulfides in the soil that can form sulfuric acid when exposed to rainwater or groundwater. This water can also dissolve toxic heavy metals from surrounding rocks. This process is called *acid mine drainage,* and it can harm the environment if not managed correctly.

>> Where mining results in clearing natural forests, wind can erode exposed surfaces and pick up toxic elements from the exposed rocks, creating air pollution.

Recycling metals can significantly reduce the negative environmental impacts of mining.

Looking at How Metal Is Recycled

As with most recycling, the process starts with collecting the waste material. When you dispose of your metal cans and other metal packaging in your curbside recycling bin, you're helping keep these metals in use and reducing our reliance on raw materials.

The steps for collecting and recycling metals are relatively consistent worldwide, although some steps may vary slightly depending on where you live. Here I describe the steps involved in recycling metals (see Figure 9-2):

1. **Consumers recycle cans, tins, and other metal items.**

   The process of recycling metal begins when you put your metal cans and tins in your recycling bin.

2. **The metal is collected.**

   Metal waste is collected through curbside recycling, drop-off centers, or a metal scrapyard. I explain more about metal scrapyards and how to use them later in this chapter.

3. **The metal is sorted.**

   Once received at the recycling facility, the metal is separated from the other recyclables. Unless your area has a multi-stream collection, in this case, you'll have already done the sorting. Sorting at the facility may be done by hand but is more likely to involve automated machines incorporating magnets, infrared scanners, or X-rays to identify the metals.

TECHNICAL
STUFF

   Steel cans are separated from recyclable material using a strong magnet. The magnet attracts the steel can and drops it into a separate container. Aluminum and other nonferrous metals are also separated using a magnet, even though they're not magnetic. When an aluminum can is subjected to a changing magnetic field, a spiraling electric current, or "eddy current," forms in the aluminum. The eddy current creates a magnetic field, which is opposed by the original magnetic field. This causes the aluminum can to fly off the conveyor.

4. **The metal is crushed and baled.**

   Metals are flattened and formed into bales for transporting to a metal manufacturer. The metals are then shredded into small pieces to aid the melting process. It also reduces the amount of energy required to melt the metal.

5. **The metal is melted and undergoes purification.**

   Metals are melted in a giant furnace. The temperature of the furnace changes depending on the metal, and the time it takes to melt can vary from a few minutes to several hours. Melting metal also helps separate any impurities. They rise to the top and can be removed easily. Electrolysis is sometimes used to remove any remaining contaminants. Once purified, the metal is cooled into different-sized bars or sheets for easy identification and transportation to manufacturers.

6. The recycled metal is manufactured.

These bars or sheets are delivered to manufacturers and used in new products. Aluminum or steel cans make their way to a factory to be filled with product, labeled, packed, and then transported to a supermarket or other retail store. As I mention earlier in this chapter, recycled aluminum can be back on supermarket shelves in only 60 days.

7. The recycled metal is purchased and used.

Consumers like you and me purchase products in cans, use them, and discard them. Then hopefully you recycle them so that the cycle starts over again.

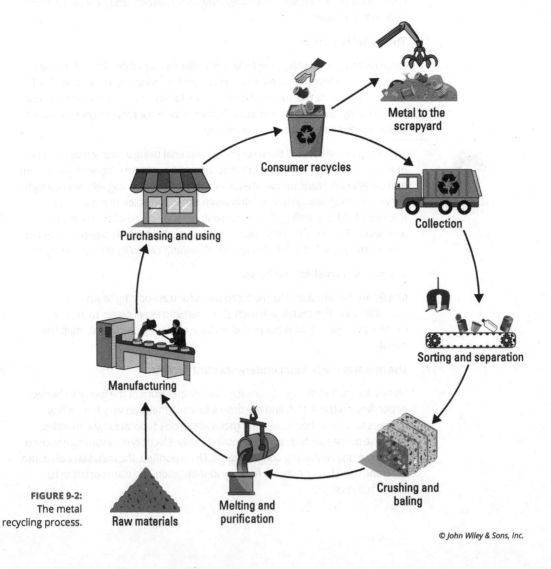

Metal to the scrapyard

Consumer recycles

Purchasing and using

Collection

Sorting and separation

Manufacturing

Crushing and baling

Melting and purification

Raw materials

FIGURE 9-2: The metal recycling process.

© John Wiley & Sons, Inc.

Knowing What Metal Items Can and Can't Be Recycled

Figuring out how to recycle your metal packaging is as simple as getting familiar with what goes in and what stays out. In the following sections, I take you through some common rules and tips to help you recycle your metals properly.

Asking about local metal rules

REMEMBER

Metal recycling is relatively straightforward, and there aren't many differences from one location to the next. There are, however, a few things worth checking in your local area, just in case:

>> **Does my curbside recycling program accept metal?** If you have access to a curbside recycling service, they will likely accept metal. Recycled metal is quite a valuable material. Despite this, it's always worth checking what your local area accepts. If you don't have access to curbside recycling, you may have a recycling center or container deposit program nearby where you can drop off your cans. If you live in an apartment, you might have a shared dumpster for metals.

>> **Do I need to separate my metal from other recyclables?** Curbside recycling services that use multi-stream collection might require you to place your metal waste in a separate bin. In other locations, metal and plastics go into the same container. There are many different bin configurations, so check your local area. For those who live in an apartment, be sure to check the rules for your complex as well. You can use the worksheet in the later section "Pulling it all together" to note what you find out.

>> **Do I need to crush my metals?** Crushing your aluminum cans before recycling them can help save space, but unfortunately, it may hinder the recycling process. It's particularly a problem in single-stream recycling. The equipment used to separate metal cans from other recyclables is designed to identify the standard shape and size of an empty can. A crushed can is potentially more difficult to separate because it has a different shape and size. As a result, the item may get missed and end up contaminating other recyclables or getting sent to a landfill. Crushed cans may also be an issue in container deposit programs where they need to be able to read the bar code. So it's best to check what your local area requires.

Why not take all of your metals to a metal scrapyard to avoid this issue? If you collect your aluminum cans and take them directly to a scrapyard, it doesn't matter if you crush them or not. Find out more about scrapyards later in this chapter.

Following a few guidelines for metal

Here are my top tips for recycling your metal packaging:

>> **Place only metal packaging in your recycling bin.** Curbside recycling services offered to homes are designed to collect and process packaging. So when it comes to recycling metals through your curbside bin, stick to packaging like aluminum beverage cans or steel tins. All other metal items found in the home are best recycled at a metal scrapyard (as I describe later in this chapter).

>> **Remove all food residue.** It's best to keep your recycling free from food residues. You don't need to scrub your tins and cans until they're spotless, but you'll want to ensure they're empty of liquids or solids. In other words, if you're recycling a food can with significant food residue, give it a quick rinse with water before throwing it in your recycling bin.

>> **Remove all parts that aren't metal.** Often products have multiple materials. For example, glass jars may have a metal lid. You must separate these parts and recycle them separately. In other chapters in Part 2, you can discover how to recycle any plastic, glass, or paper parts.

Different material types are recycled best when they are separated.

>> **Leave labels on.** There is no need to remove labels from aluminum cans or tin cans. If they can be removed very easily, like paper labels on a tin can, then go ahead; it will definitely help. However, removing them is unnecessary because they're burnt off during the recycling process.

>> **Check the size.** Curbside recycling is designed to collect only metal packaging, so if you stick to that rule, you won't have an issue with items being too big. If you're struggling to fit your old sink in your recycling bin, it's a clear sign that it doesn't belong there. Large items may be collected through a local government bulk collection or can be taken to a transfer station or metal scrapyard.

>> **Collect the small things.** Conversely, some metal items are too small and can fall through the cracks at the recycling facility. Bottle caps, pop tabs, and ring pulls from aluminum cans are perfect examples of items that are too small.

A great idea is to collect any small metal items that are too small to be processed at the recycling facility and take them to a metal scrapyard. Follow these steps:

1. First, work out whether the item is made from aluminum or steel using the magnet test. I explain how to identify ferrous and nonferrous metals using a magnet in the next section.

2. Find a can made from the same metal.

3. Collect the bottle caps, ring pulls, and other small items in the can. For example, place the steel caps in a steel can and the aluminum caps in an aluminum can.

4. Once the can is half full, squeeze the top shut so they don't fall out.

   WARNING

   Be careful not to cut yourself if the can has sharp edges.

5. Take the items to your local scrapyard.

Identifying your metals

Because curbside recycling accepts only metal packaging, only a few types of metals belong in your curbside bin. They're steel, a ferrous metal, and aluminum, a nonferrous metal. Ferrous metals are usually relatively easy to distinguish from nonferrous metals because most of them will stick to a magnet. Table 9-1 provides some examples of ferrous and nonferrous metals.

TABLE 9-1 ## Examples of Ferrous and Nonferrous Metals

Ferrous	Nonferrous
Iron	Aluminum
Steel	Copper
Stainless steel	Brass
Wrought iron	Bronze
Carbon steel	Zinc
	Lead
	Tin
	Gold
	Silver

TIP

Find a magnet around the house and place it against the metal object. If the magnet sticks, the metal is ferrous and likely steel. If it doesn't stick, then it's most likely nonferrous and aluminum.

TIP

There are some types of stainless steel that a magnet won't stick to, even though they do contain iron. However, the kinds of items you can recycle in your curbside recycling won't be made from stainless steel. If you need to dispose of an item like this, it's best to take it to a metal scrapyard if you can.

Seeing what metal items go in

In Table 9-2, I provide a list of the common metal objects you can recycle in your curbside recycling bin. If you don't have access to curbside recycling and instead use a nearby recycling center, they will likely have similar rules. However, they may accept more items than what's listed here.

TABLE 9-2 **What Metals Items Go in Your Curbside Bin**

Item	Description of items
	Aluminum beverage cans: This includes beer and soft drink cans and any other beverage in a can. Empty all the contents before recycling. Check whether your local recycling service prefers that you crush your cans or leave them intact.
	Steel or aluminum food cans: Examples include many canned foods like soups, vegetables, and beans, just to name a few. They're usually made from steel but occasionally aluminum, both of which are recyclable in your curbside bin. Make sure no food is left in them, and give them a quick rinse.
	Metal can lids: The lids on metal cans are almost always made from the same material as the can, so they're recyclable. It's a good idea to push or place the lid back into the can to ensure the lid won't get missed in the sorting process. But depending on your can opener, the lids can have sharp edges, so it pays to be careful with them.
	Aluminum foil: Did you know aluminum foil is recyclable? Make sure it's clean and dry, and then roll it into a ball. Keep rolling new pieces onto the ball until it's about the size of a baseball. Then you can toss it in your curbside recycling bin. You can even include foil trays and foil wrappers from Easter eggs. Mind you, if you used the foil to cook nachos or some other greasy food, it might have too much cheese for recycling. If that's the case, toss it in your general waste bin.

Keeping some metal items out

Curbside recycling is intended to accept only your everyday metal packaging, like tins and beverage cans. The following list of household goods made from or containing metals cannot be recycled through your curbside service. Note that if you're using a local recycling center instead of curbside recycling, be sure to check the rules. You'll find a list of these items and some tips on what you can do with them in Table 9-3.

TABLE 9-3   **What Metal Items Stay Out of Your Curbside Bin**

Item	Description of items
	Pots and pans: When your old pots and pans are at the end of their life, you cannot dispose of them in your curbside bin. Many pots and pans have a *Teflon* coating, which makes them nonstick. Unfortunately, this makes recycling them problematic. Check with your local scrap metal facility to see whether they accept them.
	Metal coat hangers: Coat hangers can easily get caught in the machinery at recycling facilities, so they're generally not accepted. Try taking metal coat hangers to your local dry cleaners to see whether they can reuse them; otherwise, take them to your metal scrapyard.
	Metal cutlery and kitchen knives: Although generally made from stainless steel, metal cutlery can be dangerous in curbside recycling collection. Imagine someone being stuck with a fork or knife while sorting through the recycling! If they're still in good condition, try donating to a charity. Or why not make your own reusable cutlery sets for the whole family? I use an old cutlery set for work. I leave it at the office so that when I buy my lunch, I always have a set on hand and don't have to rely on disposable cutlery. And if one of the pieces goes missing, I just grab another piece from home.
	Household appliances (also known as white goods): Household appliances like toasters, fridges, coffee machines, and slow cookers can have many metal parts worth recycling. But these items don't belong in your curbside bin. They're classed as e-waste or WEEE (waste electrical and electronic equipment) because they have an electrical cord. E-waste must be handled with care by a specialist recycler. Find out more about e-waste in Chapter 13.
	Electrical cords and cables: Electrical wires and cables can contain high-value materials like copper and aluminum. However, it takes specialist machines to separate the plastic insulation from the metals. They don't belong in your curbside recycling bin. Cables can get caught in sorting machines and cause safety issues. Many e-waste programs accept cables and cords, but if you can't find a nearby recycling program, then put them in the general waste bin.

(continued)

TABLE 9-3 (*continued*)

Item	Description of items
	Razor blades: Razor blades are another item that can be dangerous in curbside recycling. Not only are they dangerous, but it's also hard for the machines to pick them up because of their size. You can take them to a metal scrapyard, or why not get on board with TerraCycle's razor recycling program? Find out more at www.terracycle.com.
	Metal toys: The problem with toys is that most have many parts made from different materials. They can include plastic, metal, and even paper parts. It's a lot of work separating these different materials, so curbside recycling programs can't manage them. Teach your kids to look after their toys so they last a long time, and donate them if they're in good condition.
	Car or bicycle parts: Reuse when you can; otherwise, take your car or bike parts to a metal scrapyard. Note that motor oil cans will need to go to your local government hazardous waste drop-off location.
	Metal tools: Reuse or donate tools if they are in good condition; otherwise, take these to a metal scrapyard. Tool libraries are popping up in many locations. They're just like traditional book libraries, but instead of borrowing books, you borrow tools. If you have tools you no longer need, why not try donating them to a local tool library so they will continue to be used?
	Building materials: Metal building materials like roofing or fixtures don't belong in your curbside bins. Recycling facilities aren't built to process these sorts of items. Scrapyards are the best place to take these, and being large items, you might even make a few dollars.
	Computers, phones, TVs, and other electronic devices: E-waste like TVs, computers, monitors, phones, and other electrical devices can contain hazardous materials like lead or chromium. So these items should be disposed of at your local e-waste or WEEE specialist recyclers. See Chapter 13 for more information.
	Hazardous materials: Items like batteries or propane gas tanks need to be handled with care because they contain hazardous materials and can be combustible. When included in curbside recycling, they can pose a risk to workers and machinery. They also don't belong in your general waste bin. For example, certain types of batteries can spark and cause fires when disposed of in with general waste material. It's important that hazardous materials are handled carefully to mitigate these risks. Many town and city governments organize collection days or permanent drop-off locations for their residents. These can be a great way to dispose of many different hazardous materials you have around the home. Discover more on this and other specialist recycling programs in Chapter 14.

TIP

Keep items in use for as long as you can because a lot of time and resources were invested in creating them. When you no longer need them, try to find someone else who can use them through a secondhand market. If you have no luck selling or donating them, the next best option is to take them to a metal scrapyard to be recycled. Find more information on metal scrapyards later in this chapter.

Checking on a few unusual metal items

Acceptance of some items varies depending on whether you have access to curbside recycling or a nearby recycling center. If you live in an apartment, acceptance might also depend on the rules in your complex. Table 9-4 is a list of items you should check to see if they're accepted in your area.

TABLE 9-4   **What Metal Items to Check with Your Local City or Town**

Item	Description of items
	**Paint cans:** Some programs accept paint cans but only if they're empty and the paint residue has dried. However, many places require you to take old paint cans to a hazardous waste center or specialist recycler. Paint drop-off locations can be found in many countries. In fact, in some areas, even the old paint gets recycled. It's converted into an energy source or used in industrial applications.
	Aerosol spray cans: Many curbside recycling programs don't accept aerosol cans because they can explode. Examples include deodorants, hair sprays, insect sprays, paint cans, cooking oil, or whipped cream cans (my favorite!). Check with your local area. If they're accepted, make sure the can is empty. If it's full, then it should be treated as hazardous waste. In this case, you can either empty it or take it to a hazardous waste drop-off near your home.
	Cooking oil tins: Many curbside recycling services and recycling centers accept small cooking oil tins, like the type you keep in your kitchen pantry, but not all do. As with all metal recycling, ensure your cooking oil cans are empty before placing them in your curbside bin.
	Glass jar lids: For the majority of locations, you'll likely be requested to separate metal lids from glass jars. If the lids are larger than a credit card, you can put them straight in your recycling bin. However, smaller lids are not usually accepted, but you can collect them and take them to a nearby metal scrapyard. For more info, see the earlier section "Following a few guidelines for metal." However, some locations do ask you to leave lids on your glass jars as they will get picked up through the recycling process.

Pulling it all together

Figure 9-3 is a worksheet to help you record your local rules in one place. Use this worksheet to summarize the metal recycling rules for your area.

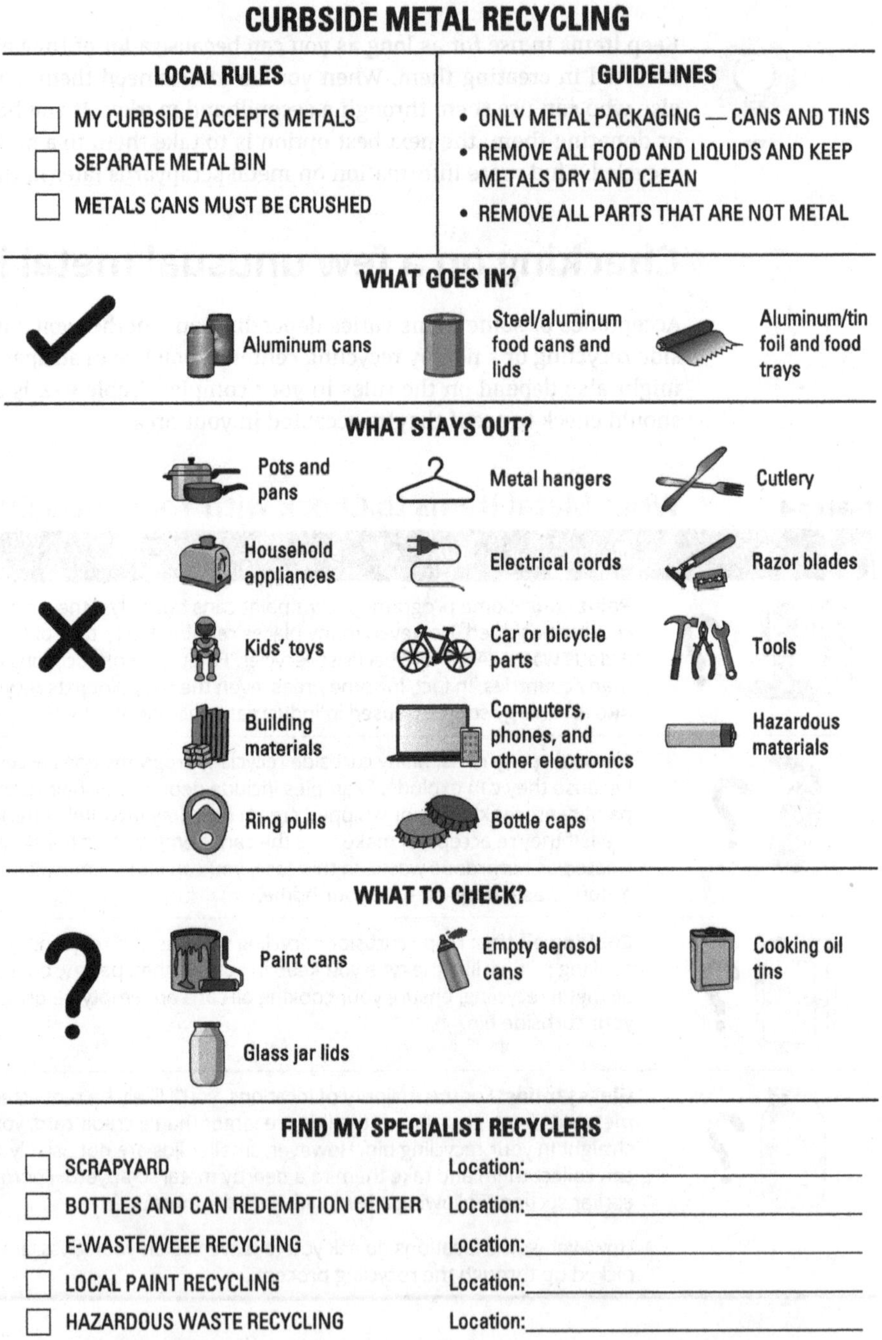

CURBSIDE METAL RECYCLING

LOCAL RULES	GUIDELINES
☐ MY CURBSIDE ACCEPTS METALS	• ONLY METAL PACKAGING — CANS AND TINS
☐ SEPARATE METAL BIN	• REMOVE ALL FOOD AND LIQUIDS AND KEEP METALS DRY AND CLEAN
☐ METALS CANS MUST BE CRUSHED	• REMOVE ALL PARTS THAT ARE NOT METAL

WHAT GOES IN?

✓ Aluminum cans   Steel/aluminum food cans and lids   Aluminum/tin foil and food trays

WHAT STAYS OUT?

Pots and pans   Metal hangers   Cutlery

Household appliances   Electrical cords   Razor blades

✗ Kids' toys   Car or bicycle parts   Tools

Building materials   Computers, phones, and other electronics   Hazardous materials

Ring pulls   Bottle caps

WHAT TO CHECK?

? Paint cans   Empty aerosol cans   Cooking oil tins

Glass jar lids

FIND MY SPECIALIST RECYCLERS

☐ SCRAPYARD   Location:_____

☐ BOTTLES AND CAN REDEMPTION CENTER   Location:_____

☐ E-WASTE/WEEE RECYCLING   Location:_____

☐ LOCAL PAINT RECYCLING   Location:_____

☐ HAZARDOUS WASTE RECYCLING   Location:_____

© John Wiley & Sons, Inc.

FIGURE 9-3: Metal recycling worksheet.

Surveying Specialist Metal Recycling Services

Many of the objects around our homes that contain metal don't belong in your curbside bin. But don't worry, there are other options. In some countries, local governments organize pickup services for bulkier items that cannot go in your curbside program. These are called bulk collection or hard rubbish services. These can be a good way to dispose of your large metal items.

However, two specialist services are available for recycling your waste metal: container deposits and metal scrapyards. And the good news is that you can make money from both of these services.

Collecting for container deposits

A container deposit scheme works by adding a small cost to the price of the can or bottle at the store, which is then refunded to you when it's returned. Although they accept only aluminum beverage cans, not food cans, they are a great option if you don't have access to curbside recycling. You can even get some money back by recycling this way. Plus, collection of recycling through container deposit schemes leads to lower contamination and a cleaner product for use by manufacturers.

Here's how to recycle cans at a container deposit depot:

1. **First, find out whether you have a container deposit depot nearby.**

2. **Check the rules on what they accept.**

3. **Start collecting your cans in a container.**

TIP You can also take glass and plastic beverage bottles to a container deposit depot, so don't forget to collect them too.

4. **Take your collection to the depot, and they will pay you the going rate for your cans.**

TIP Here are some ways to make a little extra money:

>> Ask friends and family whether they will collect cans for you.

>> Check with your local cafés or bars to see whether they would be happy for you to take theirs.

>> Keep your eyes peeled for litter around the street. Not only will you get a little more cash, but you'll also be helping to reduce litter.

How much money can you make? Most container deposit schemes offer only about 5 to 10 cents in your local currency. So how much you can make will depend on how many cans you collect. Collecting cans over time and going to the depot only when you have enough will make the trip more worthwhile.

Making money at the scrapyard

Metal scrapyards have been around for hundreds of years. Their business is to purchase various types of scrap metal from whoever wants to sell it, businesses and individuals, and then to sell it to manufacturers. They'll collect all sorts of metals, including steel, aluminum, copper, zinc, brass, and other rare metals.

In the last few years, my husband and I started collecting our waste metal, including aluminum cans and foil, and taking it to a nearby scrapyard. We don't make much money, but we feel good knowing that the metal doesn't risk being missed by the sorting system at the facility where our recycling is taken. It also means we can collect and recycle all the small pieces and different types of metals like copper, brass, and zinc that don't belong in curbside recycling.

TIP

You can pretty much take any metal item not accepted by regular curbside recycling to a scrapyard. Here are some tips for taking your metal to the scrapyard:

>> Some scrapyards require you to show ID, so bring it with you. This might seem onerous, but they must record your ID to adhere to laws regarding anti-metal-theft legislation in place in many countries. It helps discourage people from stealing street signs, copper wiring, or piping from building and other sites.

>> Scrapyards accept most metal items, but it's still a good idea to check their rules before you head there.

>> Check if there's a minimum amount of material you must have to get paid. You might need to keep collecting for a few weeks or months until you have enough.

>> For items that are encased in plastic or combined with other materials, the typical rule is the product needs to be at least 50 percent metal. If it's less than 50 percent metal, try to remove some of the nonmetal parts or separate the metal.

>> Separate metals by type if you can. You can use the magnet test to separate the ferrous and nonferrous metals (see the earlier section "Identifying your metals"). Although not essential, it can help ensure you have enough of the

different metals for a payment. Plus, it will speed up the process when you get to the scrapyard.

>> If you're not sure an item is made of metal, don't be afraid to ask at the yard. I'm sure they'll be happy to help.

Many scrapyards usually won't accept electronics or household appliances. These items are classified as e-waste because they have batteries or a power cable. Some scrapyards might accept them as long as you remove the battery. However, e-waste is best recycled by specialist recyclers. Many places have collection programs for e-waste; you can find out more about this in Chapter 13.

It can be quite a bit of work collecting enough scrap metal to make a decent amount of money. But if you're willing to work hard, it can be done. Here are a few tips to get you started:

>> Nonferrous metals, like copper, aluminum, and zinc, usually have a higher value than ferrous metals like steel.

>> Prices can fluctuate depending on market conditions, so always check on or near the day you plan to drop it off.

>> Separating the different types of metals helps you get a better price. When your metals are mixed, scrapyards may only offer you the value of the lowest-priced metal in the mix.

Reducing Your Consumption of Metals

Once you've figured out how to recycle your metal, it might be good to consider how to reduce your overall use. It's good to start with small changes here and there; over time, they will make a bigger difference than you would imagine.

In the kitchen, consider the following:

>> Reduce the quantity of food packaging you consume by making your own soups and other foods from scratch or simply using fresh ingredients.

>> Reuse aluminum foil if it's still clean. You can even wash it and let it dry if it has some food residue on it.

>> Switch to silicone baking liners that can be washed and reused.

>> Use beeswax wraps to wrap your sandwiches and other food items instead of aluminum foil, or simply place it straight into a reusable plastic container.

>> Choosing metal packaging over plastic is a good idea, but make sure you recycle it when you're finished with it.

Around your home, try the following:

>> Take metal clothes hangers back to the dry cleaner to be reused.

>> If you need new pots or pans, choose cast-iron cookware. It'll last forever and isn't coated with chemicals.

>> Look after your metallic furniture and appliances. Don't leave things out in the weather; even stainless steel will start to rust in certain conditions. Exposure to seawater or humidity can eat away at the protective layer and cause stainless steel to deteriorate. If you live near the ocean or in a humid environment, put away your barbecue or outdoor furniture when you are not using it.

>> Get items fixed instead of replacing them. If you're not great at repairing things, why not search for a local Repair Café? Volunteers in these programs will help you fix all manner of items.

>> Reuse steel or aluminum cans around your home or garage to store things in rather than buying dedicated containers. The great thing about this is that you can still recycle when you're done with them.

Because metal is so easy to recycle, it's not often advertised on a product. Steel cans are made, on average, with 60 percent recycled content. In fact, it can take just a few months for the material to be recycled, made into a new item, and be back on the shelves. This is good news because it means you are probably already using recycled metal products.

Other products that might be made from recycled metals include car and bike parts, as well as construction materials. Products you're more likely to purchase that use recycled metals are appliances, electronic gadgets, and home furniture.

One of the best things you can do is recycle your metal containers. Metals require a lot of energy and resources to create, and when they're dumped in a landfill, all of the energy and resources go to waste. Metals can be infinitely recycled, unlike paper and plastic, and should be viewed as a resource rather than rubbish.

Chapter **10**

Making Sense of Multilayer Materials

Multilayer packaging is made by laminating or gluing together multiple materials to form a single piece of packaging. You may not realize it, but a lot of food packaging you come into contact with daily is multilayer. Sometimes the layering might be obvious, like a milk carton or juice box with its paper board and plastic layers, but others are more difficult to see, like the layers of plastic and aluminum in a chip packet.

The different layers of multilayer packaging provide protection from external elements like light, air, and heat; reduce damage during transport; and in some cases can extend the shelf life of food. On the downside, these layered materials pose a significant challenge for recycling, and most curbside recycling services don't accept them.

In this chapter, I explain why we use multilayer packaging and what materials go into making them. I describe the challenges in collecting and recycling them. Finally, I provide some typical examples and discuss what options might be available for you to recycle them.

Breaking Down Multilayer Materials

Multilayer materials come in many forms, including soft, flexible packaging and more rigid types. Typical examples you might recognize are cartons, pouches, tubes, bags, and single-use coffee cups. Multilayered packaging is a popular choice for many liquids, foods, toiletries, and cosmetics. In the following sections, I describe the functions of different materials and layers, their benefits, and the challenges of recycling them.

Focusing on the functions of different layers and materials

REMEMBER

Multilayer packaging is created when two or more materials are combined to form a single layer or package. The various layers can be combined by coating one material with another, using extrusion methods with the two materials, or by laminating them together thermally or using an adhesive. There may be twelve or more layers of various plastics, frequently mixed with layers of paper or metal. Each layer plays an important role in protecting the contents from heat, moisture, or light, providing structure and the necessary space for logos and information.

Here are some examples of the different layers and their functions:

>> **Structure layer:** Helps the container hold its shape

>> **Protection layer:** Keeps the contents safe from moisture

>> **Barrier layer:** Keeps out air and light

>> **Sealant layer:** Creates a seal or barrier for the contents

>> **Print layer:** A place for logos, nutritional information, and other information

The structural layer is often paperboard-like in a frozen food box but may be a more rigid plastic. An aluminum foil or metalized layer may be included when additional protection is required. This metal layer protects against moisture and air but may also be chosen for its metallic appearance, popular for potato chip brands or chocolate confectionery packaging.

TECHNICAL STUFF

Despite the possible inclusion of paper and metal layers, plastic makes up the majority of the multilayer packaging. Common plastics include

>> **Polyethylene (PE):** Provides a heat and moisture barrier; commonly used in milk and juice cartons or to coat paper cups

>> **Polypropylene (PP or plastic #5):** Provides heat and moisture barriers or structure for toiletries and cosmetic packaging

>> **Ethylene-vinyl alcohol (EVOH):** Regularly used in many packaging types as an oxygen barrier

>> **Low-density polyethylene (LDPE or plastic #4):** Found in cartons and other packaging

>> **Polystyrene (PS or plastic #6):** Commonly used for the outer printing layer

>> **Ethylene-vinyl acetate (EVA):** A common plastic for the adhesive or bonding layer

>> **Polylactic acid (PLA):** A plastic regularly used to coat paper cups and plates

Other plastic layers may be included, particularly as research continues in the pursuit of biodegradable plastics. Find out more about plastic recycling in Chapter 6.

Understanding why products have multilayer materials

REMEMBER

There's a very good reason we use these complex multilayer materials. Multilayer materials help ensure the high quality of food and personal care products we rely on. The different layers protect the products inside in many ways, including these:

>> Extending the shelf life of food

>> Protecting food from elements like light and air

>> Keeping the contents free from bacteria

>> Protecting products from being damaged during transportation

>> Keeping insects and vermin out

>> Keeping toxic dyes from labeling out of food

>> Reducing transportation costs and lowering carbon dioxide (CO_2) emissions because multilayer packaging like soft plastics is light and thin

The solutions offered by multilayer materials are a key part of reducing food waste and feeding the world safely. You can find out more about food waste and how you can reduce your impact in Chapter 12.

Appreciating the recycling challenges

While multilayer packaging provides many benefits, there are also several drawbacks. In particular, it's extremely challenging to collect and recycle. For recycling to work, different materials must be sorted and separated from each other. This is problematic in the case of multilayer packaging because it's very hard to separate the layers. Some methods are available, but they are costly and require significant human involvement.

REMEMBER

Most curbside recycling services don't accept multilayer packaging. The mechanical recycling methods used in most recycling facilities worldwide are unsuitable for multilayered materials. First, separating them from other recyclables like glass, paper, and other plastics is difficult. Second, many multilayer materials are soft plastics, so they not only pose a risk of contamination to other recycling streams, but also, like plastic bags, they can get stuck in the machinery. Discover more about soft plastics in Chapter 11.

Even though recycling this multilayered packaging is challenging, there are some success stories. Specialist recycling of Tetra Paks or long-life milk cartons is now available in many locations. In fact, more than 50 percent of Americans have access to recycling services for this sort of packaging. The main material captured from recycling Tetra Paks is paper, but aluminum and plastic may also be captured. The recovered material can be used to make lower-quality paper products, or a type of construction board that can be used in the building industry as an alternative to traditional plywood.

SIMPLIFYING THE FUTURE WITH NEW PACKAGING

Many brands are working to simplify their packaging to increase its recyclability. One example is Colgate. They've created a toothpaste tube made from a single material instead of the multiple layers typically used in this packaging. This single material (plastic #2 or high-density polyethylene) is much easier to recycle.

Although this is a great step forward in simplifying packaging, it's unlikely that these toothpaste tubes will be accepted in your curbside recycling bin in the near future. Unfortunately, it's too hard for recycling facilities to differentiate between this tube and the regular ones made from multilayer materials. Until such time as they are accepted, you can try recycling them with TerraCycle (www.terracycle.com) in their free Colgate Oral Care program.

Recycling Common Multilayer Materials

Recognizing multilayer products and knowing how to dispose of them is extremely helpful to recycling. Most multilayer materials can't go in your curbside recycling bin, but some are recyclable through specialist recycling services. Recycling soft plastics is one example of these services; see Chapter 11 for more details.

The following sections provide some common examples of multilayer packaging and information on whether your local town or city will likely accept them.

REMEMBER

If you're unsure whether something is recyclable, you're best to discard it in your general rubbish bin. By putting it into your curbside recycling bin, it may end up contaminating other recyclables.

Cartons for liquids and Tetra Paks

A carton or Tetra Pak is a box-shaped container used to store liquids like milk, juice, soups, and stocks. Tetra Pak is a brand name but has become the generic name used by many. Other names include Tetra Briks (another brand name from Tetra Pak), long-life cartons, or simply cartons or boxes. The distinctive feature of the cartons is that they're folded from a single sheet with the recognizable corners folded on the sides.

The cartons are made with a paperboard base combined with multiple layers of plastic and aluminum to create what's referred to as liquid paperboard. There are two types of liquid cartons: shelf-stable cartons stored at room temperature, and cartons that must be refrigerated.

>> **Shelf-stable or long-life cartons:** They're typically made from paper with a thin layer of plastic and aluminum foil. These layers help protect the contents and keep them fresh. Examples include juice, milk, and soup cartons.

They typically have six layers: four layers of plastic, one of paperboard, and one of aluminum. The plastic and aluminum make it hard to recycle these containers, but it's possible, and many new products can be made from the recycled material.

You'll need to check whether your local town or city accepts these cartons in your curbside recycling or find a specialist recycler.

>> **Refrigerated beverage cartons:** The other type of carton you might come across is refrigerated liquid cartons. In a fridge, you'll find these cartons storing products like milk, juice, and cream.

Refrigerated cartons are primarily made from paper with a layer of plastic. Multilayering makes it more challenging, but many areas still accept them in curbside recycling. These containers are often recycled with paper rather than plastic, but occasionally it's the opposite. Be sure to check what your local town or city accepts.

TIP

If you live in the United States and want to see if you have access to carton recycling in your area, check www.recyclecartons.com. For the United Kingdom, check out www.tetrapakrecycling.co.uk/ to find where to recycle your cartons. Otherwise, check with your local town or city government. In Chapter 5, I provide many ways to find your local information.

Plastic-coated food cartons

You can tell whether a carton is plastic coated when it appears shiny or very smooth to the touch. The coating protects the food inside by shielding the packaging from moisture. Imagine a standard cardboard box in the wet environment inside your freezer. It's not likely to last very long. You can often see the multiple layers by tearing one of the corners of the packaging. If it's shiny on at least one side but still tears like paper, it will most likely be a multilayer material that includes a layer of paper and plastic.

Although this plastic coating helps protect the packaging from moisture and the contents from spoiling, it also prevents the paper from being recycled. These boxes can often be recycled as part of the paper recycling process, but many places still don't accept them.

TIP

You can check with your local authority to see whether your curbside service can accept this type of packaging.

Here are some examples to help you identify them:

>> **Frozen food boxes:** Frozen food boxes for foods like pizza, seafood, and prepared meals are typically made with plastic-coated paperboard.

>> **Ice cream containers:** Some ice cream containers are made entirely from plastic, so check first to see what your ice cream container is made of. If it's made from plastic, look for the plastic number on the bottom or label and check whether your local recycling service accepts it. (Chapter 6 provides more instructions on how to recycle your plastics.) If you're able to tear the ice cream container, as mentioned earlier, it's made from liquid paperboard. You'll need to check with your local town or city government if it is accepted or goes in your general waste bin.

>> **Plastic take-out boxes:** Many take-out containers are made from cardboard with a plastic coating to stop them from absorbing food. This gives them a shiny look but also makes recycling very difficult. Like other plastic-coated paper, they need to go in your general waste bin unless your local government specifically notes their acceptance.

TIP

Ask your local takeaway restaurant if you can bring your own reusable container or encourage them to switch to more recyclable containers.

Standup or squeezable pouches

Nowadays, a lot of foods come in standup or squeezable pouches. These pouches are very handy and certainly have some advantages. Because they're lighter than traditional packaging, such as cans and glass jars, they help reduce the fuel used during transportation. They're also less likely to break during transit and can increase the shelf life of food.

On the flip side, they're less recyclable than traditional packaging. They are made from multiple plastic layers and sometimes include an aluminum foil layer, making them extremely challenging to recycle. They also frequently contain a spout or lid made from a different plastic, adding even more complexity.

TIP

There is, unfortunately, no simple answer on whether they can be recycled. Here are some things to look out for:

>> **Is there a recycling label on the packet?** In Chapter 5, I explain the new recycling labels that inform you on how to recycle. Look and see whether the package has one of these labels. If it does, it may tell you that the package can be taken to a drop-off store for soft plastics. Chapter 11 includes a list of websites to help find soft plastic drop-off locations.

>> **Is the pouch or packet classified as soft plastic?** If there's no label to help, you can check online if it's accepted in your local soft plastic recycling (see Chapter 11).

>> **Look for a specialist recycling program.** There may be other specialist recyclers that take this sort of packaging. For example, TerraCycle (www.terracycle.com) has many free recycling programs for specific brands that use pouches.

Personal product packaging

Many personal products use packaging made from multiple layers of different materials, including plastic, paper, and metal. Some common examples include beauty products like moisturizers, ointments, sunscreen, and toothpaste tubes.

TIP

Most curbside services don't accept them because of the issues with the multilayer materials. But luckily, many specialist recycling programs will take this packaging and recycle it. In fact, some brands offer a take-back program where you can mail in your empty packaging. Check your favorite brand to see whether they offer this service, or join TerraCycle (www.terracycle.com), which provides many different programs.

Single-use multilayer packaging

Here I describe a number of multilayer packaging items that are single-use, meaning they are used once and immediately disposed of. Since most single-use items cannot be recycled, they are highly likely to become litter in the environment (see Chapter 3). The best course of action is to stop using these items and find alternatives:

» **Coffee cups:** In the United Kingdom alone, 2.5 billion disposable coffee cups are thrown away every year. Coffee cups are made from either white foam polystyrene (PS or plastic #6) or plastic-coated paperboard. Sadly, neither of these coffee cups are recyclable in your curbside recycling bin. However, specialist services are available in some countries.

TIP

In Australia, Simply Cups recycles plastic-coated cups, collecting them through conveniently local stores, businesses, and even schools. The plastic is separated from the cups, and materials are used in products like reusable coffee cups, garden edging, road surfaces, and lightweight concrete. Visit www.simplycups.com.au.

REMEMBER

Never put disposable coffee cups in your curbside recycling. They go in the general waste bin. Your best option is to say no to takeaway coffee cups altogether and get your own reusable cup.

» **Compostable coffee cups:** These types of cups are becoming more common as they replace regular coffee cups. They're touted as a better alternative, but be aware that many require commercial composting conditions to break down. These cups may also be accepted by the Simply Cups program mentioned earlier.

» **Paper plates, cups, and other single-use items:** Many single-use plates, bowls, and cups are made from paper with a thin layer or coating of plastic. This helps ensure the paper doesn't absorb too much food while in use. These are rarely accepted in regular curbside recycling and belong in your general waste bin.

TIP

Keep a reusable set with a plate, bowl, cup, and cutlery in your car and one at the office to make sure you never get caught out.

Envelopes and mailers

It can be really difficult to figure out which types of postal packaging you can and can't recycle. Here I describe a few common types and their recyclability:

>> **Paper envelopes padded with paper:** If the envelope is padded with paper or similar material, it's recyclable in curbside recycling.

>> **Paper envelopes or mailers padded with plastic:** When plastic padding like bubble wrap is used in mailers, separating the paper from the plastic is very difficult. For this reason, padded plastic envelopes aren't accepted in curbside recycling.

>> **Mailer bags made from plastic:** Some mailing bags are made entirely from plastic. It may be possible to recycle these with your soft plastics. Refer to Chapter 11 for more info.

>> **Biodegradable mailer bags and envelopes:** Many companies are making the switch to biodegradable delivery packaging. Check whether these are accepted in your local compost service or whether they are accepted in a home compost. Otherwise, they go in the general waste bin.

3
Finding Solutions in Specialist Recycling

IN THIS CHAPTER

» Exploring the resources that go into soft plastics

» Realizing how soft plastics damage the environment

» Unwrapping how soft plastics are recycled

» Getting to know which soft plastics can and can't be recycled

» Shifting your soft plastic habits to reduce your impact

Chapter **11**

Starting with Soft Plastics

Soft plastics are one of the fastest-growing types of packaging we encounter today. They're an increasingly popular choice for food packaging because of their protection properties, affordability, and minimal weight. As a result, a large amount of our plastic waste is made up of soft plastics. And unfortunately, no more than 10 percent gets recycled.

The other problem is that soft plastics make up a sizable portion of the plastic polluting our environment. They're thin and light, so they easily blow out of bins and dumpsters, polluting our waterways and making their way into the ocean. Once exposed to the elements, they quickly fragment into tiny pieces, amplifying their impact.

Soft plastics are currently not accepted in most curbside recycling services because they can cause contamination and safety issues at processing facilities. But that doesn't mean they're not recyclable. Luckily, many of us have access to specialist services that make it easy to ensure our soft plastics are recycled and kept out of the environment. In addition, efforts are underway in many places to introduce soft plastics collection to curbside services, so keep a look out.

In this chapter, I take you through the basics of soft plastics, what they are, how they're made, and how you can recognize them. Then I explain the typical rules for recycling your soft plastics and what is and isn't accepted. Finally, I show you what industries see recycled soft plastics as a resource and the products they make.

Defining Soft Plastics

Soft plastics, also called *flexible plastics* or *plastic films*, are thin and flexible and can easily be scrunched up with your hands. In contrast, rigid plastic is any plastic object that doesn't easily lose its shape when squeezed or pressed. I cover the recycling of rigid plastics in more detail in Chapter 6.

Markets like food and beverage, personal care, cosmetics, and pharmaceutical rely on soft plastics for their packaging. Typical examples you might be familiar with include bread bags, plastic bags, cereal box liners, chip packets, bubble wrap, and resealable zip-top bags (like Ziploc).

Soft plastics are popular as a packaging material because they're flexible, lightweight, durable, and highly cost-effective. They're employed in various socially beneficial ways, such as lowering food waste and maintaining the hygienic standards of medical equipment.

In the following sections, I explain the materials and steps needed to produce soft plastics.

Resources used to make soft plastics

Soft plastics generally use the same resources as rigid plastics, including

>> **Base material:** Most plastic is made from fossil fuels but may also be made from renewable plant sources like corn and sugarcane. (Plastics made from plant materials are called *bioplastics*. You can find out more about bioplastics in Chapter 6.)

>> **Water:** All stages of plastic production require water. In fact, it can take around 22 gallons of water to produce one pound of plastic.

>> **Energy:** Every stage in the production of plastic products demands energy, from the extraction of fossil fuels to the manufacture of products and the delivery of those products to stores.

>> **Chemical additives:** Chemicals are added to plastic to create various properties and to protect them from the elements. For example, plasticizers are commonly added to make the film more flexible and pliable.

TECHNICAL STUFF

I'm sure you read "plasticizers" and, just like me, wondered why we need to add plasticizers to plastic. Different plastics have quite different properties. Some are more rigid and brittle, while others are softer and more flexible. A manufacturer may want to use a particular plastic with a unique property, but the plastic may be too rigid or hard to shape. In this case, they add plasticizers to make the material easier to work with or to improve its flexibility. Plasticizers are used in many products, including epoxy resins, water piping, plastic food containers, dental sealants, and food packaging.

>> **Added layers:** Soft plastics often have multiple layers of different plastics, but they also can include layers of aluminum foil. The various layers provide different levels of protection or strength to the packaging, keeping the contents fresh and safe. This chapter covers soft plastic with multiple layers; you can discover more about other types of multilayer packaging in Chapter 10.

How soft plastics are made

TECHNICAL STUFF

Flexible or soft plastic packaging is made from a wide variety of plastics. The most common include plastic #2, #3, #4, and #7 (see Chapter 6). Each of these plastics provides different benefits to the packaging. For example, plastic #4, low-density polyethylene, is a popular choice because it's already very flexible. Another common choice is plastic #2, high-density polyethylene, which offers exceptional chemical resistance.

Much like other plastic packaging and products, soft plastics are made from pellets produced through the plastic-making process. I explain how plastic is made from fossil fuels in Chapter 6.

Blown film extrusion is the most common method used to make soft plastics or plastic bags. In this process, plastic pellets are melted down and pushed through a small circular hole, creating a tube shape. The tube is pulled up high above the machinery and filled with air, so it expands. As it's drawn up, the tube is pulled through rollers that compress it into thin sheets of plastic film. The faster the plastic is pulled through and drawn up, the thinner the film.

The plastic film is then cut into the desired width and put onto a large roller. Logos, instructions, warnings, and other information are then printed onto the plastic film. After this is complete, the plastic film roll is fed into various machines that produce the desired end product. For example, to make a plastic bag, the film is cut into shape and heat-sealed to create the bag shape.

Soft plastic packaging can use more than one type of plastic or come from more than one material. For example, plastic can be layered with aluminum foil, as in chip packets. The aluminum foil forms a barrier that protects the food against oxidation and light damage. These layered materials are great for preserving food and protecting the contents, but the multiple layers can make them more challenging to recycle.

There are also multilayer materials that have paper layers, but these aren't categorized as soft plastic. I explain these in more detail in Chapter 10.

Understanding the Benefits of Recycling Soft Plastics

It's become increasingly apparent as the world wrestles with a plastic crisis that a large percentage of the plastic waste we create consists of soft plastics. Millions of tons of soft plastics are sent directly to landfills annually. In the United Kingdom, it's estimated that more than 300 thousand tons of soft plastics are thrown out every year, but only 6 percent are recycled.

It's just as disheartening in the United States, where according to the U.S. Environmental Protection Agency (EPA), Americans generate nearly 9 billion pounds of soft plastics annually, but only 10 percent is recycled. That equates to more than 8 billion pounds being sent to landfills or entering the environment annually. No wonder we're struggling with plastic waste.

While we were busy focusing on recycling rigid plastics (see Chapter 6), soft plastics were quickly becoming the fastest-growing packaging material on the planet. They're light, cheap, and really good at protecting the food inside. But the problem is they're challenging to collect and separate from other plastics in typical recycling systems. Services are available that collect soft plastics from supermarkets or other convenient locations, but unfortunately, many people are still unaware of these services and how to use them.

WARNING

So why should you make the extra effort to sort your soft plastics and drop them off at your local supermarket? Well, it turns out these thin, flimsy pieces of plastic are capable of causing significant harm to the environment. Soft plastics are blown around by wind and water and get caught in waterways and eventually the ocean, where they're mistaken for food by marine animals or birds. (Discover more of the damaging effects in Chapter 3.) Even when sent to landfills, these plastics can be trouble. They take hundreds of years to degrade, and when they do, they break down into microplastics that can escape landfills and negatively impact the environment.

REMEMBER

On the other hand, recycling your soft plastics helps reduce landfills and keep plastic waste out of the environment. By recycling your soft plastics, you help save energy and resources that would typically go into making new plastics. And once recycled, soft plastics can be made into many new and useful products.

The impacts of soft plastic waste

Soft plastics cause many different issues when they get into the environment, including the following:

>> **Polluting the environment:** Lightweight bags and wrappers are easily picked up by the wind and transported into waterways and environments, ultimately ending up in the ocean.

>> **Breaking out of landfills:** Soft plastics can also escape from landfills, especially mismanaged ones.

>> **Sticking around forever:** No different from regular plastic, soft plastics take hundreds of years to degrade. However, because they're thin, they are more likely to break into smaller and smaller pieces. These small pieces of plastic are called *microplastics* and are recognized as a significant environmental problem (see Chapter 3 for more details).

>> **Impersonating food:** Mistaken for food, soft plastics in the environment pose a serious threat to marine life and seabirds. A plastic bag floating in the ocean looks very similar to a jellyfish when you're a sea turtle. Or a small piece of plastic can appear like regular food to fish or birds.

>> **Trapping animals:** The flexible nature of soft plastics can result in animals getting trapped and tangled when they encounter them in the environment. It can cause significant injuries to the animal, hinder its ability to feed, and eventually lead to its death.

>> **Leaching toxins:** Once in the environment, plastics can release toxins. These chemicals can be absorbed by the soil and groundwater around landfills or enter waterways and the ocean.

>> **Using energy:** Soft plastics have a carbon impact, just like any other material. It takes energy to create plastic products and packaging. It's such a waste when we use it once and throw it away into a landfill.

How recycling soft plastic helps the environment

Similar to the benefits of rigid plastic, recycling your soft plastics helps minimize the negative impacts of plastic production and waste. A plastic bread bag that gets recycled can't end up blowing away from a landfill to become waste on the beach or be eaten by a sea turtle mistaking it for food. But it can become a new product and continue its life cycle.

REMEMBER

Recycling your soft plastic can

>> Reduce waste sent to landfill.

>> Conserve resources and keep them in use.

>> Keep plastic waste out of the environment.

>> Protect wildlife.

>> Save energy.

>> Support the circular economy.

Soft plastics are very useful and probably won't disappear from the supermarket shelves any time soon. While improvements to simplify packaging, remove unnecessary parts, and devise better recycling outcomes are progressing, you can still do a lot to protect the environment. Recycling your soft plastics is a simple step you can take that will have a considerable impact.

TIP

Many people are unaware that soft plastics are recyclable, so be sure to spread the word.

Seeing How Soft Plastics Are Recycled

Given that soft plastics are one of the fastest-growing plastic categories, many governments and organizations are trying to find a solution for our soft plastic recycling challenges. In the past, the focus has been on excluding soft plastics from curbside recycling because of the problems they cause. Soft plastics can cause safety issues by getting caught in machinery and can contaminate regular recycling streams. More recently, however, the focus has shifted to capturing and recycling these materials. In the following sections, I explain how soft plastics are recycled.

The steps of soft plastic recycling

Just as with most materials, recycling soft plastics starts with the collection of waste and ends with the creation of a new product:

1. **All that plastic is collected.**

   Collection is one of the most challenging steps to recycling soft plastics. This is because it's very hard to separate them from rigid plastic packaging. The majority of recycling facilities lack the appropriate equipment to separate them. Fortunately, specialist services have been developed that provide drop-off points at convenient locations.

2. **The soft plastic is shredded.**

   Once the soft plastic has been collected from the drop-off locations and taken to a recycling facility, it's put through a shredder to cut it into small pieces.

3. **The soft plastic pieces are cleaned.**

   Contamination is removed by manual sorting or by mechanical processes like float tanks and magnets.

4. **The soft plastic pieces are turned into pellets.**

   The plastic is forced through an extruder and formed into pellets.

5. **The soft plastic pellets are mixed with other materials.**

   More robust recycled plastic or sometimes virgin plastic is added to increase the strength of the material. Other compounds like UV stabilizers and light fasteners may be added to improve the longevity of the new products.

6. **The new soft plastic is molded and extruded.**

   Finally, the plastic pellets are melted again and molded into new products. Manufacturing soft plastics into new products can be tricky, because there are many different types of plastics mixed together. One of the challenges can be achieving uniform results in color and texture. As a result, this material is more suited to outdoor and commercial applications. I look at some of these products later in this chapter.

BANNING THE BAG

One of the great campaigns to reduce the amount of single-use plastic we waste is the introduction of plastic bag bans across the world. These bans have also motivated us as individuals to rethink our daily use and change our habits. In my hometown, most people now bring their own reusable bags to the supermarket. It took time for everyone to form the habit, but it's now part of our regular routine. I even take along reusable produce bags for my fruit and vegetables now.

The first plastic bag bans were introduced in Bangladesh back in 2002. The bags were causing significant issues clogging drainage during flooding. Other countries with similar issues followed suit, including Kenya, which has the strictest laws. They ban the manufacture, importation, and sale of all plastic bags. And breaking this law can result in a $40,000 fine or a stint in jail for up to four years.

Today more than 70 countries have implemented some sort of plastic bag ban or partial ban. Many countries like Kenya have outright banned the bag, but others have replaced them with compostable ones or require customers to purchase thicker reusable bags. The United States and Australia stand out as lacking consistent bans across the country, although individual states have implemented their own bans.

Why most curbside programs don't include soft plastics

WARNING

The majority of curbside recycling programs are currently designed to process and separate rigid plastic packaging, metals, glass, and paper. They're not intended to recognize and separate soft plastics. These plastics jam equipment and cause safety issues, resulting in delays and potentially shutting the entire plant. Workers may be required to manually remove material wound around machinery before starting it up again. Figure 11-1 shows a Kent County employee cleaning plastic bags and other soft plastics from the machinery. It's not a job I would want to be doing!

Even if soft plastics don't create a catastrophe at the facility, they can't be adequately sorted and end up mixed with other unrecyclable contaminants that are sent to landfills.

REMEMBER

Soft plastics and other potential items that could get tangled in the machinery, like cables, ropes, clothing, and textiles, don't belong in your curbside recycling bin unless your curbside service specifically caters for them.

Images thanks to Kent County Department of Public Works, Michigan, USA

FIGURE 11-1:
A Kent County
Department of
Public Works
employee
cleaning plastic
bags and other
soft plastics from
the sorting
machinery.

Despite these problems, a lot of curbside recycling programs are trying to figure out how to collect soft plastics. In late 2021, householders in Ireland were introduced to a new rule permitting them to place all plastics, both rigid and soft, into their curbside recycling bin. Homeowners can put all plastic packaging in their recycling bins because Ireland has invested in advanced sorting machinery. They are able to separate the different types of plastics regardless of whether they're soft or rigid. This is a significant step forward in how we collect plastics for recycling and will help Ireland reach their target of recycling 50 percent of plastic packaging by 2025.

And it's not just Ireland making advances in their collection of plastics. Some curbside services in the United States and United Kingdom allow you to place certain soft plastics into a bag and put them at the top of your recycling bin. These are hand-picked off the line at the recycling facility and processed separately. In Canada and Australia, pilot programs using a similar manual collection process are also underway.

TIP

Keep an eye out for changing rules with your local town or city government so you'll know when they're implementing soft plastic recycling.

Knowing Which Soft Plastics Can and Can't Be Recycled

For the majority of us, using a specialist recycler's drop-off location is the only way to recycle our soft plastics. The types of soft plastic your local specialist recycling service collects depend on what equipment they have and the end markets for their products. In the following sections, I take you through the typical rules, tips, and examples of commonly accepted items for these specialist services.

Identifying soft plastics versus rigid plastics

TIP

The distinction between soft and rigid plastics is one of the most important things to understand when recycling your plastic. It's easy to figure out whether something is a soft plastic or a rigid plastic using the following tests:

>> **Do a scrunch test.** A scrunch test helps determine whether a plastic item is rigid or soft. Try to scrunch the plastic piece with your hand, like in Figure 11-2. If the plastic pops mostly back into shape like a plastic milk bottle would, then it's rigid plastic. If the piece of plastic scrunches into a ball and stays that way, like the plastic bag on the left in Figure 11-2, then it's a soft plastic.

>> **Do a tear test.** Try to tear the packaging. If it tears like paper, it will most likely be a multilayer material that includes a layer of paper or cardboard. This can't be recycled with your soft plastics and commonly belongs in the general trash. You can find out more about multilayer material in Chapter 10. If the item doesn't tear easily, it's most likely a soft plastic.

>> **Do a poke test.** If you can poke or push your finger through the plastic like you might a plastic bag, then it's soft plastic. If you can't poke your finger through the plastic, then it's rigid plastic.

REMEMBER

In summary, here's what to do with your plastics:

>> Rigid plastics go in your curbside recycling bin. Note that not all types of rigid plastic are accepted in every location, so be sure to check your local rules and head to Chapter 6 for help to work it out.

>> Soft plastics go to specialist recycling drop-off.

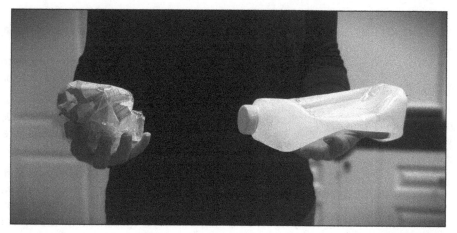

FIGURE 11-2:
How to do the
scrunch test to
identify soft
plastics.

Asking about the local rules for soft plastics

REMEMBER

You'll want to look out for these rules in your local area to ensure you recycle your soft plastics correctly:

>> **Can I put soft plastics in my curbside bin?** The answer is no, unless you have solid evidence that you're in one of the rare places where soft plastic is accepted in curbside services.

>> **Don't bag your recyclables.** Avoid using plastic bags to hold your recyclable bottles and containers in the curbside bin. Recycling facilities are designed to process loose bottles, cans, and jars, so there's no need to bag unless specifically requested by your town or city government.

>> **Do I have access to a soft plastic recycling service?** Check the relevant websites later in this chapter for your location to see whether you have a drop-off point nearby. If you don't have a store drop-off for soft plastics in your area, they need to go in your general waste bin.

Following a few soft plastic guidelines

Here I list several tips that will help you recycle your soft plastics the right way:

>> **Check the rules with your local soft plastic recycler.** Not all recycling facilities are the same, so the rules and what's acceptable vary from place to place. Make sure you check your local specialist recycler's website for their dos and don'ts.

>> **Look for a recycling logo.** Keep an eye out for packaging displaying the How2Recycle, the Australasian Recycling Label (ARL), or the UK On-Pack Recycling Label (OPRL) labels. These labels help tremendously to work out what goes in which bin or to a drop-off center. Discover more on recycling logos in Chapter 5.

Not all packaging displays these labels. If a package doesn't have these new labels, try out the tests described earlier in this chapter to figure out whether or not it's a soft plastic.

>> **Make sure they're clean and dry.** Remove all food scraps from the plastic and let it dry. I usually give it a quick rinse depending on what was contained inside. If you can't clean it easily — this can be the case for meat wrapping or sticky cheese wrap — throw it in your general waste bin. Plastic film or bags heavily soiled with dirt, paint, or food can't be recycled and can contaminate other recyclables.

Make sure your soft plastics are dry before dropping them off. If they're wet, the plastic can become moldy. If you do get it wet, simply let it dry on the sink overnight.

>> **Cut it down to size.** Many services ask you to cut any large soft plastics into smaller pieces. This is because these large pieces can become tangled in the machinery. If you have a large bag like a dry cleaning bag, cut it into a few smaller pieces.

>> **Remove receipts, labels, or other items.** If the label is a small paper label, you can leave it, but larger labels, bigger than about 6 inches, should be removed either by peeling them off or cutting that section away and throwing it in the general waste bin.

>> **Bag your soft plastics.** I recommend you collect your soft plastics in a grocery or retail plastic bag. That way, you can place the whole thing into the soft plastics drop-off bin.

Many services don't let you put your soft plastics into a black or dark green garbage bag or similar bags. It's hard for the collection crew and workers at the processing plant to see what's inside, so it gets rejected. They use this visual check to help reduce contamination.

Remembering to take your soft plastic recycling with you can be hard. When my soft plastic bag is full, I put it by the front door or straight into the car along with my reusable grocery bags. Don't worry if you forget, though. Sometimes I finish my supermarket shopping only to return to the car and discover my soft plastics still sitting on the back seat! You can always take it next time.

Knowing what soft plastics go in

Here are examples of what packaging is typically accepted in soft plastic recycling:

>> Plastic shopping bags, grocery and retail

>> Bread, pasta, and rice bags

>> Outer plastic packaging from toilet paper, paper towels, napkins, and other sanitary products

>> Plastic wrapping on cases of water bottles and soda bottles

>> Reusable shopping bags

>> Zip-top or other resealable bags like sandwich bags

>> Newspaper and magazine wrapping

>> Dry cleaning bags

>> Furniture and electronic wrap

>> Plastic shipping envelopes or courier packs — only the plastic variety, not the ones made from paper and bubble wrap

>> Garden potting or soil, manure, and compost bags

>> Empty ice bags — must be empty and dry

>> Road salt bags — must be dry

Keeping some soft plastics out

Here are some examples of items that commonly don't belong in soft plastic recycling:

>> **Other recyclables:** These include items that go in your regular curbside recycling bin like glass, tin cans, paper, cardboard, and rigid plastic packaging.

>> **Food waste:** Food shouldn't be placed in soft plastic recycling drop-off bins.

>> **Biodegradable/compostable bags:** Compostable packaging is usually not accepted in your soft plastic recycling. These materials are likely to degrade before they're processed. I explain in Chapter 6 how biodegradable and compostable plastics are designed to break down.

>> **Bioplastics:** Made from plant materials instead of fossil fuels, they usually can't be recycled with other conventional plastics.

>> **Rigid plastics like cookie trays or strawberry punnets/containers:** Items like these are made with very thin plastic, so although they're classed as rigid plastics, they are quite flexible and soft. You can even scrunch some of them. Most soft plastic recyclers don't accept this type of packaging. However, some curbside recycling services allow you to place them in your recycling bin with rigid plastic.

>> **Disposable face masks, gloves, and other medical-related items:** Medical-related items can't be placed in soft plastic recycling.

>> **Beach balls and blow-up pool toys:** Plastic beach and pool toys are made from polyvinyl chloride (PVC or plastic #3) and, unfortunately, are not easily recycled. They don't go in your soft plastic recycling or your curbside recycling bin and for now are best placed in your general waste bin.

>> **Thick vinyl plastics:** Many linen and bedding companies use flexible vinyl (PVC or plastic #3) for packaging their products. This material isn't accepted at facilities that recycle soft plastics.

>> **Nylon:** Most collection services don't accept fishing lines or nylon netting.

>> **Balloons:** Leave them out. They're either made from rubber or multilayered material using aluminum and plastic. See Chapter 10 for more information on multilayer materials.

>> **Other miscellaneous items:** Other items that usually don't belong in the soft plastic bins at drop-off locations include

- Plastic strapping from boxes or pallets
- Clothing or textiles of any sort
- Polystyrene (or Styrofoam) or any other foam-type plastics
- Wrapping paper, ribbons, or bows
- Adhesive tapes
- Pool covers or tarpaulins

Noting what soft plastic items to check

Rules vary depending on where you live, so I've listed some items that you should check with your local service about before including in your soft plastic recycling. These include

>> **Confectionery bags and candy wrappers.** There are many different materials used for candy wrappers, so checking what is accepted is important.

IS COMPOSTABLE PACKAGING BETTER THAN SOFT PLASTIC?

The rise of compostable packaging materials feels like the right thing, but it's not as simple as it seems. Compostable plastics require certain conditions to break down. These conditions may be present in home composting but sometimes are achievable only in industrial composting facilities.

With industrial composting facilities not always available, compostable plastics are often sent to landfills. The problem is that materials in properly run landfills are deprived of oxygen, but oxygen is an essential ingredient in composting. Because of this, compostable plastics don't always decompose in a landfill.

They are still a great choice. You just need to make sure you have access to a commercial composting facility. Or if you have your own compost, make sure they state "home compostable." Flip to Chapter 12 for more about home composting.

>> **Fresh produce bags.** This includes net bags for fruits and vegetables and woven bags for rice.

>> **Frozen food bags.**

>> **Bubble wrap and packing air pillows.** Pop the packing pillows to deplete them before putting them in.

>> **Foil-lined plastic packaging.** Potato chip bags and chocolate wrappers are examples.

>> **Food and drink plastic squeeze pouches.** Where accepted, you may also be able to include the rigid plastic lid with the pouch.

>> **Dog and cat food bags.** If you buy large bags, cut them into smaller pieces for recycling.

>> **Cling film.** Different brands of cling film are made of various plastics, so acceptance can vary.

>> **Prewashed salad mix bags.**

>> **Six-pack rings.** For an alternative, check out www.ringrecycleme.com/ to find recycling services for six-pack rings in the United States, Canada, and the United Kingdom.

>> **Cellophane.** An example of cellophane is the plastic used to wrap flowers and gifts.

>> **Coffee bags.**

>> **Cereal box liners.** Some cereal box liners are multilayer with a layer of paper while others are simply plastic.

TIP

Many more items may or may not be included in your soft plastic recycling, so be sure to check in with your local soft plastics recycler before you drop them off.

Locating soft plastic recycling facilities

In Table 11-1, I provide a list of soft plastic recycling services available across a few countries. This will help you find your nearest drop-off location so you can start recycling your soft plastics. If your location isn't listed, try a Google search by typing "soft plastic recycling near me" or talk to your local town or city government.

TABLE 11-1 **Soft Plastic Recycling Facilities by Country**

Location	Website
United States and Canada	www.plasticfilmrecycling.org/ www.bagandfilmrecycling.org/ Some retail stores providing in-store drop-off locations include Walmart, Staples, Target, Home Depot, Wegmans, and Safeway along with many other retail stores.
United Kingdom	www.recyclenow.com https://flexibleplasticfund.org.uk/ Typical retail stores involved in collecting soft plastics are Tesco, Marks and Spencer, and your local co-op store.
Australia	www.redcycle.net.au/where-to-redcycle/ **Note:** At the time of writing this book, the REDcycle program in Australia is temporarily closed. Much work is underway to get the program back up and running, so check their website to get the latest status. Until they are up and running again, soft plastics will need to be placed in your general waste bin unless you have access to a service through your local town or city government.

Pulling it all together

In Figure 11-3, I've provided a checklist to help you check what soft plastics are accepted in your local area.

SOFT PLASTIC RECYCLING

LOCAL RULES

☐ MY CURBSIDE ACCEPTS SOFT PLASTIC

☐ SOFT PLASTIC DROP-OFF LOCATION

_____

GUIDELINES

- LOOK FOR A RECYCLING LOGO
- KEEP THEM CLEAN AND DRY
- CUT UP LARGER PIECES
- REMOVE RECEIPTS AND LABELS IF POSSIBLE
- CHECK YOUR LOCAL RULES

WHAT GOES IN?

✓
- Plastic shopping bags
- Bread, pasta, and rice bags
- Outer plastic packaging or wrap from toilet paper or cases of bottled water
- Reusable shopping bags
- Zip-top or other resealable bags
- Newspaper and magazine wrapping
- Dry cleaning bags
- Furniture and electronic wrap
- Plastic shipping envelopes or courier packs
- Garden potting or soil bags
- Empty ice bags
- Road salt bags

WHAT STAYS OUT?

✗
- Other recyclables like glass, cans, paper, and rigid plastic packaging
- Food waste
- Biodegradable/compostable bags
- Bioplastics
- Disposable face masks, gloves, and other medical-related items
- Beach balls and blow-up pool toys
- Thick vinyl plastics
- Nylon
- Balloons
- Plastic strapping from boxes or pallets
- Clothing or textiles
- Polystyrene (or Styrofoam) or any other foam-type plastics
- Wrapping paper, ribbons, or bows
- Pool covers or tarpaulins

WHAT TO CHECK?

?

☐ Confectionery bags and candy wrappers
☐ Fresh produce bags
☐ Frozen food bags
☐ Bubble wrap and packing air pillows
☐ Foil-lined plastic packaging
☐ Food and drink plastic squeeze pouches
☐ Dog and cat food bags

☐ Cling film
☐ Pre-washed salad mix bags
☐ Six-pack rings
☐ Cellophane
☐ Coffee bags
☐ Cereal box liners

FIGURE 11-3: A quick guide for recycling soft plastics.

Using Less Soft Plastic

An excellent way to reduce how much soft plastic packaging you use is to run a waste audit. A waste audit is where you sort through your waste to find out what plastic packaging (or other type of item) you regularly throw away. You can then figure out ways to reduce that waste. I explain how to do a waste audit in Chapter 17.

TIP

Whether or not you do a waste audit, there are many ways you can reduce the amount of soft plastics you use. Here are some ideas to get you started:

>> Take reusable bags to the supermarket or other store. Buy extras and leave them in the car for when you forget to bring the ones from home. If you normally carry a handbag, perhaps keep a reusable bag in there so you'll always have one with you.

>> Choose unwrapped produce when it's available. Many supermarkets wrap fresh fruit and vegetables in plastic to keep them fresh through their long journey from grower to store. This is good because food waste is a big problem (see Chapter 12), but it produces more plastic waste. Avoid these packaged fresh foods whenever possible.

>> Get yourself some reusable produce bags for fruit and vegetables. These bags are made of netting, are reusable, and can even be washed in your washing machine. The ones I use from a brand called Onya are even made from recycled plastic (www.onyalife.com).

TIP

If you regularly use single-use plastic produce bags, don't throw them out. You can rinse, dry, and reuse them the next time you go to the supermarket or at home for packaging sandwiches and other snacks.

>> Grab some reusable wax or silicon covers as a good replacement for cling wrap, or simply put your leftovers into a glass or plastic container.

>> Have you tried your local bulk food store? I only just discovered mine recently. I was a bit nervous about how it would work at first, but it's been great. We eat a lot of nuts and dried fruit in my household, so I've saved a huge amount of packaging by buying them in bulk.

>> Bubble wrap is so often used once and then tossed away. Reuse your bubble wrap, or try dropping it off at your local postal store or giving it away through a local Buy Nothing group.

You can find more ideas to reduce your plastics in Chapter 15.

Purchasing Recycled Soft Plastic Products

There are many uses for recycled soft plastics. They use recycled material and replace raw materials that would inevitably require energy and resources to make. Some examples of products currently available include

» Composite timber for decks, park benches, outdoor sports equipment, playground sets, and dog agility equipment

» Fencing, fence posts, bollards (short posts), and signage

» Garden products like edging, crates, pallets, containers, and veggie garden beds

» Outdoor furniture

TIP

Many of the products made from recycled soft plastics are suited to home renovations, landscaping, and commercial uses. If you're planning a project at home or for your business, why not consider using a recycled plastic product instead of conventional timber or other material?

TECHNICAL STUFF

Recently soft plastics have found their way back into soft plastic packaging. Amcor, the packaging company for Nestle, created the first soft plastic made with recycled content from the recycling of soft plastics. The KitKat wrapper uses 30 percent recycled content, achieved by processing the soft plastics back into oil and then remaking the plastic from the primary ingredients. That way, the plastic can be classified as food-grade quality.

Imagine if all our soft plastics could be recycled and reused as new plastic packaging, creating a closed-loop process. Keep your eye out for more soft packaging with recycled content in the future, and head to Chapter 18 for more on the future of recycling.

Purchasing Recycled Soft Plastic Products

Chapter **12**

Composting to Reduce Food Waste

t least one-third of the food produced worldwide currently goes to waste. In developed nations, that equates to the average person throwing away about one pound, or half a kilo, of perfectly edible food every day. Not only could this food have potentially helped feed more people, but it also required resources such as land, water, energy, fertilizers, and pesticides to be produced. Food production harms the environment by degrading vast areas of land, threatening biodiversity, using precious water, and contributing to climate change. It uses an enormous amount of resources, all of which go to waste when that food is tossed in the bin.

Most food waste that's thrown away winds up in landfills, where it emits greenhouse gases as it decomposes, increasing its overall impact on climate change. In fact, in the United States alone, food waste results in more greenhouse gas emissions into the atmosphere than 37 million automobiles. If you want to have an impact on climate change, then food waste is an excellent place to start.

In this chapter, I explain why the food we waste is such a big problem for the planet. I describe how food labeling really works before offering you plenty of ideas for how to cut down on food waste. The next best thing for minimizing your food waste is to recycle it and turn it into useful compost, but there are other options if you don't have a green thumb. I list all these options, and if you're interested in starting your own home compost, I provide everything you need to know.

Defining Food Waste

REMEMBER

The definition of *food waste* is food that was intended for human consumption that instead is discarded or wasted in some way. It includes both uneaten food and inedible parts like fruit peels and vegetable offcuts. Food waste can occur anywhere along the food supply chain. If it's discarded between harvest and retail stores, it's called *food loss*, while *food waste* refers to anything tossed out by consumers at home or in restaurants or other retail businesses.

Food loss is a big issue for developing countries, while food waste is more of a problem in developed countries. Food loss deserves an entire book of its own, so here I'm going to focus on food waste created by consumers and small businesses.

Food waste can happen in a few different ways:

>> **Food spoiling:** This can occur at any stage: at the store, in transit, or even in our fridges at home. At restaurants and other retail businesses, it can be caused by problems with the processing of food, fluctuating demand, issues in delivery, equipment malfunction, or damage by vermin, insects, or bacteria.

Food can also spoil when we improperly store it at home or simply because we purchased too much of it and can't use it all.

>> **Food aesthetics:** Store standards can result in imperfect produce being tossed in the bin.

TIP

Choose the ugly fruit; don't just pick the perfect fruit and vegetables. This will send a message to the retail store that we don't care what our fruit and veggies look like.

>> **Overstocking:** Food waste can result from overstocking food. An example is a restaurant that must throw away food that wasn't sold to customers by the end of the day.

>> **Overordering:** Sometimes our eyes are too big for our stomachs, and we order too much at the restaurant but can't eat it all.

>> **Labeling:** Date labels on food can confuse and lead to wholesome food being thrown out unnecessarily.

Most people are unaware of how much food they throw away every day. It goes into our bins as small pieces through the day. But if we were to collect it for a whole week, we would be shocked by how big the pile would be.

Knowing Why You Should Care About Food Waste

And you thought the plastic problem was a big problem! Food waste is also one of the biggest environmental problems we face today. Around one-third of the food produced worldwide goes to waste. That's the equivalent of about 1.3 billion tons of food annually, enough to feed one-third of the world's population. This is especially alarming given that the U.S. Environmental Protection Agency (EPA) predicts that global food production will need to expand dramatically by the year 2050 to close the food gap and reduce hunger.

As consumers, we throw away, on average, the equivalent of around one pound, or half a kilo, of perfectly good food every day. It's like throwing out a whole loaf of bread each morning. But it's not just the perfectly good food we're throwing out that's a concern. We also waste all the resources — including land, labor, water, and energy — needed to cultivate, gather, process, transport, and store food.

When discarded, most food waste ends up in landfills, creating another environmental issue. Many of us presume the food will simply rot away and break down. But the problem is that when food waste breaks down, it releases large amounts of greenhouse gases, particularly methane, a potent greenhouse gas. Landfills are a significant contributor to climate change.

If you're looking for an easy way to protect the environment and help tackle climate change, then you've only got to look as far as your fridge. You can make many changes to reduce the amount of food waste you create. You might even save some money while you're at it. I describe some ways you can help later in this chapter. In the following sections, I discuss the resources used to make food and the impacts of food production on the environment. Getting a handle on these topics can go a long way in understanding why you should care about food waste.

Resources used in making food

Food is vital for humans to live, but it's so readily available and convenient that we can easily discard it with little thought of the effort to produce it. Advancements in agriculture over the last century mean we no longer need to work hard to get food. We simply go down to the supermarket and buy what we need. It's easy to forget all the effort that goes into producing food.

Here I detail the resources required to produce food:

>> **Land:** About 50 percent of the world's habitable land is used for farming and animal husbandry. Land provides the soil necessary for crops to grow or animals to forage. It also provides space for collecting, processing, storing, and transporting food materials from farms to processing plants to retail stores.

>> **Water:** Producing food requires a lot of water. Agriculture accounts for the largest amount of water use through irrigation of crops and livestock farming. But water is also used throughout the entire life cycle of foods. Water is essential in cleaning and processing raw foods, as an ingredient itself, and in producing packaging like plastic (see Chapter 6).

>> **Energy:** According to the Intergovernmental Panel on Climate Change, food loss and waste were responsible for 8–10 percent of global anthropogenic greenhouse gas emissions between 2010 and 2016. In fact, the Food and Agriculture Organization of the United Nations says that if food waste was a country, it would be the third top producer of greenhouse gases, producing almost as much as China and the United States.

The energy used in the production of food includes energy used to

• **Transport food and get it to us:** Food is usually grown in country areas and must be transported to where you, the customer, are located. Today we expect different sorts of food to be available even when it's out of season or can't be grown in our local climate. As a result, food is often transported long distances, possibly even internationally, to fill these gaps in the market.

• **Process food:** Food processing methods can range from grinding or milling grains to mixing and packaging ingredients. All of these activities require energy.

• **Store food and keep food fresh:** Once food has been grown, processed, and transported, it must be stored to keep it fresh. This includes refrigerated transport, cool stores, and all those open freezers lined up in your local supermarket.

>> **Pest control:** Pesticides are substances used to kill pests, such as insects or vermin, unwanted plants, bacteria, or fungi. There are several different kinds, including insecticides, herbicides, bactericides, and fungicides. Pesticides are made from natural ingredients such as plants like chrysanthemum but are also made synthetically from petroleum or other chemicals. Proper pest management is vital in food production; however, producing pesticides requires resources and energy.

>> **Fertilizers:** We must feed plants so they can feed us. Fertilizers provide nutrients for crops that may not be present in the soil. Most fertilizers are made from nitrogen, phosphorus, and potassium, but other nutrients like zinc, calcium, or magnesium may be added. The raw ingredients used for fertilizers include natural gas, compost, or waste material like sewage.

>> **Other additives:** There are many additives used to produce the foods we buy. Salt is a good example, but other additives include preservatives, flavors, colors, sugars, fats, and nutrients. All of these ingredients must be grown as a separate crop, mined, or processed in a factory.

>> **Food packaging:** The majority of food produced must be packaged. Packaging comes in many different shapes and sizes and may include plastics, glass, paper, metals, or a mix of these. As I explain in Chapters 6 to 11, all these materials require their own list of resources to produce.

REMEMBER

When you throw out perfectly good food, you also throw out the resources required to produce that food. It might seem like just a small piece of food, but you're also wasting the energy and resources required to grow, produce, process, transport, store, and discard the food. It's a lot when you add it up.

TIP

Consider the resources required to produce food while you're planning your next supermarket shop. It might help you buy only what you need. I talk more about this planning later in this chapter.

Food production's impacts on the environment

Feeding the world is taking its toll on the environment. Our excess food production systems are leading to land degradation, deforestation, disruption of ecosystems, and loss of biodiversity. The impacts of food waste are twofold. There's the impact of producing the food in the first place, and then there is the impact of the wasted food if it's not disposed of correctly.

>> **Soil degradation:** Our soils are overworked. They are tired and haven't got much left to give. Soil degradation is when soil no longer has sufficient nutrients for growing anything. It may also be contaminated by pollutants. Soil degradation can affect soil biodiversity, promote erosion, and result in the loss of organic matter and fertility.

>> **Overuse of water:** Much of the water used in food production is extracted from surface water like creeks, rivers, or lakes. But it may also be extracted from bores (wells) or other subsurface water bodies. This can deplete groundwater, affecting habitats and biodiversity, causing loss of vegetation,

erosion, poor soil conditions, and overall water quality, and may even lead to land subsidence.

>> **Greenhouse gases:** Decomposing food waste in landfills emits methane, a nasty greenhouse gas that is 25 times more potent than carbon dioxide in trapping heat in the atmosphere. Landfills are the third largest source of methane emissions in the United States and many other countries.

TECHNICAL STUFF

The EPA estimates that the effects of food waste in the United States, excluding landfills, contribute the equivalent of 170 million metric tons of carbon dioxide (CO_2) per year. That is almost equal to the emissions from 42 coal-fired power plants.

>> **Landfill space:** Waste food takes up a significant amount of space in landfills. In fact, according to the EPA, 5.3 million tons of wasted food were sent to U.S. landfills in 2018. That's 24.1 percent of all municipal solid waste sent to landfills.

>> **Loss of biodiversity:** In the name of food production, natural habitats are transformed into farmland. Vegetation is cleared, fertilizers and pesticides pollute the soil, and waterways are diverted or depleted. These changes present one of the biggest threats to biodiversity.

Clearing Up Confusion Over Labeling

I have a terrible sense of smell, whereas my husband has a very sensitive nose. So whenever a use-by date has passed on a food item in my fridge, or it looks suspicious, I call my husband. Before I met my husband, many food items were tossed out because the use-by date had passed and I was unsure if it was safe to eat. Though the "sniff test" isn't as foolproof as my husband would like to think, it's certainly true that some foods continue to be safe to eat for somewhat longer than their labeling might suggest.

It's typical to believe that food is no longer edible once the expiration date has passed. Unfortunately, as a result, many usable and safe foods are thrown out. The following sections explain standard food labeling in more detail.

Grasping food date meanings

REMEMBER

What do the dates on food products indicate if they aren't alerting us that the food is bad? These date labels are actually intended to indicate the last date when food is still at its peak freshness and quality. They're not designed to signal that the food is unsafe. In fact, none of these dates are related to safety or provide a guarantee the food will be safe before the date.

These dates are chosen by the manufacturer and offer a guide to help us know when it's more likely a product will go off, assuming the food has been stored properly. Regardless of the date provided on food products, you should make yourself aware of food safety and the signs to look out for. I provide some tips in the following section.

Here are the most common examples of date labels:

>> **Best-by or best-before date:** "Best by" or "best before" indicates the date when the product is likely to start going bad. It doesn't mean it will go bad. It's just a time from which you should be more cautious and check the food for typical signs before using it. Other versions of this date might be "best if used by," "best enjoyed by," or "best used by."

>> **Sell-by date:** This date is primarily for retailers and indicates when they should remove the product from the shelves. It's also not a safety date.

>> **Use-by date:** This refers to the last date for using the product at its peak quality. In some countries, however, it indicates the estimated date after which the food should not be consumed and can no longer be sold.

WARNING

Use-by dates on infant formula are a little different from the rest. Infant formula should not be used if its use-by date has passed. Refer to the appropriate government guidelines for the country in which you reside.

>> **Closed dates:** These are found on canned foods and represent the date the product was manufactured. Some products may also display a use-by date. Unless the date you're reading includes the words "use by" or "best before," then it will be a closed date.

>> **Freeze-by date:** This indicates the date you should freeze a product to keep it as fresh as possible.

>> **Baked-on or baked-for date:** Bread items may include a date "baked for." It refers to the current date if the bread was baked before midday and the next day if it was baked after midday.

REMEMBER

Expiration dates for food products aren't always regulated. This is why there is limited consistency in the labels. Check with your local or federal government to find out more about labeling requirements where you live.

Figuring out when food is no longer edible

Excluding infant formula, if the date has passed on a product in your cupboard or fridge, it may still be safe to eat. Assuming you have stored it properly as recommended on the label (for example, refrigerate after use), then you just need to keep your eyes peeled for signs that it's spoiling.

Even if the best-before date hasn't passed, you should examine the food. Trust your eyes and nose (or, in my case, my husband's nose!) when it comes to checking if your food is okay to eat. Here are a few ideas:

>> Pay attention to odd smells or funny tastes.

>> Look for discoloration.

>> Check for mold.

If none of these exist and the food has been stored appropriately, then it should be okay to eat. If not, it may be best to throw the food out. Always use your common sense and good judgment, and when you have doubts, it's best to err on the side of caution, particularly with more perishable foods such as meat, fish, poultry, and dairy. Keep reading to find out what you can do with your discarded food.

REMEMBER

Food safety and regulations can vary from country to country, so be sure to contact your local government or the manufacturer if you have any questions.

Reducing Your Food Waste

The best way to reduce food waste is not to create it in the first place. It's interesting to consider why we buy more food than we need. I used to buy a lot of fruit but never ended up eating it. It wasn't to do with excess or indulgence; it was because I knew I should eat fruit to be healthy. I had good intentions, but then I'd fall back into my old habits, and it would all start to rot and end up in the bin. Understanding the problems with food waste and its associated issues has helped encourage me to stop buying food I know I won't eat, even if it's healthy.

You can do many things to reduce the amount of food waste you generate. The added benefit is it will help reduce your overall carbon footprint too. In the following sections, I detail some of the most effective tips. I also provide a checklist to help you put these steps into action and reduce your food waste.

Planning ahead

REMEMBER

One of the best ways to reduce your food waste is to plan ahead. Planning what you'll eat for the week can reduce the chance you will overpurchase and end up with food you can't eat. A lot of cooking blogs and apps can help you plan your meals, but here are a few pointers to get you started:

>> Write down the ingredients you will need.

>> Note which items are already in your cupboard or fridge.

>> Include quantities so you can make sure you don't buy too much.

>> Plan for days when you'll be too busy by cooking in bulk and reheating foods.

Saving your leftovers

These are just a few examples of ways you can use your leftovers:

>> Make a pasta bake with leftover pasta.

>> Freeze all your leftovers, even if it's only a few veggies. You can add them to your dinner the next night or throw them in a soup.

>> Leftover vegetables can be mixed with mashed potato to make bubble and squeak (a British favorite!) or added to an omelet.

>> Juice your leftover fruit before it starts to rot, and freeze the juice.

>> Make an apple pie or banana bread when fruit is almost out of date.

>> Make bread crumbs from leftover bread.

>> Give leftovers to your dog or chickens.

WARNING

Some foods, including certain fruits and vegetables, artificial sweeteners, and food additives, can be toxic to animals. Always check to ensure that any leftover food you give animals is suitable for them.

>> Use offcuts like the stems of your food. It may seem less attractive, but you can eat broccoli and cauliflower stems. But if you prefer not to, you can use them to make stock.

>> Join a Buy Nothing group or other local community group and donate good-quality food you can't finish. In my local group, it's not uncommon for someone to list excess fruit or vegetables.

Switching to frozen foods

Fruits and vegetables that have been frozen are often considered inferior, but this isn't always the case. Many frozen foods are immediately frozen after being harvested, which increases the likelihood that their nutrients will be preserved. My father, for example, now freezes passionfruit and lemons whole when he has too many from the garden.

The best part about frozen foods is that you use only what you need, and the rest stays in the freezer for your next meal. One of the common ways we waste food is when we use only a part of the vegetable. For example, if we buy a cabbage but need only half for a recipe, the chances of the other half going to waste is quite high. Frozen vegetables help solve this issue. However, switching to frozen vegetables leads to more soft plastics. Be sure to read Chapter 11 to find out how to recycle your soft plastics.

Preventing spoilage

REMEMBER

If left alone, food will decompose sooner or later, but it can spoil prematurely if we don't store our food properly. This can lead to wasted food but can also be a health risk in some cases. Make sure you follow the handling and preparation instructions on the food label to ensure it retains its quality.

Understanding how to correctly store food in your fridge can make a difference. Different parts of the fridge (including shelves and drawers) can have different temperatures, so you can keep your food fresher by storing it in the right spot. Figure 12-1 provides some easy-to-follow tips on where to store different foods in your fridge. But first, here are some basics:

>> Check your fridge and freezer temperatures. Your fridge temperature should be about 40 degrees Fahrenheit, 4 degrees Celsius, or a bit lower. Your freezer should be set at 0 degrees Fahrenheit or –18 Celsius.

>> Foods that should definitely be stored in the fridge include dairy foods, eggs, and green vegetables like broccoli, green beans, leafy greens, and spinach.

>> Foods that are best stored outside of the fridge include bananas, nectarines, pears, onions, tomatoes, and potatoes.

REMEMBER

For more information on health risks associated with mishandled or spoiled foods, refer to your local or federal government or contact the manufacturer.

TIP

Our mothers and grandmothers were superstars at making food go a long way. Unfortunately, many of us have forgotten these methods due to modern conveniences and our busy lifestyles. Why not chat with your mother or grandmother and see what tricks they can teach you? I'm sure they'd be happy to share them. Zero waste living blogs and books are also a good source of tips to make your food last longer.

You can use the checklist in Figure 12-2 to help make changes to reduce your food waste.

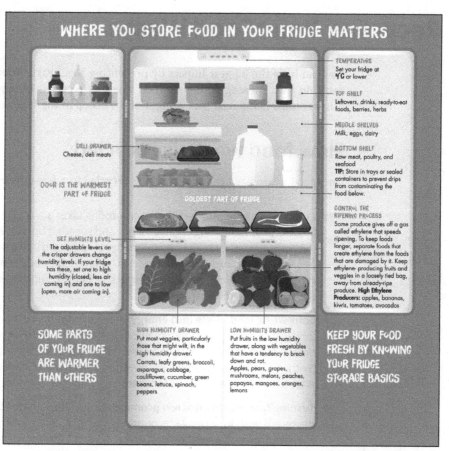

FIGURE 12-1:
Reduce spoilage
by storing your
food in the right
place in your
fridge.

Image provided by Love Food Hate Waste Canada (www.lovefoodhatewaste.ca)

Ways to Reduce Your Food Waste

☐ Plan ahead and make a shopping list

☐ Buy only what you need

☐ Buy local and in season

☐ Buy the ugly fruit and vegetables

☐ Use the food you already have

☐ Store your food properly

☐ Freeze your leftovers

☐ Get to know the meaning of food dates

☐ Share your extra food with others

☐ Compost your food waste

FIGURE 12-2:
A checklist of
ways to reduce
your food waste.

Recycling Your Food Waste

You can have the biggest impact by preventing food waste altogether. But if you can't do this, making sure your food waste is recycled through composting or other options is the next best thing. Get the scoop in the following sections.

How food waste is recycled

Once food waste has been collected, it's recycled in a few different ways:

>> **Composting food into fertilizer:** Composting takes advantage of the natural process of decomposing organic matter and speeds it up a little by creating the perfect conditions. The organic matter is converted into a nutrient-rich fertilizer called *compost*. Waste food can be recycled through commercial composting facilities, anaerobic digesters, or home composts (which I describe later in this chapter).

>> **Converting food waste into energy:** *Anaerobic digestion* is a process where food waste, along with other organic materials like manure or waste crops, is broken down in the absence of oxygen. When it breaks down, it releases methane, which is captured and converted into biogas and used to generate electricity or to make fuels or fertilizers.

>> **Turning food waste into new products:** One of the fantastic outcomes of the recent push for a circular economy is that innovation is thriving. Here are a few examples of ways that food waste is being transformed into something new:

- **Wrapping food with food:** The brand Great Wrap in Australia has developed compostable cling wrap using the skins of potatoes left over from making potato chips. They convert the potato waste into compostable bioplastic. It's even home compostable once you have finished with it. Check it out at www.greatwrap.co.

- **Vegan leather from pineapples:** Making leather from pineapple leaves is an example of reinvigorating an age-old technique. The leaves from the pineapple plant are processed into a soft leather-type material that's a great ethical and vegan leather substitute. Keep an eye out for the many brands using it in their products.

- **Going bananas over textiles:** Using bananas to make environmentally friendly fabric has long been used in Asia. Textile industries looking to support a circular economy are now taking advantage of this process and making textiles from banana waste. The natural textile is made from the stem or peel of the banana plant. The inner fiber is delicate, smooth, and silky, and the outer fiber is coarser.

Research is ongoing into various discarded fruit and vegetable parts in various applications, from pharmaceuticals and food preservatives to new bioplastics to replace conventional plastic. While we should continue to focus on reducing food waste overall, these new innovations are exciting.

Curbside recycling services for food waste

Food composting services are expanding in many countries, and in some places, local authorities even collect food waste through curbside services. Some curbside programs have a separate bin for food waste (also referred to as food organics), while others allow you to put it into your green waste or garden waste bin.

REMEMBER

Rules for what is accepted and how you should collect your food waste vary from location to location. As with recycling plastics and glass (see Chapters 6 and 8), it depends on what equipment and processes are available at nearby facilities. Always check with your local curbside composting company or your local town or city government to get familiar with their rules.

Options for recycling at home

Here I list some options for those who don't have access to a local collection service to recycle their food waste:

>> **Home composting:** Starting your own compost at home is the best way to make sure your food waste isn't wasted. Composting is a natural process where food scraps are broken down into organic material that is rich in nutrients. I take you through setting up your own home compost in the next section.

>> **Bokashi bin:** Developed in Japan, this method requires that you to collect your food scraps in a reusable bin for a few weeks. Every time you put more food in, you spray a fermenting agent that helps break down the food. As the food breaks down, it produces a liquid referred to as *bokashi juice*. It's full of nutrients and great for your garden or any potted plants. After a few weeks, you bury the contents in the garden and start a new batch. It can be a good option if you live in an apartment or condominium as long as you can find a way to dispose of the solids once they have broken down. I describe some options later in this section.

>> **Worm farms:** Worm farms are a bit like compost bins, except the food waste is broken down by earthworms. Earthworms are extremely good at breaking down food and garden waste. They basically eat up all the organic matter and convert it into fertilizer that can be used in the garden. It's packed full of

nutrients and helps the soil retain moisture, all the stuff our gardens need. Worm farms don't take up much room and are reasonably priced. Plus, if you have kids, they're fantastic for teaching them about natural processes.

TIP

» **Donating your food scraps:** If you don't have the means to compost your food waste, there are other alternatives like those listed here:

- You might know an enthusiastic composter or someone who owns chickens who would be happy to take your food waste.

- Check if you have a local compost hub, community garden, school garden, or farmers market that will take your food waste.

- Look for local food scrap drop-off programs. For example, in New York City you can sign up for GrowNYC, a nonprofit that provides over 200 drop-off locations for food waste across the city (www.grownyc.org/compost).

- There are various mobile phone apps available that match you with people who want your food waste. One example is ShareWaste (www.sharewaste.com), which is available worldwide. About six months ago I used the ShareWaste app and found a local couple with a home compost and chickens. They live about five minutes away from me, and I've been dropping off our food waste to them once a week ever since. It's significantly reduced our general waste.

» **Paid composing services:** There are paid services available that will come and pick up your food scraps from your home and compost it for you. This is particularly great if you don't have access to curbside composting or a community location. CompostNow is a good example (www.compostnow.org); they have services operating across the United States and Canada and will even pick up from apartments.

TIP

If you want to find out more about these options, Compost Revolution is a good source of information. They have some great tutorials available on their site here: www.compostrevolution.com.au/australia-wide/tutorials/.

Starting a Home Compost

Composting can be quite a rewarding practice. It not only reduces your impact on the environment but also saves money and resources. Plus, it will have your garden looking amazing. Compost provides everything gardens need and keeps the soil in good condition. Your plants will love you for it. Plus, you will be keeping this material out of the landfill.

Composting has so many benefits:

>> It improves soil. Healthy soil contains nutrients and living things that help hold those nutrients.

>> Plants depend on the nutrients in the soil to thrive. Composting will help feed your plants and keep them healthy.

>> It's the best way to reduce food waste and prevent it from being sent to landfills.

>> It lowers greenhouse gas emissions.

>> It's a circular economy process right in your own home.

How do you set up a compost at home?

Follow these steps to set up your own home compost:

1. **Choose a composting bin.**

   You'll find plenty of different types of composting bins. You can choose a simple standup bin with a lid or use the advanced option with a mechanism to turn the unit. If you prefer, you can simply set up your compost in the corner of the garden or in a hole (without a bin) or build your own box.

   Look out for a recycled plastic compost bin to help support recycling while doing your bit to reduce food waste.

2. **Find a good location for your compost.**

   This will depend on the size of your garden and the landscaping you might already have. Make sure access to the site is easy, and keep in mind that you need access to water to keep your compost moist.

   Composts can get a bit smelly, so you might want to make sure it's not too close to the house or back veranda.

3. **Get together the ingredients.**

   For a successful compost, you need a source of carbon and nitrogen. Bacteria need both to grow and multiply. Some materials are carbon rich, while others are nitrogen rich. To achieve and maintain a reasonable carbon-to-nitrogen ratio, simply use a 50:50 mixture of browns and greens, as described here and later in this chapter:

   - **Browns:** Materials with higher carbon than nitrogen include straw, sawdust, dried leaves, twigs and branches, paper and cardboard, and cotton fabric. As well as contributing carbon, browns help provide gaps throughout the compost to allow airflow.

- **Greens:** These are ingredients with high nitrogen content and lower carbon. Examples include kitchen food scraps, fresh lawn clippings, green leaves or weeds, and chicken poop. Items are mostly green in color, but not always.

TIP

Cut your veggie scraps into small pieces; this makes it easier for the organisms and worms to get to them.

4. **Place some sticks and other woody material in the bottom of your compost bin to help with drainage.**

5. **Add equal proportions of browns and greens.**

6. **Give it some time.**

   Maintain your compost by keeping it moist and turning it over weekly to introduce oxygen. Keep adding ingredients as the compost reduces, and you have room in the top.

TIP

Keep the moisture level right. Too much moisture will cause the mixture to go moldy and smell pretty bad, but too little moisture will mean it's too dry, and the organisms can't break down the food. If you put your compost in a sunny spot, keep a closer eye on it, because regular sunshine can cause it to dry out quicker.

WARNING

Temperatures in composts can get pretty hot, so much so that they can start smoldering or even catch fire. Although this is pretty rare, you can stop your compost from becoming a fire hazard by keeping it moist. See the nearby sidebar "Steaming or smoking?" for more information.

Composting times will vary and can take up to 12 months, depending on where you live and your ingredients. The compost should have no visible food scraps when it's done and should be crumbled and dark.

7. **When the compost is ready, you can lift the bin or scoop it out and start spreading it over your garden.**

   Dig it into your garden, choosing different areas every time to ensure your whole garden benefits. Then simply sit back and watch your garden thrive, knowing you're reducing your impact.

STEAMING OR SMOKING?

Some of the moisture in compost piles may be converted to water vapor or steam by the heat. This can often happen on chilly mornings. You might think your compost is smoldering and at risk of catching on fire, but usually it's just the steam.

Smell the air near your compost. If it smells like burning vegetation or smoke, get the hose out and wet it down; if not, it's more likely it's just steaming.

What can go in your compost?

Although not extensive, Table 12-1 and Figure 12-3 give you an idea of what you can put in your compost.

TABLE 12-1

What Goes in Your Compost: Brown versus Green

Browns	Greens
Dried leaves, branches and twigs	Grass clippings and plant trimmings
Straw	Fruit scraps (some people avoid citrus scraps)
Sawdust	Vegetable scraps
Paper or cardboard	Eggs and eggshells
Cotton fabric	Animal manure (not from household pets)

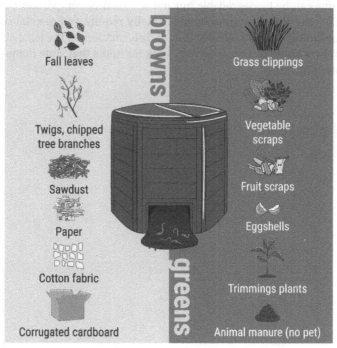

FIGURE 12-3: Use 50 percent browns and 50 percent greens to maintain a healthy compost.

browns

Fall leaves
Twigs, chipped tree branches
Sawdust
Paper
Cotton fabric
Corrugated cardboard

greens

Grass clippings
Vegetable scraps
Fruit scraps
Eggshells
Trimmings plants
Animal manure (no pet)

m.malinika/Adobe Stock

What can't go in your home compost?

Many items can slow the composting process and attract vermin or undesirable bacteria. Some examples include

>> Liquids such as milk or cooking oil

>> Dairy products like cheese

>> Cardboard or paper with a plastic coating

>> Citrus and onions (will slow the composting process)

>> Cooked or raw meat, fish, and bones

Although many of these items can't go in a home compost, some commercial or curbside services will accept them.

It's also important to understand the definitions of *biodegradable* and *compostable*. Items can be biodegradable but not necessarily compostable. Plus, many things that state they are compostable actually require commercial composting conditions to break down. Always look for information on the label or with the brand to confirm an item is compostable. Look for items that state home-compostable and avoid the others.

IN THIS CHAPTER

» Grasping the meaning of "electronic waste"

» Exposing the problems with e-waste

» Explaining how e-waste gets recycled

» Getting guidance on responsible disposal

» Breaking down battery recycling

» Making choices to minimize your e-waste

Chapter **13**

Exploring E-Waste Recycling Solutions

Most of the comforts we enjoy in life are made possible by technological devices and appliances. These devices save us time, keep us connected, and entertain us. But all of this convenience comes at a price. E-waste, or electronic waste, is considered the world's fastest-growing waste stream. It's not surprising, given how easily we're convinced to give up our perfectly good, working devices for the latest update. Our obsession with the newest style or model, paired with inherent obsolescence and increased accessibility, has created a complex and challenging waste stream impacting human health and the environment.

The term *e-waste* refers to electronic devices and appliances with a cord or battery. Often they are labeled as items that have reached the end of their useful lives, but sadly, many still function and could continue to be useful for a long time. Changing how we perceive electronic gadgets and appreciating their worth is perhaps the most fundamental way to deal with our growing e-waste issue. We should keep using and, when necessary, repair our e-waste before we consider recycling it.

In this chapter, I explain what e-waste is, providing plenty of examples to help you identify the e-waste in your home. Then I take you through the problems caused by e-waste and how recycling can help. Finally, I give you the tools to dispose of your e-waste responsibly and discuss ways to cut down on the amount of electronic trash you create.

WARNING

E-waste is one of the most complex categories of waste. Not only does it contain a mix of metals, minerals, and plastics, but it also contains many harmful compounds, such as brominated flame retardants, lead, arsenic, and mercury. When e-waste is disposed of incorrectly, these substances can pollute the soil, water, and air and pose a risk to human health.

Defining E-Waste

E-waste is short for *electronic waste,* a term used to describe electronic products near the end of their "useful life." Other terms used to describe this sort of waste include e-scrap, end-of-life electronics, and WEEE, which stands for "waste from electrical and electronic equipment."

REMEMBER

The best definition I've come across for what constitutes e-waste is "any household or business item with a plug, cord, battery, or electronic component."

Typical examples of e-waste are mobile phones, computers, and televisions, but e-waste encompasses many common everyday items. Table 13-1 gives you an idea of the items included.

TABLE 13-1   **E-Waste Items by Category**

Small Home Appliances	Large Household Appliances
• Microwaves • Irons • Toasters, kettles, and coffee machines • Sewing machines • Power tools • Lights/lamps, flashlights	• Refrigerators and washing machines • Cookers • Electric fans • Heaters and air conditioners • Electric lawnmowers • Solar panels
Personal Devices	**Other E-Waste**
• Mobile phones/smartphones • Power supplies • Watches, including smartwatches • Cameras • Hairdryers, curlers, and straighteners • Electric shavers • Electronic cigarettes	• Medical devices • Automatic dispensers • Thermostats • Massage chairs • Diabetic testing equipment • Heart monitors • Defibrillator

Home Entertainment	IT and Telecommunications
• CD, DVD, & Blu Ray players • CDs and DVDs • Televisions • Stereos • Video game systems • Remote controls • Video recorders • Amplifiers • Musical instruments • Radios • Hand-held video games • Kids' toys	• Home and office telephones • Desktop computers • Laptops and tablets • Printers and scanners • Copy machines and fax machines • Circuit boards • Hard drives/CD ROM/computer disks • Monitors (CRT, LCD, plasma) • Network hardware like modems, routers, and servers • UPS systems • Audio and video equipment

Tackling the E-Waste Problem

TECHNICAL STUFF

As I mention earlier, e-waste is the fastest-growing waste stream in the world. And it's not surprising, considering our addiction to the latest technology. According to the Global E-waste Monitor (https://ewastemonitor.info/), backed by the United Nations, 53.6 million metric tons of e-waste were generated worldwide in 2019, an increase of 21 percent since 2014. And they predict the annual amount will reach more than 74 million metric tons by 2030.

Unfortunately, less than 20 percent of the world's e-waste gets recycled. The 80 percent not recycled is sent to local landfills or developing nations, where it's either incinerated or dumped, causing pollution and health hazards. The U.S. Environmental Protection Agency (EPA) estimates that every year, up to 60 million metric tons of e-waste is discarded in landfills in the United States alone.

Yet many of the materials found in e-waste still have value. E-waste contains valuable raw materials that can be recovered and reused. For example, circuit boards contain precious metals like silver and gold. On the flip side, toxic materials are lurking in these devices that, if left unchecked, can cause significant environmental pollution. Recycling e-waste not only keeps materials in use and decreases demand for mining raw materials but also enables the safe management of these toxic materials.

The e-waste problem is complex, and solving it requires a concerted effort from consumers, businesses, and governments. As a consumer, you have the power to make a difference, and you should be willing to use it. The best way is to put off buying new devices and instead use what you already have, repair broken devices or donate them for reuse, and make sustainable and ethical choices when buying a new device. Don't worry if that sounds like a lot to take in; I describe all of these later in this chapter. But before we get to that, in the following sections I explain the benefits of recycling e-waste and what can happen when it ends up in the wrong bin.

Understanding how recycling e-waste helps the environment

Here are a few important reasons why we should recycle our electronic waste:

>> **Keeping materials in use and decreasing demand for new materials:** Digging up new deposits of rare metals and precious minerals is a surefire way to cause environmental damage. Mining not only takes a heavy toll on the environment but also risks the health of the individuals working in the mines. Every time you recycle an old device, the minerals and other materials in the device can be recovered and reused, thereby reducing the demand for new resources. In fact, according to the EPA, for every million cell phones recycled, you can recover around 35 thousand pounds of copper, 772 pounds of silver, 75 pounds of gold, and 33 pounds of palladium.

TECHNICAL STUFF

Electronic products can contain both rare earth minerals and precious metals. Despite their name, rare earth metals are relatively abundant in the earth's crust, but they occur in very small concentrations and are extremely difficult and expensive to extract. On the other hand, precious metals are rare, and because they are usually lustrous and beautiful, they are desirable and very valuable.

>> **Minimizing the risk of toxic pollution:** When landfills are mismanaged, toxic chemicals can leach into soils, groundwater, and nearby waterways. These chemicals can damage vegetation, wildlife, and humans that rely on those water sources. While e-waste accounts for only a few percent of the waste by volume, it accounts for more than 70 percent of the toxic compounds accumulating in landfills.

>> **Saving energy and resources:** Materials reclaimed from e-waste often have a smaller carbon footprint than equivalent materials extracted from the ground and processed through traditional methods. In fact, according to the EPA, we could power 3,500 homes for a whole year with the energy saved by recycling one million laptops.

Mining materials in electronic devices

Electrical goods, like phones and computers, can contain precious metals. These metals are usually rare, difficult to extract, and have a high economic value. Keeping these metals in use minimizes the need to extract more resources, saving energy and reducing the overall environmental impact. Plus, precious metals are nonrenewable, so they won't be replaced or replenished once we've extracted the last of them from the earth.

Some of the precious metals found in electronic goods include the following:

>> Gold occurs in small amounts in mobile phones, laptop computers, calculators, cameras, and microwaves.

>> Silver can be found in printed circuit boards, television screens, mobile phones, and computer chips.

>> Platinum is used in almost every electronic gadget you can think of. Some examples are anything with an LCD screen, computer hard disks, and circuitry.

>> Copper is a valuable mineral used in the circuitry and wiring of many electronic products.

REMEMBER

The good news is that these precious metals can be recovered and reused. Each electronic gadget has only a tiny amount inside, but when recycled by specialists, it's sufficient to make a difference.

Recognizing that toxic materials lurk in your gadgets

WARNING

E-waste might seem safe on the outside, but toxic substances are lurking inside many of our electronic goods. If allowed to leach into the environment, they can be very harmful. What might start as a small quantity can accumulate in soil or water, reach dangerous levels, and impact ecosystems and potentially lead to health problems for humans. Because the risks from toxic chemicals are so high, many states and countries have established laws banning the disposal of e-waste in landfills.

Examples of toxic substances found in e-waste include the following:

>> Lead is known for its dangerous health effects, particularly in children. Despite being banned in many consumer products, it's still found in some electronic gadgets like mobile phones and computers. The cathode-ray tubes in older televisions contain large amounts of lead; however, luckily most new televisions no longer use cathode-ray tubes.

>> Mercury can be toxic, with significant environmental and human health issues, even in very low doses. Mercury is found in LCD screens and monitors, some button-cell batteries, and older appliances.

>> Arsenic is used in electronic parts like LCD screens, computer chips, and circuit boards. When e-waste is burned through informal recycling methods in developing countries, arsenic can get into the air and create significant health issues for surrounding communities.

>> Cadmium is found in many batteries, particularly rechargeable nickel-cadmium batteries, but is also present in cathode-ray tubes. Cadmium is another material often burned by informal recyclers when they are trying to extract valuable materials from e-waste.

>> Brominated flame retardants help reduce fire risk in many electronic gadgets. However, they are known to have many adverse human health risks if not handled appropriately.

REMEMBER

Recycling your e-waste responsibly through specialist services can significantly reduce the risk of these hazardous substances escaping and affecting communities and the environment.

Knowing that e-waste doesn't belong in the bin

WARNING

Electronic waste shouldn't be placed in your general waste bin. It doesn't break down easily and can release hazardous chemicals into the environment, leaching into soils and waterways and potentially impacting human health. Putting e-waste in your general waste bin is like throwing toxic chemicals straight into a creek or river. Plus, these hazardous materials are valuable and very useful, so letting them sit in landfills and not reusing them is a waste of resources.

REMEMBER

E-waste also doesn't belong in your curbside recycling bin. Electronic waste is unlike other waste you create and must be handled by a specialist recycler. If placed in your recycling bin, e-waste items can become hazardous during transportation and at the recycling plant, leading to unsafe conditions for workers. It can also contaminate other recyclables and result in them being sent to landfill.

So, what should you do with your e-waste? Later in this chapter I provide a list of drop-off locations and collection services. If none of those are available to you, try searching Google for "electronic waste recycling near me," or get in touch with your local town or city government. Unfortunately, if you live in a more remote setting, you may need to travel a bit farther to a drop-off point. In this case, why not team up with your neighbors and take turns making the trip to the drop-off location or look for mail-in options?

Exploring How E-Waste Is Recycled

You thought recycling plastics was difficult! The wide range of devices classified as e-waste, varying proportions of materials like glass, metals, and plastic, and the presence of toxic materials make recycling e-waste a significant challenge.

Safely recycling e-waste is very labor-intensive and expensive. As a result, e-waste is often shipped to low- or middle-income countries for processing, where they lack the infrastructure and safety standards to manage the toxic materials. The impact on the environment and communities has been disastrous.

Since the introduction of the Basel Convention, described in more detail in the nearby sidebar "Banning the illegal trade of hazardous waste," and the public outcry over environmental and human health issues associated with the processing of e-waste, things have started to change. Many governments have stepped up and cut exports of these hazardous materials. Meanwhile, private companies are rising to the challenge of recycling e-waste and creating accessible certified programs. But there's still work to do to stop the legal and illegal shipping of waste to other nations. The following sections describe the least desirable and most preferred way to recycle e-waste.

BANNING THE ILLEGAL TRADE OF HAZARDOUS WASTE

The Basel Convention, adopted in 1989, was designed to reduce the movement and disposal of hazardous waste between developed and developing countries. Basel Convention rules dictate that exporting e-waste to a country requires explicit permission from that nation. The Basel Ban, an amendment to the original Basel Convention treaty, also prohibits the export of hazardous wastes from member countries to non-member countries. It was added in 1995 but didn't become law until 2019. Generally, the Basel Convention Ban Amendment now makes exporting e-waste to developing nations illegal for those countries that have signed up.

Unfortunately, despite signing the Basel agreement, the United States has not yet ratified it. About 25 states have established e-waste recycling legislation, but no federal laws directly address the issue. This means it is still legal for e-waste to be shipped overseas from the United States.

Seeing the dangers of informally recycling e-waste

Informal recycling refers to recycling by individuals, groups, or small businesses that aren't typically associated with government or authorized recycling centers. Informal recyclers undertake a significant proportion of waste recycling globally, and typically they are located in developing countries. Their rudimentary methods and lack of environmental safeguards in treating e-waste can introduce toxic chemicals to the surrounding environment and risk the health of nearby communities.

Methods often involve burning devices to melt away nonvaluable material, including dangerous plastics or other toxic substances like mercury or lead, or using acids to recover gold from devices. Unfortunately, in many of these locations, environmental laws offer minimal protection for the environment.

But it's not just the environment that suffers; workers are often exposed to these dangerous chemicals all day long without protection. Figure 13-1 provides an example of workers' conditions in processing e-waste. Labor laws or their enforcement are often inadequate and don't protect the workers. And typically, many informal recyclers are poor or marginalized and depend on the income from this dangerous job to survive.

FIGURE 13-1: Close-up of immigrant workers cooking circuit boards to remove the solder, exposing themselves to toxic solder fumes.

David Fedele/www.e-wastelandfilm.com/www.david-fedele.com/last accessed February 21, 2023

The Basel Convention, which governs the trade of hazardous waste (see the nearby sidebar "Banning the illegal trade of hazardous waste"), and the implementation of the China Sword Policy restrictions on the importation of recyclable materials (see Chapter 4) have helped reduce the amount of e-waste exported to developing countries. But even with restrictions and laws in place, exporting e-waste remains cheaper than responsibly recycling it, so rogue scrap dealers are willing to risk fines. One way you can help is by making sure your e-waste goes to certified e-waste recyclers. Find out more in the next section.

Recycling e-waste the right way

Responsibly recycling e-waste is complex and labor-intensive but not impossible, and techniques are advancing. Safe recycling requires disassembling the gadgets into their individual, marketable components while maintaining appropriate working conditions to prevent exposure to harmful compounds.

REMEMBER

The first thing that happens in recycling e-waste is to assess an item for reuse. Using products as initially intended for as long as possible is the best outcome. It ensures that the maximum possible value is obtained from the energy and resources invested in designing, manufacturing, and delivering the product. When items cannot be repaired or are too costly to repair, they are taken apart or shredded. Each material will then be collected, processed, and sold to manufacturers for use in new products. Of course, the process depends heavily on the type of object.

Here are the most common steps in recycling e-waste:

1. **The e-waste is sorted into categories.**

   Sorting the various types of e-waste is an essential first step in the process, and often recyclers will get you to help by putting your e-waste into different bins at the drop-off location. At a facility, manual workers will sort items further.

2. **The e-waste is reverse manufactured.**

   E-waste items are dismantled in the reverse order in which they were built. This process helps capture valuable materials and components for reuse; however, it's extremely labor-intensive. It requires trained technicians who understand the manufacturing process and can follow dismantling instructions. Plus, some items must be treated more carefully when taken apart, particularly those that contain hazardous waste. The process of reverse manufacturing is shown in Figure 13-2.

3. **The e-waste is shredded.**

   Parts that can't be reused are shredded. The resulting mixture is sorted into different materials using mechanical or manual separation, similar to what happens at a regular materials recovery facility (MRF) or recycling facility. For example, magnets are used to extract ferrous metals, and infrared detectors help identify the different plastics.

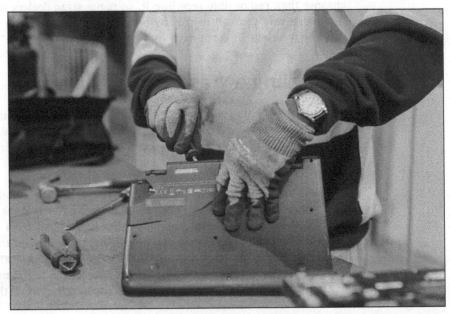

FIGURE 13-2: Reverse manufacturing e-waste at a factory.

Scipher Technologies Pty Ltd/www.scipher.com.au/last accessed February 21, 2023

4. **The materials are sold to a manufacturer.**

   Once separated, the materials may require further treatment to remove any remaining contamination before they can be sold to a manufacturer.

Unfortunately, most mobile phones don't get turned back into new mobile phones. Instead, the individual materials find their way into many manufacturing processes. These individual materials are used in different products like cabling, circuit boards, new batteries, keyboards, toys, and jewelry. Any plastics, metal, and glass might find their way into regular reprocessing streams to be incorporated into various new products.

Responsibly Disposing of Your E-Waste

Electronic and electrical items take a significant amount of energy and resources to make. They're not designed to be used and thrown away in a short period of time. Before discarding an electronic device that you believe has outlived its usefulness, you might ask yourself a few probing questions, which are described in the following sections.

Considering selling or donating your item

The sooner an unwanted electronic device is given away to someone who will use it, the better. Leaving it sitting in your drawer will only lead to it being outdated and no longer useful to someone. Here are some options:

>> If the item is still functioning, try selling it to someone who will continue to use it. You can sell many used e-waste items at garage sales, or on eBay, Facebook, or Craigslist.

TIP

If you're selling an item, make sure it works and has all the required cords for charging. For transparency, always clearly state the condition and age of the item for the buyer.

>> You can also give your gadgets away to someone you know will use them. Ask your family and friends to see whether anyone needs such a device. If not, try donating it to someone in your local Buy Nothing group or local community charity shop.

TIP

Not all charities accept electronics, even if they are still working. Check before dropping off any old devices.

Before selling or donating your devices, delete all personal information. Find out more later in this chapter.

Repairing your item to keep it in use

Many decades ago, we would have repaired an item repeatedly before discarding it. Today we throw that item away far too quickly without considering if it's repairable. But even if we try to repair an item, we quickly find it's not easy. Companies limit the availability of information and specialist tools, making it difficult to repair their products and, in some cases, impossible. This makes finding a repairer difficult and makes repair costs very high. Sometimes, it can even cost us more to repair an item than to purchase a new product.

But change is on its way, with countries looking at passing laws to ensure that the information and tools to repair our devices are readily available. These laws are starting to switch things around, making device repair more accessible. Find out more about this idea in the nearby sidebar "The Right to Repair movement."

Here are some existing repair options worth looking into:

>> Send the item back to the manufacturer for repair.

>> Visit local repair shops.

>> Follow online tutorials and instructional videos via YouTube.

>> Try dedicated repair websites like www.ifixit.com.

>> Look for a local Repair cafe at www.repaircafe.org (find out more about these community events in Chapter 17).

Recycling your item responsibly

Once you've exhausted all of the other options or the item is broken beyond repair, it's time to look at recycling your e-waste. Depending on where you live, you might have access to one of the following:

>> There may be local town or city permanent designated drop-off locations like waste depots or recycling centers.

>> Special collection events may be organized by the government or businesses.

>> Some brands have free in-store drop-off programs or mail-in services. For example, companies like Apple, Dyson, and Dell will take back your old devices and appliances and recycle them for free.

THE RIGHT TO REPAIR MOVEMENT

Things are changing for the better, even if slowly. Consumers want to have the ability to repair items they've spent their hard-earned money on. A movement called the "Right to Repair" has arisen out of this frustration, and governments are taking notice. The movement advocates government legislation to guarantee that customers can modify and repair products they have purchased without being subject to limitations imposed by the manufacturer.

The Right to Repair movement was initiated to end the monopoly car manufacturers had on repair information, giving them an unfair advantage over independent auto-repair businesses. It has since expanded to many other products, focusing primarily on electronics.

For example, New York recently passed legislation requiring digital electronics manufacturers to provide information and tools to third-party repairers. Plus, more than 25 U.S. states have introduced or are considering introducing Right to Repair bills. The European Union (EU), which already has several laws in place, is looking to bolster these laws and make repairs more accessible. And despite leaving the EU, the United Kingdom has mirrored its Right to Repair laws. These measures will make it easier to repair old devices, extending their life and helping to reduce e-waste.

Add your voice to the Right to Repair movement by calling or writing to your local legislator and letting them know you support your right to repair. Find out more about the campaign at www.repair.org.

>> Some metal scrap yards accept e-waste.

>> When purchasing a large electrical item like a fridge, you can sometimes arrange for the retailer to collect your old one during the delivery.

>> Independent specialized businesses collect and process e-waste.

I provide many examples of these recyclers in Table 13-2 in the next section. But before you drop off your gadgets, consider the following:

>> **Check if the e-waste recycler is certified.** It's crucial to ensure the recycler you use has the appropriate certification to manage your e-waste responsibly and ethically. With no certification, there's no guarantee the waste will be processed appropriately and through the correct channels. You can check certification through E-Stewards (https://e-stewards.org/), or contact your local government environmental protection agency or department for help.

- **Check the rules for safe battery disposal.** In some places, batteries must be dropped off separately. However, you should remove the battery only if it's safe and easy. You can discover more about recycling your batteries later in this chapter.

REMEMBER

- **Don't try to separate materials yourself unless it's safe.** Pulling out a battery or taking off a plastic cover might be okay, but don't try to separate parts or materials unless you're certain that it's safe to do so. E-waste recyclers are trained and have the equipment to assist in safely pulling things apart and dealing with hazardous or toxic materials. If you're unsure, talk to your local e-waste recycler and ask for their advice.

REMEMBER

- **Remove your personal data.** It's important to ensure you've removed any personal data from the electronic equipment. There's a risk of identity theft if you don't. Some service companies will clean the data from your devices for you, but often this may come at a cost. However, in many cases, it's a relatively simple process, and you can find ways to remove your data through online guides for each device. This blog post from Compare and Recycle provides some simple guidelines for removing personal information from your mobile phone: www.compareandrecycle.co.uk/blog/how-to-remove-data-from-iphone-android.

- **Check what items the recycler accepts.** Before you head down to your local drop-off location, check online or call them to ensure they accept all the items you plan to drop off. For example:

    - Some programs don't take LCD TVs and monitors because they can contain mercury or lead, a hazardous material.

    - Larger e-waste items like washing machines or ovens may need to be disposed of through specialist programs.

    - If you plan to donate computers or mobile phones to a charity, they may have rules concerning the condition and age.

Finding an e-waste recycler near you

To help you discover a recycler in your country, I've included in Table 13-2 as many alternatives for recycling e-waste as I could find. However, if you don't find one nearby, I encourage you to search your local area by checking the resources provided at the end of Chapter 5, running a Google search for "electronic waste recycling near me," or contacting your local town or city government for help.

REMEMBER

If the device is at the end of its life and you need to recycle it, please don't put it in the general rubbish bin or your curbside recycling bin. Try to find a local e-waste recycler or drop-off point.

TABLE 13-2   **E-waste Recycling Locations by Country**

Country	E-waste Recycling Locations
United States	**Recycling services:** Greener Gadgets **Charities:** World Computer Exchange, Free Geek, Goodwill **Retail drop-offs:** HP, The Home Depot, Lowe's, Best Buy, LG, Samsung, Toshiba, Apple, Sprint, Office Depot, Staples, Amazon
Canada	**Recycling services:** Electronics Recycling Association, EPRA/Recycle My Electronics, Free Geek Vancouver **Retail drop-offs:** Staples, Best Buy, Canadian Tire, HP, The Home Depot, Lowe's, LG, Samsung, Toshiba, Apple, Sprint, Office Depot, Staples, Amazon
United Kingdom	**Recycling services:** Household Waste Recycling Centres. Check your local rules as some local authorities accept small electric items in your curbside collection. **Charities:** WeeeCharity website (https://weeecharity.com/), Salvation Army Retail Shop **Retail drop-offs:** Currys PC World
Australia	**Recycling services:** National Television and Computer Recycling Scheme, TechCollect, eCycle Solutions, Mobile Muster **Charities:** Brotherhood of St. Laurence, St. Vincent de Paul Society, and GiveNow. Or turn your gadget into a meal for someone in need by donating it through the "PonyUp for Good" Emeals program. **Retail drop-offs:** Amazon, Apple, Samsung, Dell, LG, HP

Examining Battery Recycling

Our lives would slow down and possibly come to a standstill without batteries. They power our phones, computers, clocks, TV remotes, and many e-waste devices around the house. They even power the future through electric cars and solar energy. Batteries are integral to our current quality of life and very important for a more sustainable future. Therefore it's just as important that we recycle our batteries. Find out the details about battery recycling in the following sections.

Understanding why you should recycle batteries

Most of the chemicals used in batteries are toxic to humans and damaging to the environment. In landfills, the outer casing of batteries will degrade, allowing the contents to escape. Worse still, these chemicals can contaminate adjacent streams and groundwater, endangering both the environment and people's health.

Recycling batteries keeps these toxic substances from leaking into the environment and ensures they get collected and reused. In fact, many of the materials and chemicals can be recycled and reused in new batteries. Here are examples of metals that can be recovered from old batteries and how they get reused:

>> Lead can be recovered from lead-acid batteries and is used to make new batteries.

>> Cadmium can be used to make stainless steel products.

>> Lithium from lithium-ion batteries is used in lubricants, glass, and ceramics.

Knowing which batteries can be recycled

REMEMBER

Battery recycling is straightforward, but there are a few rules that you should consider, including:

>> **Most batteries can't go in your general waste bin.** In some locations, like Australia and some states in the United States, all batteries are classed as hazardous waste and can't be placed in your general waste bin.

Although in other locations, some batteries are classified as nonhazardous, they are still recyclable. Given the many drop-off locations available, there's no reason to send these valuable materials to a landfill.

>> **Never put batteries in your curbside recycling bin.** Batteries should never go in your curbside recycling bin. Curbside recycling services aren't designed to handle batteries, and as a result, they can cause safety issues. Lithium-ion batteries from phones, laptops, and power tools are particularly problematic as they can cause fires and even explosions in waste trucks or recycling facilities.

The following sections describe the types of batteries that can be recycled.

Disposable batteries

Disposable batteries are also called single-use batteries because they are no longer useful once their charge is spent. You can dispose of all these batteries through a specialist recycling service. Here are some examples:

>> **Common household batteries:** These are the type that power your home electronics like flashlights, clocks, toys, games, smoke alarms, and TV remotes. They are commonly alkaline or zinc-carbon batteries, but you might recognize them as AA, AAA, D-cell, or 9-volt batteries.

Single-use batteries that are leaking can cause chemical burns. Avoid skin contact when handling them by using gloves and protective eyewear. If in doubt, contact the manufacturer for safe handling instructions.

>> **Button-cell batteries:** You'll find these small round batteries in devices like watches, car remotes, hearing aids, or small flashlights (also known as torches). They can be either alkaline or lithium batteries. However, some contain silver, cadmium, or even mercury, especially if purchased from a less reputable supplier.

It's a good idea to store button-cell or coin batteries out of the reach of young children to prevent swallowing hazards.

Rechargeable batteries

Rechargeable batteries are designed for repeat use and can be recharged many times. However, even rechargeable batteries eventually expire. When this happens, you can recycle them through the many specialist services listed in the next section. Here are a few different types of rechargeable batteries you might encounter:

>> **Car batteries:** Cars generally use lead-acid batteries, also referred to as 12-volt batteries. When you buy a new battery for your vehicle, the store will usually take your old battery and dispose of it for you. Electric or hybrid cars use lithium-ion batteries, which should only be removed from the vehicle by specialists. (Find out more about lithium-ion batteries in the nearby sidebar.)

>> **Phone or laptop batteries:** The battery in your phone or laptop is lithium-ion (Li-ion). But these batteries are also found in power tools, children's toys, scooters, and vaping devices.

These batteries can be hazardous and should never be placed in your curbside recycling or general waste bin.

>> **Nickel-cadmium batteries (NiCd):** These are found in rechargeable packs in electronics, photography equipment, and power tools. They should always be recycled through specialist programs.

Finding your nearest drop-off point

You can recycle your batteries through specialist programs, recycling centers, drop-off points, or even at well-known stores. I list numerous options in Table 13-3. If you don't find one nearby, check the resources provided at the end of Chapter 5, try a web search for your local area, or check with your local government.

TABLE 13-3

Battery Recycling Locations by Country

Country	Battery Recycling Locations
United States	**Recycling services:** Call2Recycle, RecycleNation, The Big Green Box **Stores and brands:** Battery Solutions, Batteries Plus, Staples, Lowe's, The Home Depot, Best Buy
Canada	**Recycling services:** Call2recycle.ca, Free Geek Vancouver **Stores and brands:** Staples, Lowe's, Best Buy, The Home Depot
United Kingdom	**Recycling services:** Recycle Now **Stores and brands:** Aldi, Co-op, Marks and Spencer, Tesco, WHSmith, Valpak
Australia	**Recycling services:** Australian Battery Recycling Initiative, B-cycle Battery Recycling, Recycle Mate **Stores and brands:** Aldi, Battery World, Officeworks, Bunnings

Using fewer batteries

Here are some simple ways to reduce how many batteries you use:

>> Switch to rechargeable batteries where you can. You can save some money this way too.

WATCHING OUT FOR LITHIUM-ION BATTERIES

Improper battery disposal has led to fires at several material recovery facilities and in garbage trucks across the United States and other countries. Lithium batteries have also been the culprits behind exploding or spontaneously combusting consumer devices in recent years, including e-cigarettes, hoverboards, and Samsung Galaxy Note 7 smartphones.

Products containing lithium-ion batteries include mobile phones, headphones, cordless vacuum cleaners, earbuds, power tools, and laptops. Most of the time, lithium-ion batteries are relatively safe inside your devices; it's only when they are damaged, or some parts are exposed to the air, excessive heat, or other metals that issues arise.

Keep an eye out for signs of a bad battery, and don't try to remove the batteries yourself. Where applicable, consult the manufacturer's instructions for safe handling requirements. Always recycle lithium-ion batteries at a specialist recycler.

TIP

>> Use up the charge in single-use batteries until there's nothing left. You can do this by moving the battery to an object that doesn't need as much power, like a wall clock or a computer mouse.

Buy a battery tester to help check how much life your batteries have left.

>> Store your batteries at room temperature, because heat and cold can make them wear out faster.

>> Don't store batteries with other metal objects like coins, because this can cause a short circuit.

Reducing Your Overall E-Waste Impact

E-waste is a complex mix of products and materials, and as I explain earlier in this chapter, recycling it can be complex and costly. The following sections describe some things you can do to reduce e-waste and your overall impact.

Taking care of your devices

TIP

You can help make your devices last longer by looking after them. Here are a few things you can do to keep them in top shape:

>> Keep them clean. Dust and dirt can get into electronics or the mechanism of devices and cause issues. Using protective covers can help with this.

>> Remove batteries from toys, decorations, or other devices you use infrequently. Batteries can leak if left unattended for a long time, damaging the device.

>> Put your electronic devices away after use, particularly if they are used outside. The sun can degrade the outer casing and lead to an early demise.

>> Teach your kids to look after their toys so they can be handed down to a family member or friend, or donated to a charity.

>> Don't let your laptop or mobile phone overheat. If your phone overheats, turn it off for a while until it cools down.

Deciding whether to purchase a new device

We often throw away devices at the first sign of trouble, whether it be a malfunction, speed, or just the appearance of a newer model. New devices are designed and sold when there's nothing wrong with the old device, while marketing encourages us to replace things like smartphones or TVs before their useful life is over.

If you think you need a new device, try asking yourself the following questions before making the purchase. You can find a summary version in Figure 13-3.

>> Can you do without it? Perhaps it's an item you rarely use, so test if you can get by without it.

>> Do you have a device that already solves your needs?

- Does your old device do everything you need? It's easy to get caught up in the latest functionality but consider, for a moment, if you really need to upgrade.

- Can the old device be repaired to keep it in use longer?

- Is there another device you already own that can solve the problem?

>> Can you borrow or rent a similar item?

>> Can you buy the same item secondhand?

REMEMBER

The most effective way to reduce your impact is to use your products and postpone upgrading them as long as possible. You can save money and help reduce your impact by buying only what you need and not what companies tell you that you need.

Choosing the right device

Even if you do all the right things by taking care of your devices and repairing them, unfortunately, sooner or later, you'll need to replace them. Or perhaps you've discovered that you require a new device for a particular purpose. When planning to purchase a new device, considering a few things upfront can help lessen the impact later. Finding good-quality, repairable, and recyclable products takes a little extra time, but it's well worth it and might even save you money in the long run.

Here are a few things to consider before you start shopping. Take a look at Figure 13-3 for a flowchart to help your decision process.

Decision Process for Buying Electronics

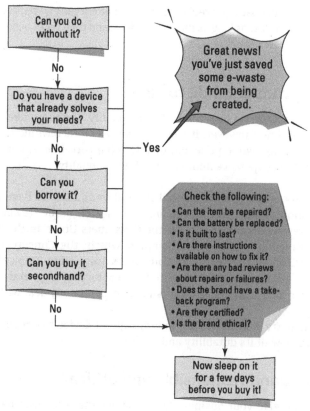

FIGURE 13-3:
How to decide whether to buy a new electronic device.

Is the product easy to repair?

Before you buy, do some research and see whether the item is repairable and parts are readily available:

>> Look for instructions on how to fix the item on YouTube, Google, and websites like iFixit.

>> Check the availability of parts on the brand's website or with other suppliers.

>> Look for reviews that specifically discuss product warranty, replacement, and repairability.

>> Search your local area for repair services and see whether they can service the device.

>> Check if the battery is replaceable. If the battery can't be replaced in a device, it will only last as long as the battery does, and then you'll need to buy a brand-new device.

Is the product made to last?

As with anything we buy, the better the quality, the more likely the product will last a long time. However, it's not always easy to determine the quality of items these days. And while price and quality often correlate, it's not always the case that the most expensive item is of the highest quality.

The beauty of being so connected these days is that we have access to a lot of information online. To find the answers, search online review websites or use official review organizations like the Consumers Union in the United States, the United Kingdom's consumer champion Which, the Consumers' Association of Canada (CAC), or the Australian Consumers Association (Choice) in Australia. You may also get some good information by contacting a general repair service and asking for their insights on the brands they commonly deal with.

TIP

If possible, try waiting several months after a device has been released to get an accurate view of its durability and quality.

Is the brand responsible and ethical?

If you can, give your business to companies that use sustainable resources and have a defined process for their product's end-of-life. A few things to consider include the following:

>> Are they using recycled content in their products?

>> Do they have a take-back or recycling program for the product's end-of-life?

>> Do they offer transparency in their supply chain?

>> Does the company have EPEAT certification? (See the nearby sidebar for more information.)

CHECKING FOR PRODUCT CERTIFICATION

The Electronic Product Environmental Assessment Tool (EPEAT) is a global ecolabel for electronic devices. It's designed to help consumers, businesses, and retailers to buy and sell environmentally preferable electronic products. Each device is assessed by criteria covering material selection, product design, energy conservation, and end-of-life management and rated as bronze, silver, or gold. The EPEAT ecolabel was launched in 2006 and was adopted by U.S. federal agencies the next year. It's now accepted worldwide and used by many online sellers to inform customers. You can search for products on www.epeat.net.

» Check how ethical a brand or product is:

- Check out the Guide to Greener Electronics Report Cards by Greenpeace at www.greenpeace.org/usa/reports/greener-electronics-2017/.

- Another option is Ethical Consumer. You can search their website for different devices and other items (www.ethicalconsumer.org/). You'll need to subscribe to get their full information, though.

Chapter **14**

Scouting Other Recycling Programs

You might be surprised to discover how many recycling programs are available besides your regular curbside service or local recycling center. Many of them take hard-to-recycle items that build up in landfills and can contain plastics or other toxic materials. These items may also have many valuable materials that can be recovered and used in new products.

In this chapter, I list some of the available specialist collection and recycling programs. I describe what items are included, what they can be recycled into, and how you can find these services.

Scrapping Your Household Metal Items

TIP

Most metals can be recycled infinitely, so finding a place to recycle them is an excellent way to keep the materials in use and not send them to a landfill. Scrap metal comes in many shapes and sizes around the home, including metal fixtures and fittings, appliances, electronic devices, jewelry, and toys, to name a few. Here are a few ways to recycle your metal items:

>> **Metal scrapyard:** A metal scrapyard is a good solution for recycling the metal scrap you accumulate in your house. They'll collect all sorts of metals, including steel, aluminum, copper, brass, and other rare metals. And you can even make a few dollars from your scrap. You can find more about recycling your metal at a scrapyard in Chapter 9.

>> **Government take-back programs:** Many local town or city governments will organize collection programs for bulky household items, including those made from metal.

>> **Paid services:** You can contact local junk removal companies who, for a fee, will pick up metal items from your home.

>> **Commercial collection or take-back:** Some companies take old or outdated appliances or devices for recycling. For example, some may take away old appliances like washing machines or dishwashers when they deliver a new one to you.

>> **Recycling your precious metals:** If you have small amounts of gold or silver in jewelry or other items, you can recycle them through specialist metal recyclers. Typically, you can mail in these metals, but you can also drop them off at certain locations, like coin shops.

REMEMBER

If you have access to curbside recycling, put only metal food packaging like steel and aluminum cans and tins in your recycling bin.

Safely Disposing of Hazardous Waste

Around every home, there will be some type of hazardous waste. You might have old paint, strong cleaners, flammable liquids, garden sprays and chemicals, or spent batteries lying around. These items are classified as hazardous. In other words, they can harm the environment or human health if not dealt with responsibly. They require careful handling to mitigate these risks.

Many town and city governments will organize collection days where you can drop off your hazardous waste for free at an easily accessible location. If your local area doesn't provide this service, you may need to find a paid service. You can find some examples of recycling services that will pick up all sorts of specialist items in Chapter 4.

REMEMBER

You should always check the rules for your local hazardous waste service. Many have specific safety guidelines for different chemicals and may even limit how much you can drop off. Hazardous waste doesn't belong in your general waste bin or your curbside recycling bin. In many places, you're likely breaking the law if you dispose of your hazardous waste this way.

Typical examples of household hazardous waste include the following:

>> Painting supplies like paint, paint strippers and removers, aerosol cans, stains and finishes, solvents, inks, glues, and adhesives

>> Flammable products like fuels, kerosene, lighter fluid, and propane tanks

SAFELY GETTING RID OF UNUSED OR UNWANTED MEDICATIONS

Many of us have a medicine cabinet full of out-of-date drugs or medications we no longer need. Unfortunately, medications aren't recyclable, but by disposing of them responsibly, you can prevent them from harming the environment.

When you dispose of medications down the toilet or sink, they can make their way into waterways and even into the ocean, where they can impact the environment. Research suggests that the buildup of drugs in aquatic environments can affect the behavior of fish and other animals. Plus, medications disposed of in landfills can leach into the surrounding soil or groundwater and have similar impacts.

Here are the best ways to dispose of your unwanted or out-of-date medications:

• Try to find an organized take-back program. Check with your local or federal government for drug take-back programs in your area. These can either be permanent collection sites or regularly scheduled events.

• Contact your local pharmacy and see whether they collect unwanted or out-of-date medications. It doesn't have to be the one where you made your purchase. For example, Walgreens in the United States provides take-back bins.

Your first option should always be to find a take-back program; however, if you don't have access to one, follow the instructions on the package, contact your doctor, or get in touch with your local government agency for assistance.

>> Medical supplies like hypodermic needles (sharps) and human and pet medications (see the nearby sidebar for more information on how to get rid of medications)

>> Personal products like nail polish, some home hair color kits, and aerosols

>> Household cleaners like bleaches, oven cleaners, pool chemicals, and wood or metal polishes

>> Automotive products like antifreeze, fuel additives, and motor oil

>> Garden products like herbicides and insecticides

>> E-waste, including anything with a power cord or a battery (read more about the impacts of e-waste and how to dispose of it in Chapter 13)

>> Batteries (see Chapter 13 for information on different battery types, how to recycle them, and a long list of drop-off locations)

Recycling Light Bulbs and String Lights

There are numerous recycling options for the different light bulbs in your house. Here is a list of the most common bulbs and how to dispose of them responsibly:

>> **Incandescent light bulbs** are one of the easiest types to dispose of and can safely go in your general waste bin. However, they are also accepted in some recycling services.

>> **Halogen bulbs** can also go in your general waste bin because they have minimal environmental threats, but it's worth checking if your local recycling center accepts them.

TIP

If incandescent or halogen light bulbs break, wrap them in newspaper to make them safer and so they don't tear your garbage bags.

REMEMBER

>> **Fluorescent tubes and compact fluorescent light (CFL) bulbs** should never be thrown away in your general waste bin; they contain mercury, which is toxic to both humans and animals. In landfills, mercury can leach into groundwater and waterways, endangering surrounding communities. The good news is they can be recycled, and the mercury and other materials, such as glass, can be recovered.

>> **LED bulbs** use less energy and last much longer. However, LED bulbs contain electronic components with tiny amounts of lead and arsenic, two very nasty compounds. In some locations, they're categorized as hazardous waste, but this isn't always the case due to the small quantities involved.

TIP

Regardless of whether you're required by law, I recommend recycling your LED bulbs through a hazardous waste collection so the materials can be recovered and reused. I discuss hazardous waste earlier in this chapter.

TIP

Here are several ways to find out where to recycle your light bulbs:

>> Local government hazardous waste collections

>> Your nearest transfer station or recycling center

>> Specialist recycling schemes like www.lightbulbrecycling.com or www.lamprecycle.org in the United States, www.recolight.co.uk in the United Kingdom, or www.fluorocycle.lightingcouncil.com.au in Australia

>> Collection points at local retailers like The Home Depot, Ikea, and Lowe's, or possibly your local lighting and lamp stores

One special type of light to consider for recycling is string lights. I'm a sucker for a gorgeous string of lights in a tree or decorating a house during the festive season, or anytime really! The problem is they sit outside in the weather for long periods, and depending on where you live, there could be long periods of snow or heat. But these string lights aren't usually made to handle such extremes. Try as you might, it's hard to keep Christmas lights in top condition. Putting them away as soon as the season is over and making sure they are clean, dry, and wound up neatly will help keep them in good condition. But what do you do when they no longer twinkle?

TIP

You can recycle old Christmas or other string lights through e-waste recycling programs, at recycling centers, or through retail programs. The lights are shredded, and the other materials like glass, PVC, and copper are separated and then processed. Many retailers even offer a mail-in recycling service; for example, in the United States you can try Christmas Light Source (www.christmas-light-source.com/pages/christmas-lights-recycling-program) and Holiday LEDs (www.holidayleds.com/free-light-recycling).

Ensuring That Your Car Tires Get Recycled

Most of us drive a car or motorbike and sooner or later need to replace our tires. In addition to being made from rubber, tires include materials like metal, fabric, and synthetics like carbon black (a material made from residue generated by combustion of fossil fuels). They also contain an assortment of chemicals.

TECHNICAL STUFF

Dumped tires are not only an eyesore, but they can also leach chemicals as they break down. If they are set on fire, they'll release dangerous gases into the air. And it's not much better in landfills. Tires are bulky and take up a lot of space, but they can also trap methane gases in the gaps they create. This causes them to become more buoyant and float toward the surface, potentially damaging landfill liners and allowing leachate to escape. For these reasons, tires are banned from landfills in many countries.

Some recycled tires are shredded for use on the rubber surfaces of playgrounds and sports grounds. Others are burned as fuel for manufacturing. However, bans on sending tires to landfills have fostered innovation, and new techniques are under development. These methods look at breaking down the different components of the tires for better reuse of the materials.

TIP

The best option for recycling your old tires is to check whether the retailer you're buying your new tires from will recycle them. If you don't need new tires but have tires you need to dispose of, they may still take them for a fee. Otherwise, depending on where you live, your local recycling center may accept them, or you can consult your local town or city government to find other options. A few countries have stewardship programs, like the one in Australia that allows you to search for your nearest retail business (www.tyrestewardship.org.au).

Recycling Other Stuff in and Around Your House

In the following sections, I list a number of specialist recycling services for items that you might have in and around your home. There are specialist recycling services available for everything from old mattresses to dirty diapers and many more that I don't have the space to list here. I encourage you to use the resources I provide in Chapter 5 or to search the internet to find other recycling programs that may be available.

Fashion and other textiles

The production of clothes generates a significant carbon footprint, even before you dispose of them. Americans throw out around 80 pounds of clothes per person per year, and very little of this gets recycled. The shocking reality is that globally, the equivalent of one garbage truck's worth of clothing is burned or disposed of every second.

Unfortunately, recycling clothing isn't all that simple, and the best thing to do is reuse and repurpose items before you turn to recycling options. Refer to the nearby sidebar for tips on how to prevent old garments from going to waste.

TIP

After you've explored all other possibilities to keep the item in use, it's time to look for recycling options. Textile and clothing recycling is still in its infancy, but a few programs are available that turn your old clothes and textiles into valuable materials. Here are a few places to start your search:

>> In the United States, try the American Textile Recycling Service (https://atrscorp.com/).

>> Upparel (https://upparel.com.au/) is available in Australia and New Zealand.

>> In the United Kingdom, you can take clothes to most recycling centers.

Recycled clothing can be transformed into fibers that can be used as insulation, as furniture padding, as carpet backing, or to provide structure in fiberglass. In some cases, it's made back into new clothing. Discover more about buying recycled clothing in Chapter 16.

PREVENTING OLD GARMENTS FROM GOING TO WASTE

A great way to start reducing the impact of your wardrobe is to ask yourself a few questions before tossing away your clothes:

- **Do you need to replace it?** Can you keep wearing it? Fashions come and go, and our bodies change shape over time. Sometimes it's worth holding onto an item.

- **Can you mend it?** A small tear or a broken zipper can usually be repaired if the item's still well-loved. If you don't know how or don't have access to a sewing machine, ask a friend for assistance, find a Repair Café nearby (find out more in Chapter 17), or try a paid service.

- **Can someone else use it?** Try to find someone else who wants to wear the item. You can give it away, sell it, or donate it.

- **Is there a way to upcycle it?** If you can't reuse it and no one wants it, look for ways to use the fabric or material and make something else. You might turn it into handkerchiefs or cleaning cloths.

REMEMBER

Clothing or textiles, such as linens, towels, cushions, and rugs, don't belong in your curbside recycling bin. They will contaminate the recyclables and cause safety issues at the recycling facilities.

Mattresses

Mattresses contain many materials, including metals, fabrics, plastic, and timber. Recovering and recycling some of these materials for use in new products is possible. Not only does this reduce our dependence on virgin resources, but it also saves a great deal of energy.

Unfortunately, currently most mattresses don't get recycled. For example, only about 16 percent of mattresses are recycled in the United Kingdom. The rest are sent straight to landfills. It's a similar story in other countries, with the United States sending more than 18 million mattresses to landfills every year.

Fortunately, there are many government-run collection programs for mattresses. In fact, in many places retailers will recycle your old mattress when you purchase a new one from them. Here are some useful examples:

>> In the United States and Canada, extended producer responsibility laws for mattresses have existed for almost ten years in some states. This is where producers fund programs to collect and recycle discarded mattresses. Participating stores collect your old mattress for recycling, or you can drop it off at a nearby site. Check whether your state has signed up at www.byebyemattress.com.

>> The Australia Bedding Stewardship Scheme provides a locator to help you find local retailers that recycle your mattress; try it out at www.recyclemymattress.com.au.

>> In the United Kingdom and other countries, you're best to start by asking your local town or city government or your local recycling center. Otherwise try running a web search to find a mattress recycler near you.

Old plant pots

If you've been doing any landscaping lately, you might have a pile of plastic pots piling up in the garden shed. These plant pots are often made from plastic #5 (polypropylene), which is highly recyclable (see Chapter 6). Unfortunately, curbside recycling programs don't always accept plastic #5 or more specifically these pots, so be sure to check your local rules before placing them in your curbside recycling bin.

TIP

To find a local specialist recycling program, check with your local garden center to see whether they will take back the pots. For example, in the United States, Lowe's will accept your empty pots and the trays and the tags that go with them. In Canada, Home Depot has a "plant it again pot recycling program." And in Australia, you can try the PP5 recycling program; there's a location map at www.pp5.com.au to help you find your nearest drop-off.

Toner ink cartridges

Ink and toner cartridges contain chemicals that can harm human health and the environment. These items are classified as hazardous waste, so you can't put them into your general waste bin or curbside recycling bin. Find out more about disposing of hazardous waste earlier in this chapter. A better option is to use a specialized printer cartridge recycling collection like one of the services here.

TIP

You'll find drop-off points for recycling ink cartridges in well-known stores across the globe. Here are a few examples:

>> **Australia:** Officeworks stores, Australia Post, Cartridge World, Harvey Norman, The Good Guys, JB Hi-Fi, Office National, and Office Depot

>> **United States:** Staples, Target, Walmart, Office Depot, HP, and Best Buy, or Cash4Toners (cash4toners.com/), a program that gives you some cashback for your surplus toner cartridges

>> **United Kingdom:** Currys PC World, Tesco, and your local Household Waste Recycling Centre

Polystyrene

Polystyrene, or Styrofoam as it's commonly known, is a plastic material commonly used in disposable food packaging like coffee cups or clamshell containers (see Chapter 6). It's also widely used as packing foam. Although it can technically all be recycled, it's not always easy to find a recycling service. Some programs are available to capture and recycle Styrofoam packaging, those large pieces of white foam that you get in delivery boxes.

Here are some websites to help you find nearby polystyrene recycling:

>> **United States and Canada:** www.homeforfoam.com/recycling/

>> **United Kingdom:** www.eps.co.uk/recycling/eps_recyclers.html

>> **Australia:** www.epsa.org.au/where-can-i-recycle-eps/ or run a search on www.recyclemate.com.au

Polystyrene is pervasive in the environment. It's incredibly lightweight and can be carried easily by wind and water, spreading throughout waterways and into the ocean. It also breaks apart into small pieces that are easily mistaken for food by animals. If you don't have access to a polystyrene recycling service and must place it in your general waste bin, make sure it's secure and can't blow out easily.

Crayons

Crayons are essentially made of paraffin, a waxy substance usually made from petroleum. As a result, just like plastics, they take many years to biodegrade, possibly even up to 25 years. Every day, more than 12 million crayons are created, and the majority of them end up in landfills once they are no longer wanted.

But there's a way you can keep them from a landfill. Recycling collection programs for crayons are available in many locations. You can either drop them off or mail them in, whatever is more convenient. You may even consider organizing your own crayon collection drive as a fundraiser event for the local school or charity.

Find your nearest program through www.crazycrayons.com in the United States and Canada or www.crayoncollection.org in the United Kingdom. If you don't have access to a recycling program, plenty of online guides show you how to remelt your leftover crayon pieces into new ones. Oh, and don't forget to consider buying recycled crayons to help close the loop.

Diapers

If you want to dispose of your diapers responsibly, then they definitely don't belong in your curbside recycling bin. They belong in your general waste bin unless you're lucky enough to live in a location where diaper recycling is available. Yes, it's a thing. The fibers are used to make kitty litter, floor tiles, rubbish bins, household furniture, and even paper napkins, although even I'm a bit squeamish at this last idea! They've even been used to pave roads in Wales in the United Kingdom. More than one hundred thousand recycled diapers were mixed with asphalt and laid along a 1.5-mile stretch of highway.

Switching to reusable cloth diapers is the best change you can make, but if you have trouble doing so, search for specialized recyclers. DiaperRecycle (https://diaperrecycle.com/), based in Australia, will pick up your used disposable nappies and use the plastics and fibers in new products like kitty litter. It's a paid service, but not only do they recycle your diapers, but they'll also pick them up from your home. For a similar service in your local area, check with your local town or city government.

Carpets

Some communities are lucky enough to have access to carpet recycling. You might not have thought about it before, but carpets are made from many layers of materials. Even natural-fiber carpets, like wool, have plastic-based backing. When sent to landfills, carpets can leach chemicals into the soil and groundwater and take hundreds of years to decompose.

Diverting carpets from landfills is important because many of them contain plastic fibers. But it's even better if they can be recycled and made into something new. Old carpets can be made back into carpets, carpet backing, insulation, or traffic signs. They are even used to create a fabric called Econyl, used in many new products like swimsuits and leggings. Find out more about this and other amazing recycled products in Chapter 16.

TIP

Carpet America Recovery Effort (CARE) is a nonprofit organization backed by industry and government in the United States. If you're looking for a collection site, check out carpetrecovery.org/. If you live somewhere other than the United States, you can check with your local town or city government to see whether they have a similar initiative for recycling carpets. You might also talk to your local carpet retailers and ask them if they have a program. If not, maybe they will be interested in setting one up.

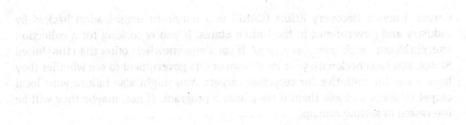

4

Knowing That Recycling Won't Save the Planet on Its Own

Safeguard the planet for future generations by finding new ways to reduce, reuse, and recycle.

Harness your consumer voting power and find out how you can start buying back your recycling to complete your cycle.

Get the latest tips and tricks on other ways you can get involved in solving the world's waste problems.

See what the future looks like. Hint: It includes intelligent robots, plastic-eating organisms, and powerful policies that drive change.

Chapter **15**

Changing Our Behaviors for the Sake of Future Generations

There's more to reducing waste than just recycling. Remember the waste hierarchy from Chapter 2? It provides a simple-to-follow road map for solving the world's waste problems. The first and most important step is to address the source of our waste or "turn off the tap," as some say.

Reducing our consumption has many positive impacts. It lessens our reliance on the extraction and processing of natural resources and, as a result, lowers our energy use and the associated greenhouse gas emissions, both of which also greatly benefit future generations.

The simplest answer to reducing waste is that we stop buying more stuff. Second, we need to keep using the things we already have for longer and keep them out of landfills. These two steps alone can make a huge difference. Then we add recycling as a vital part of the solution.

In this chapter, I describe many things that will complement recycling and help you reduce your overall waste impact. After some tips to help you get started, I explore ways you can change your consumption habits and reduce how much you buy. I then show you what you can do to keep things in use as long as possible. Finally, I offer some tips on how you can apply the reduce, reuse, and recycle principles while shopping.

Reducing How Much You Consume

Our current take-make-waste linear approach is failing. When you consider what it actually means, you start to understand the flaws in this model. There is only a finite amount of resources on the Earth, so if we simply keep taking and taking, sooner or later these materials will run out. Using so much land, water, and energy also puts a lot of pressure on our ecosystems. And once we've satisfied our needs, we let these materials pile up in landfills, leaching toxins and harming the natural environment.

The difference you can make by reducing how much you consume is significant. And all you have to do is make use of the things you already own. You can even try using what someone else has. No, I'm not suggesting you steal it! But you might consider borrowing, renting, or searching for a secondhand version. The following sections give you plenty of ideas for reducing how much you consume.

Saying no when it matters

REMEMBER

People often ask what advice you might give your younger self. With what I have learned in the last few years, I would say, *"Stop buying stuff!"* In addition to having less clutter in my home, I would also have more free time and, even better, more money. If we can all buy a little less stuff, there will be a lot less waste in the world.

Retailers, product manufacturers, and marketers are all eager to tell us we need the latest gadget or product. Their goal is to get you to buy their stuff so that they make money. However, you can employ several strategies to resist this pressure.

TIP

Try asking yourself the following questions before you buy a new item:

>> **Do I need it or want it?** This question is essential when you're trying to reduce your consumption. Understanding your motivations can help you make better decisions. If you struggle with the answer, wait a few days to try and get some clarity.

>> **Can I get by without it?** If you really need an item, then it's doubtful you can survive without it, but if you simply want it, take a moment to consider what

might happen if you don't get it. Will it make a difference in your life? One thing is for sure: you will save money if you don't buy it.

>> **Can I repurpose something else?** Often you may have something that will solve your problem just as well as a new item. Consider what you have around your home, hiding in cupboards or gathering dust somewhere.

>> **Can I borrow or rent one?** Is there an option to rent or borrow from a friend? This is an excellent option if you need to use the item only once or for a short time. That way, you don't end up with an item taking up space in your house. Renting may not always save you money now, but it will save you the hassle and time of needing to dispose of the item later.

>> **Can I get one secondhand?** Applying the principles I describe earlier in this book, it's always better to keep things in use as long as possible. Buying secondhand helps you do exactly that. Many different secondhand markets are available to check out. You might even get it free.

>> **Can it wait?** Take a couple of days to think about your purchase plans. There's usually no real rush. Retailers and brands like to make you feel like you'll miss out if you don't buy an item immediately, but there will always be another product or another sale. Waiting might give you more time to consider the preceding questions and your options.

Addressing our throwaway lifestyle with reusable items

With the development of plastics in the 1950s, the idea of the throwaway or disposable lifestyle came to life. It was marketed as a convenient way to live that could eliminate chores. Simply buy plastic plates, bowls, and cutlery and throw them out once you're done with them — no need to wash them. There was even a throwaway aluminum fry pan.

We now see the impact this throwaway lifestyle has had on our planet. The negative impacts of our addiction to single-use convenience are multifaceted. We're using resources at a drastic rate, tearing them out of the Earth to make a new plastic bottle or paper cup as quickly as we toss the one in our hand in the bin. On the other end, waste is piling up and polluting our waterways and oceans, leaching toxins and harming wildlife.

Almost half of the 380 million tons of plastic we produce yearly goes into single-use items. That equates to more than 500 billion plastic cups, 482 billion plastic bottles, and 5 trillion plastic bags — all used just once and then tossed away. It's also important to realize that single-use items aren't exclusively plastic. Many paper products are single-use too. Items like cardboard food packaging, paper grocery bags, paper cups and plates, paper towels and napkins, and even receipts are all single-use.

TIP

A great way to understand what single-use items you can eliminate from your day-to-day life is to consider doing a waste audit. In Chapter 17, I describe what you need and how to complete a waste audit of your bins. I recommend you give it a go.

REMEMBER

Here are some ways to rethink your throwaway lifestyle:

>> Change your view of convenience. Carry your own reusable cutlery kit and water bottle; see that as your convenience. Check the nearby sidebar "Considering some single-use swaps" for ideas.

>> Always bring your own bags with you when you shop.

>> Avoid products with excessive packaging or items packaged in hard-to-recycle plastics. Look for simple packaging that uses only one type of material.

>> Purchase fresh produce loose rather than packaged in plastic. Or invest in reusable produce bags.

>> Try out your local bulk food or supply store.

>> Consider switching to refillables for cleaning and personal products. To discover more about this great option, keep reading.

Exploring refillable products

The best impact you can have is to use less, particularly when it comes to plastic. But how do you do that and still run a ship-shape home? A great option is to switch to refillable products. I made the switch a year ago and am so glad I did. I use refillable cleaning products and some personal products like shampoo, conditioner, and hand cream.

Since I started using refillable containers, I estimate I've saved close to 50 plastic bottles — that's 50 bottles that didn't have to be made or recycled. What about the refill containers, you might ask. The company I use sends me the refills in soft plastic pouches. Once they're empty, I collect them and when I have about ten, I send them back to the company. Then they're washed, refilled, and ready to be sent to a new customer. It's a zero-plastic cycle. It feels great knowing that I'm making a real difference.

CONSIDERING SOME SINGLE-USE SWAPS

Here are ten single-use swaps you can make today. They may inspire you to think of others!

Single-Use Item	New Reusable Item
Single-use coffee cup	Plastic, glass, or metal reusable takeaway coffee cup
Plastic straws	Bamboo, metal, or plastic straws
Plastic cutlery	Metal or reusable bamboo cutlery
Plastic or paper plates and bowls	Reusable metal or bamboo plates and bowls
Plastic grocery bags	Reusable cotton or fabric bags
Plastic water bottle	Refillable water bottle
Paper towels	Fabric reusable towels or just a regular cloth
Zip-top bags	Reusable silicone snack bags or beeswax wraps
Plastic cotton swabs/buds	Washable bamboo and cotton swabs/buds
Plastic balloons filled with helium	Paper lanterns or recycled bunting

So how can you get on board? Why not choose a brand and give it a go? Each brand has different products and sometimes a slightly different model. You've got nothing to lose by simply trying it out.

TIP

If you're interested in giving refillables a go, here are some brands to check out and see whether they are available in your area:

>> Loop (https://exploreloop.com/)

>> Common Good (www.commongoodandco.com/)

>> Blueland (www.blueland.com/)

>> Supernatural (https://supernatural.com/)

>> ZeroCo (www.zeroco.com.au/)

>> Grove Collaborative (www.grove.co/)

>> Smol (https://smolproducts.com/)

>> ReturnR (https://returnr.org/)

>> Method (https://methodproducts.com/)

>> Tirtyl (https://tirtyl.com.au/)

If you don't like any of these brands, then try searching "refillable products near me" online to see what else comes up. You may also find refillable options through your local bulk store; see the nearby sidebar "Buying in bulk."

Finding what you need secondhand

Buying secondhand is a great way to reduce your impact and get a bargain. I always look for a secondhand option before I purchase anything now. Some things I've bought have lasted a very long time. I remember a pair of secondhand shoes I bought — I wore them every day, and they lasted me years. I have bought many other secondhand items over the years, including exercise equipment, handbags, books, furniture, musical instruments, and secondhand cars and motorbikes.

TIP

Buying secondhand clothes is also a great way to reduce your impact and help extend the life of old clothes. You might be surprised by what bargains you can find. Some great sites to check out include

- » ThredUP (www.thredup.com)

- » Poshmark (https://poshmark.com/)

- » VarageSale (www.varagesale.com/)

- » eBay (www.ebay.com)

- » Etsy (www.etsy.com)

- » The RealReal (www.therealreal.com/)

- » Tradesy (www.tradesy.com/)

TIP

But there are other ways to get what you need that can be even cheaper than buying secondhand. The Buy Nothing Project is a global movement of community-based groups that encourage donating or giving away household goods. No money changes hands in the transaction. It's simply a way to give away items you no longer need. Or, if you're looking for a particular item, you can make a request. Recently someone in my local group requested a hat stand, and I had one I was no longer using. It's the best scenario because someone needs something, and someone else wants to get rid of it. For more information, check out https://buynothingproject.org/.

Borrowing things when you need them

The Library of Things is a social enterprise aimed at helping to reduce waste while saving people money. Consider the concept of a library for books. A library of things is much the same, except you can borrow a whole range of different things. There are libraries for kitchen appliances, tools, kids' toys, seeds, musical instruments, electronics, and arts and crafts.

Many of us have items in our homes that see the light of day only once every five years or so. What if you could borrow something and return it when you're done instead of buying a new item?

TIP

You can find a good library of things list on the Wikipedia page for the Library of Things (https://en.wikipedia.org/wiki/Library_of_Things), or if you live in the United Kingdom, try www.libraryofthings.co.uk/. And if you can't find one nearby, why not consider starting your own? You can find out more at www.shareable.net/how-to-start-a-library-of-things/.

Renting what you need

Many new rental models are being created to help solve the world's waste problems. You can rent many things that you may not have considered before. Here are a few examples to get you thinking:

» **A wardrobe or just one piece of it:** It's a great way to refresh your wardrobe regularly without the waste and expense. Plus, you can give brands and styles a go without investing significant money. Take a look at

- Rent the Runway (www.renttherunway.com/)

- Nuuly (www.nuuly.com/)

- Armoire (https://armoire.style/)

- By Rotation (https://byrotation.com/)

- My Wardrobe HQ (www.mywardrobehq.com/)

» **Computers, gaming gadgets, and other devices:** No need to own that latest device that will turn into e-waste in a few years when you can rent it. One good example of this model is Grover (www.grover.com). They'll even cover most of the repair costs if the item gets damaged. When you no longer want it, you can return it free of charge.

» **A Christmas tree:** You rent a real pine tree, return it after Christmas, and the company plants it. Companies include Rent-A-Christmas.com and RentXmasTree.com in the United States or Loveachristmastree.co.uk and Green Elf Trees (www.greenelftrees.co.uk/) in the United Kingdom.

» **Tools:** So often we buy items, use them once, and then store them in our garage until we finally find a new home for them or throw them out. Consider renting the tools you need before spending big and filling your garage with stuff you'll never use again.

Keeping Materials in Use

One main principle of a circular economy is to keep products and materials in use as long as possible. When we use an item once and toss it away, we not only create waste but also throw away all the energy and resources that went into making it. That's why it's better to keep using objects as they were originally intended for as long as possible. I explore the different ways you can keep materials in use in the following sections.

Looking after what you already have

Take a moment to pause and consider the things you currently own. Appreciate the energy and resources that have gone into producing them. What materials do they contain? How were those materials acquired? Ask yourself what they're made of, how they were formed, and what effects their production may have already had on the environment.

REMEMBER

If you take better care of your possessions, they might last longer and save a great deal of waste. You may even save money because you won't need to replace stuff as often.

We live in a disposable society, but that doesn't mean we need to treat all our objects as disposable. Consider the materials and energy that went into making items and show respect for those resources. Regardless of what an item costs you, it's worth considering what it costs the Earth.

TIP

Treat your low-cost items as if they're priceless, and treat your high-cost items just the same. Here are some tips for taking care of your possessions:

>> Keep things clean. When dirt and grime get ingrained in items, the dirt can get into moving parts and cause issues.

>> Read the maintenance guidelines from the brand and follow them as best you can.

>> Don't leave things out in the weather. Rain, sun, and wind can be harsh and cause a lot of damage. Metal rusts and plastics fade and break down.

>> Plan regular maintenance for major appliances. For example, if you have a lawn mower, take it to be serviced regularly to extend its life.

>> Keep computers and other devices clean and protected. Make sure you keep them cool with enough ventilation.

>> When it comes to clothing, read the labels and follow the care directions. Avoid dryers and air-dry your clothes whenever possible. And make repairs when necessary.

>> Teach your kids to look after their toys so they will last longer and can be handed down or donated when they have outgrown them.

Finding a new home for items

If you no longer need or want an item, there are many ways to find a new home for it. Here are some ideas:

>> Check with family or friends if they have a use for the item.

>> Sell it on eBay, Etsy, Facebook Marketplace, via a garage sale, or at swap meets.

Some retail stores have also established resale programs. The best example is Patagonia's Worn Wear, a marketplace for secondhand Patagonia gear (https://wornwear.patagonia.com/).

TIP

>> Join your local Buy Nothing group and see whether anyone in your community needs the items. Find out more in the earlier section "Finding what you need secondhand."

>> Donate to a charity store. They will take items and either give them to those in need or sell them to fund support programs.

REMEMBER

Nobody wants to wear your worn-out or stained clothing or use your broken crockery. If you wouldn't use it or wear it again, there's a good chance that no one else will want to. Charities often end up with many unwearable or unusable items that must be disposed of in landfills at a cost. Donated goods may also be packed up and shipped to developing countries, where these low-quality pieces are dumped in poorly controlled landfills. Be considerate when you donate to charities. If an item is no longer wearable or in poor condition, look for alternative options to recycle it.

Giving items a second life

Many decades ago, we would have repaired an item repeatedly before sending it to its grave. Today we're guilty of throwing that item away far too quickly without considering if it's repairable. But even if we try to repair an item, we quickly find it's not easy. Companies frequently make it difficult and, in some cases, impossible to repair their products. This can make finding a repairer challenging. In addition, repair costs can be high, and in many cases, they cost more than the price of a new product.

However, things are changing for the better, even if it's relatively slowly. Consumers expect to be able to fix the things they paid for with their hard-earned money. A movement known as the "Right to Repair" has been fighting for consumer rights. Get more info on the work the Right to Repair movement is doing in Chapter 13.

TIP

Finding a repairer may seem difficult, but the effort is worthwhile, considering the positive benefits on our environmental impact. Here are some ideas to help you find a repair option:

>> **A local Repair Café:** This is a place where volunteers help fix items that community members bring in. Skills can vary depending on the volunteers present on the day, but they range from electronics to mending clothing. You can find your local Repair Café via www.repaircafe.org or read more in Chapter 17.

>> **Local repair shops:** Depending on where you live, you may have access to repair shops for various items. The most common tend to be for computers and household appliances or mending services for clothes.

>> **Manufacturers' repair services:** Despite many manufacturers making it hard to repair their products, many do offer a service to repair your product, particularly if it's still under warranty.

Giving Zero Waste a Go

You might have heard of the zero waste movement. My first introduction to it was seeing people presenting a small jar representing the amount of waste they had generated in a whole year. I couldn't believe it. How did they do it?

The concept of a zero waste lifestyle is not so much that you create no waste, but rather that you send no waste to a landfill. This is accomplished by embracing the concepts of the waste hierarchy; I explain this in detail in Chapter 2. The waste hierarchy encourages you to focus on reducing, reusing, and recycling. But zero waste goes beyond these behaviors and helps you consider your consumption behavior and the material possessions in your life.

I was a little scared of the concept of zero waste myself. I couldn't imagine how I could possibly reduce my waste down to that one small jar. Yet in the last few years, I've made many changes that could be considered zero waste living, and my garbage bin's pretty empty. I still couldn't fit all my waste into a tiny jar! But I'm living more sustainably and taking more responsibility for my impact.

All of the changes I describe in this chapter and throughout this book are elements of a zero waste lifestyle. By embracing just one of these, you're already on your way to reducing your waste.

If you're interested in giving zero waste a go, I recommend checking out some of the following blogs for more help:

>> Zero Waste Home (https://zerowastehome.com/)

>> Going Zero Waste (www.goingzerowaste.com/)

>> Trash Is for Tossers (https://trashisfortossers.com/)

Recognizing That Recycling Starts at the Store

We regularly make purchasing decisions based on quality, price, or our emotions. Buying sustainably simply means adding a couple more questions to that decision process. As a consumer, you can help shape the future by voting with your wallet. When you spend your money with companies and products that align with your values, you're sending a message saying this is the way you want things to work. I dive into this further in Chapter 16.

Time is your friend. There's no rush to buy, so take as long as you need to research and make your decision. Here are a few questions to ask yourself before making a purchase that will help reduce your impact:

>> **Is it made to last?** Buying good-quality products helps ensure they will be used for a very long time.

>> **Where and how was it made?** What's its backstory? Consider what the item is made from and where these materials came from.

>> **Is there recycled content in it?** I explain the benefits of buying recycled in Chapter 16.

>> **Can it be recycled?** What will happen at the end of its life? Can the item be recycled easily, or will it end up in a landfill?

>> **How is the item packaged?** Does it have excessive packaging? Look for products with minimal packaging or recyclable packaging.

Be curious, and don't be afraid to ask questions of brands and manufacturers. Favor transparent brands that tell you what materials they use and how to dispose of them correctly.

Maintaining Your Efforts for the Long Haul

REMEMBER

Our waste problem isn't going away in a hurry. In fact, it's still growing fast, so it's going to require everyone's help. You can keep the momentum going by considering the following:

>> Be sure to start small and conquer one change at a time. Do your best, and know that every bit helps.

>> Spread the word and share your discoveries with friends and family.

>> Make some noise. Write to companies about their packaging to encourage them to make changes. Let the government know you care.

Chapter **16**

Buying Recycled: Supporting Brands Turning Trash into Treasure

Y ou might have heard this expression: "If you're not buying recycled, you're not truly recycling!" This means that nothing is truly recycled until it's made its way into a new product and someone buys it. Recycling doesn't stop at the recycling bin. Nor does it stop at the transfer station or recycling plant. It doesn't even stop at the manufacturer that uses recycled content in their products. It goes full circle and comes back to you and me. We complete the recycling loop when we buy a new product made from recycled material.

Recycled material has to go somewhere. We can't keep recycling without actually using those materials in new products. From toilet paper to leggings, backpacks to sunglasses, you can find products made from recycled materials for every element of your daily life. Purchasing products made from recycled materials helps create a market for the waste material we discard. In turn, it motivates companies to increase their efforts in developing a circular economy and using recycled content. The more we purchase products made using recycled content, the louder the message we send to manufacturers and brands that we want change.

This chapter encourages you to take action beyond recycling. I explain that recycled products aren't more expensive than those made from raw materials. They range in price just as much as any other product. Their quality is also just as varied, similar to nonrecycled goods. Finally, I list many different products that are being made from recycled material and give you some tips on how to find them.

Voting with Your Wallet

"Voting with your wallet" is an expression that refers to your power as a consumer. You might not be aware, but when you purchase an item, you send a message that the product and the way it's made are acceptable to you. When that purchase aligns with your values, you're voting for the things you believe in. But when we unthinkingly make purchases from those offering the lowest cost, the most alluring advertisements, or the most eye-catching packaging, we're voting for a future where anything goes.

You're possibly already voting without even realizing it. Here are some examples that might sound familiar:

>> Buying from a local fresh food market to support local fruit and vegetable growers

>> Not supporting a brand because they use sweatshop labor overseas

>> Choosing to shop at stores that offset their carbon footprint

Voting with your wallet is an easy way for you to have your say. So how does this relate to recycling? We all need to start voting for recycled content in our products, to tell brands that we want them to use the material we place in our recycling bins. It will help increase the demand for our recyclables and build a stronger recycling industry.

WARNING

Be cautious of brand greenwashing. In Chapter 5, I describe how to spot greenwashing and provide several scenarios to help you identify it.

Knowing That Recycled Is Just as Good

Throughout this book, I highlight the benefits of recycling and how recycling reduces landfills, saves energy, and decreases our reliance on raw resources. All these things benefit the environment significantly. And it's in recycled products where this all comes together. When we buy recycled products, we help do the following:

>> Save energy and reduce greenhouse gas emissions.

>> Reduce our reliance on fossil fuels and mineral deposits and therefore reduce the negative impacts of extracting them.

>> Reduce the need for landfills.

>> Save water and other resources.

>> Support brands making an effort to change.

>> Create a more robust recycling industry.

>> Build a market for our recyclables.

Despite these benefits, many people are concerned that recycled products are inferior in quality or cost more to purchase. However, this is simply not true. In this section, I look at some of these misconceptions in more detail.

Evaluating quality

Recycled products have come a long way and can no longer be considered lower quality than products made with virgin materials. A few decades ago, recycled products were not common; those products that did exist were more often low quality or substandard. I remember the recycled paper in our office years ago. It wasn't as white and was slightly rougher than the standard paper. It was definitely seen as inferior and only used for specific applications.

REMEMBER

The idea that products made from recycled materials are inferior to those made from virgin materials is still prevalent. However, processes have progressed significantly in the last decade or so. And today, recycled products must undergo the same stringent tests that all products must pass. Nowadays, you would be unable to distinguish between recycled and nonrecycled paper and would be surprised at the quality of many other recycled products. In fact, you might not even be aware that you already have many different recycled goods in your home.

Comparing costs

Recycled products aren't more costly than products made from virgin materials. Just like any product, prices can range from cheap to expensive. Yes, there are some high-priced recycled products, but this often has more to do with the designer or brand name than the fact that it contains recycled content. There are plenty of excellent examples of reasonably priced recycled products.

Prices can vary depending on the availability of recycled material, but they are also affected by the typical cost factors of any product: markup, overheads, freight, packaging, quantities purchased, and even the time of the year. Other considerations may cause limitations and result in higher prices. However, keep in mind that occasionally these restrictions may exist because the brand is making every effort to guarantee that its suppliers uphold ethical standards and are consistent with their overall sustainable ideals. Discover more about these good brands later in this chapter.

TIP

Don't forget to apply the reduce and reuse principles first and buy something only if you really need it. It's not about buying recycled products for the sake of it. It's about choosing recycled products over virgin products when you can. Check out Chapter 15 for questions to ask yourself before you buy a new item.

It's also important to consider the impact of a product throughout its entire life cycle. You can find out more on this topic in Chapter 4. A product might require less maintenance or be more easily disposed of at the end of its life. Or maybe it replaces your need to buy many more products. Considering the overall impact of a product might make a higher price actually worth it.

Finding Recycled Products

The variety of available recycled products is enormous. You can find recycled products for the kitchen, bathroom, office, garage, garden, and even your wardrobe. Regular everyday products that can have recycled content include toilet paper, aluminum, and plastic bottles. In addition to these everyday household items, many other products use recycled content, like leggings, swimwear, outdoor wear, furniture, and beyond.

In the following sections, I explain a few terms to help you identify different types of recycled material, and then I give you some tips on finding products. Plus, I provide a list of many items in the later section "Examples of recycled products."

Some handy terminology

It's good to get to know a few different terms before you go looking for recycled products. They include the following:

>> **Virgin materials versus recycled materials:** Virgin materials are raw resources that haven't been used in a product before. Nonvirgin materials, or recycled materials, have already been used in a product, recycled, and then made into a new product.

>> **Recycling, upcycling, and downcycling:**

- **Recycling:** This is the process of collecting, sorting, and processing materials that would otherwise be wasted and turning them into materials that are roughly the same as the original product. An example is an aluminum can that is recycled and made into a new aluminum can.

- **Upcycling:** More akin to reuse, upcycling takes a discarded item and makes it into a new product of equal or greater value. The product is not broken down into base materials but instead reused in its existing state. An example is taking the inner tubes of bikes and turning them into a backpack. In upcycling, the materials can sometimes still be used again, prolonging their life.

- **Downcycling:** This is turning recycled material or discarded items into products of a lower value or quality. A typical example of downcycling is using plastic #1, PET, to make fabric for clothing instead of using it to create new plastic bottles. It's referred to as downcycling because it's less likely (at this point in time at least) that the clothing will be recycled at the end of its life, whereas a plastic bottle can be recycled again. Another example is paper that may be recycled into cardboard. Even though the cardboard can still be recycled after its use, the product is of a lower value or quality than the original paper.

>> **Recycled content versus recyclable:** "Recyclable" is when an item is able to be collected and processed, or recycled, to collect the materials. "Recycled content" means the item was made with materials that have already been collected and reused in the product. An item can be both recyclable and made from recycled material, but neither is a guarantee of the other. In other words, just because a product has recycled content doesn't mean it can be recycled at the end of its life.

REMEMBER

Always check the label and your local town or city government's recycling guidelines to see whether you can recycle an item.

- **Preconsumer versus postconsumer:** These terms describe the source of the recycled content (what is often referred to as *recyclate*):

  - **Preconsumer** is waste that results from the manufacturing process. For example, when fabric is cut for a particular pattern, some pieces become waste. It may also refer to defective items like glass jars with impurities. Often this waste, as is the case with glass or metal, is put straight back into the manufacturing process. For other materials, there may be secondary manufacturers that can use the leftover materials.

  - **Postconsumer** recycled content has been collected from our homes, schools, or offices through curbside or other specialist collection services.

Tips for finding recycled products

TIP

Finding recycled products is easier than you think. Given the size of the list provided in the later section "Examples of recycled products," you'll most likely find them in your daily life. To help you along a bit, here are some tips:

- Many popular grocery and department stores, including K-Mart, Walmart, Target, The Home Depot, Marks and Spencer, Harrods, Aldi, and Whole Foods, stock some recycled products, so keep your eye out. If you can't find any, then chat with the store manager. It might help them realize how important it is to their customers.

- Try doing an internet search by simply entering "recycled" before the product you want to buy (for example, "recycled plate"). If that doesn't work, try "recycled content" plus the product instead.

- Your local town or city government may provide "buy recycled" guides.

- When opening a store's website, always search for "recycled" to see what options they have for recycled content products.

- Look for products that say "made with recycled content" or postconsumer content.

- Check for the recycled content logo. In Chapter 5, I explain the different labels for recycling. The well-known recycling symbol or Mobius loop signifies recycled content when its colors are inverted (a white symbol in a black circle). It's often combined with the words "recycled content" or a number indicating the percentage of recycled content. You can see this example and some others in Figure 16-1.

- Take a look at the brand directory on my website www.everydayrecycler.com for some great ideas.

Recycled   MADE FROM   50% Recycled
            RECYCLED PAPER

FIGURE 16-1:
Example of
symbols showing
that a product
has recycled
content.

100% Recycled   MADE FROM
                 RECYCLED MATERIALS

© John Wiley & Sons, Inc.

Packaging with recycled content

You might be able to switch to recycled products in other parts of your life, but what about when it comes to food packaging? In many cases, we have a limited choice, especially when we consider other criteria like health, flavor, appearance, and quality. Change can seem slow, but some brands are making their packaging more sustainable, whether to make the packaging more recyclable or compostable or to include recycled content. Some examples include the following:

>> Berry, Viva, and Dove all have options for deodorant sticks that use recycled plastic.

>> Many hair care brands are starting to make changes to include recycled content in shampoo or conditioner bottles, including Head and Shoulders and TRESemmé.

>> Nestle introduced their first food-grade recycled soft plastics wrapper for their KitKat chocolate bar in Australia last year.

TIP

Many brands have set goals to include recycled content in their packaging within the next five to ten years, so keep your eyes peeled.

Examples of recycled products

Table 16-1 is a list of many different types of products I found that have recycled content options. I hope you find something that inspires you to make the switch.

TABLE 16-1   **A Sampling of Products with Recycled Content**

Bathroom	Kitchen
Combs	Coasters
Toothbrushes	Bowls, plates, and cups
Reusable razors	Trash bags
Hand soap bottles	Paper towels and napkins
Homewares	**Gardening**
Blankets and throws	Garden pots
Cushion covers	Garden edging and beds
Electronics	Worm farms
Bedding	Compost bins
Carpets, mats, and rugs	Outdoor lawn furniture
Mattresses	Playground equipment
Couches and chairs	
Cleaning	**Kids**
Toilet paper	Toys
Serviettes (paper towels for cleaning)	Clothes
Tissues	Backpacks and bags
Laundry detergent and cleaning bottles	Kids' sippy cups
Cleaning cloths	
Clothing	**Accessories**
Leggings	Backpacks
Denim jeans	Daypacks, totes, shoulder bags, and handbags
Jackets	Jewelry
T-shirts	Belts
Stockings and pantyhose	Shoes and sandals
Loungewear, day wear, and evening wear	Suitcases and travel accessories
Lingerie, underwear, and pajamas	Hats and caps
Socks	Watches
Scarves and sarongs	

Sportswear	Sports Gear
Swimsuits and beachwear	Hand planes for surfing
Swim trunks	Skateboards
Skiing pants	Bike accessories
Hiking or climbing pants	Yoga mats
Outdoor jackets	Sleeping bags
	Hammocks

Pets	Reusables
Dog leads	Water bottles
Kitty litter	Cutlery
Dog and cat toys	Plates and bowls
Dog bags	Mesh bags
Dogs' wear	Shopping bags

At the Office or School	Electronic Gadgets
Pencils, pens, and highlighters	Keyboards
Office stationery and storage solutions	Mouse and mouse pads
Rubbish (trash) bins	Computers
Postage satchels (mailing envelopes)	Monitors
Backpacks	Laptop bags

Food Packaging	Construction and Renovations
Recycled aluminum cans and foil	Fencing and decking
Plastic bottles	Building boards, lumber, and house siding
Cardboard	Carpet and carpet underlay
Steel cans	Insulation
Egg cartons	Kitchen benches
Cereal boxes	Floor tiles
Glass containers	Asphalt
Rubbish, recycling, and compost bins	Roofing materials
Garbage bags	Traffic cones

Seeking Out Good Brands

In addition to using recycled content, many brands are working hard to lessen their environmental impact and improve the sustainability of their business practices and offerings. Many of these companies have big hearts as well as their sustainable ambitions. They participate in beach cleanups, pull trash out of the ocean, or support local initiatives like helping the homeless. (Find a list of some good brands to check out in the nearby sidebar.)

Some of the initiatives brands are engaging in are listed here:

>> Ways that brands give back to the community or environment can include

- Planting a tree or removing a pound of trash from the ocean for every purchase.

- Supporting local or international nonprofits.

- Joining in or organizing beach cleanups.

- Reducing their carbon footprint.

- Donating a percentage of their profits to environmental causes. A well-known organization that assists brands in donating to good causes is 1% for the Planet (www.onepercentfortheplanet.org).

>> Brands may establish a take-back recycling program to ensure their products are disposed of appropriately at the end of their life.

>> Some brands work hard to minimize the amount of packaging they use by eliminating plastic and switching to recycled, recyclable, or compostable packaging.

>> Using recycled content is important, but so is truth. Brands that embrace transparency will

- Readily share information on their supply chain. Check a brand's website to see whether they have a dedicated page that describes their supply chain.

- Be willing to answer your questions if they don't have information available. Always be kind and give them a fair chance to answer you.

>> Producers and manufacturers can display their commitment to good environmental, social, and ethical practices by earning sustainability standards and certifications voluntarily. Some of these include the following:

- **Certified B Corporation (B-Corp):** Brands can become a B-Corp only when they meet high transparency, accountability, and performance standards.

- **OEKO-TEX certification:** Certifying that every product component, from textile and leather to accessories, has been tested against the OEKO-TEX standards for safety, social responsibility, and transparency.

- **Bluesign:** A sustainability standard that considers the chemical composition of textiles. Those that are certified have met stringent standards for pollution control of both water and air.

- **Fair Wear:** Focusing on worker health, safety, and dignity, they review a brand's supply chain to ensure a transparent and honest environment for consumers and workers.

TIP

Get to know more about the certifications and standards on my website at `www.everydayrecycler.com/eco-certifications`.

TIP

If your favorite brand doesn't tick all these boxes, don't be afraid to make some noise. Ask them what they are doing to be more sustainable.

SOME GOOD BRANDS YOU MAY WANT TO CHECK OUT

Here are some examples of brands that are not only making products using recycled content but are doing many other good things. These brands give back to the community, reduce their impact on the environment, embrace transparency, and use recycled content. This list is only the tip of the iceberg; when you start exploring, you'll find many more good brands. But keep a look out for potential greenwashing; Chapter 5 provides more guidance on how to spot it.

- **Batoko:** They produce recycled swimwear that helps support the Cornish Seal Sanctuary, the National Lobster Hatchery, and rebuilding reefs in French Polynesia (`www.batoko.com`).

- **Coalatree:** They make outdoor gear and apparel using recycled and repurposed materials while giving back through many community programs like A.N.E. (Adopt a Native Elder) and providing blankets for the homeless (`www.coalatree.com`).

- **Logitech:** As well as introducing recycled content to their products and reducing their carbon footprint, Logitech has a recycling program. They also get third-party validation to provide certainty in their claims (`www.logitech.com`).

(continued)

(continued)

- **Patagonia:** They use recycled content in many of their products. Plus, Patagonia established Worn Wear, which is a set of tools to help customers extend the life of their products by supporting the principles of caring for, repairing, reusing, reselling, and recycling their clothes (https://wornwear.patagonia.com/).

- **Rothy's:** They make recycled shoes and handbags while offsetting their carbon footprint, caring for their workforce, reducing waste at their facilities, and creating a circular production by taking back preloved products for recycling (www.rothys.com).

- **Sabai:** By building their couches to order and offering plastic-free delivery, using upcycled and recycled fabrics, and offering repairs and trade-in services, they demonstrate their dedication to minimizing waste (www.sabai.design).

- **Solgaard:** Not only are their suitcases made from recycled materials, but every purchase helps remove plastic waste from the ocean through their partnerships with organizations like Prevented Ocean Plastic, Lonely Whale, and Next Wave Plastics (www.solgaard.co).

- **Tentree:** This clothing line plants ten trees for every purchase you make and demonstrates great transparency and traceability on all their claims (www.tentree.com).

- **Waterhaul:** The company is recovering ghost fishing gear from the oceans to protect marine life and transforming it into valued products like sunglasses (www.waterhaul.co).

- **Wishbone:** This is a modular, repairable bike that can grow with your children and is made from recycled and ethically sourced materials (www.wishbonedesign.com).

- **Wolven:** They make recycled sports and yoga wear with transparency, carbon offsets, and preloved products for sale. Plus, for every order, they support the Blue Monday Project in removing 10 pounds of ocean-bound plastic along the rivers of Cambodia (www.wolventhreads.com/).

- **Zero Co:** The company offers a reusable solution for your personal care and cleaning needs while committing to untrashing the planet through their 100-year cleanup initiative (www.zeroco.com).

Sending a Message in Other Ways

TIP

If you want to help increase the demand for recycled products and make sure your recycling gets turned into something useful, here are a few other ways you can help:

>> Write to your local government representative and ask what they are doing. Governments can help increase demand for recycled products by setting goals within their procurement strategies.

>> Encourage your local school or community center to look into switching to recycled products. It's an excellent way for kids to discover the importance of recycled materials.

>> Talk to your boss and see whether you can change your stationery or other procurement policies to switch to recycled products.

>> Discuss the issue with local businesses or restaurants that you frequent. You never know; they may not have considered switching to recycled products or are unaware of the options.

Chapter 17

Highlighting Other Ways to Get Involved

Like most people, I'm sure you want to make a positive difference in the world. Recycling is an easy action that makes a real difference in minimizing your environmental impacts. But if you're interested, there are many other ways to get involved and be a part of the solution. Changing your daily habits or volunteering your time for a project like a beach cleanup can also have a beneficial impact.

In this chapter, I help you explore other ways you can get involved in reducing the impact of your waste. I look at ways you can get more familiar with your trash, discover the reality of what and how much you throw out, and help you develop action plans to reduce it. Then I lead you through a list of other great community-based activities you can join.

Stepping Up Your Personal Efforts

There are many ways you can make positive steps toward changing your habits to reduce waste. But before you can reduce waste at home, you need some data to help you create your plan of attack. In the following sections, I take you through how to run your own waste audit, optimize your recycling setup, and even organize a community collection campaign.

Organizing a waste audit

A waste audit is a great way to discover the type and quantity of waste you throw away every week. And once you've got the data, you can evaluate the results and formulate a plan. The following sections explain how to prepare for and conduct your audit, and how to analyze its results.

TIP

A waste audit isn't just for the home, either. You can run a waste audit at your office, school, or community group; just be sure to consider the appropriate safety requirements or get some help from a waste consultant.

Preparing for your waste audit

To run a waste audit at your home, you need to gather only a few items. In most cases you'll likely have these items around the house already. Here are the supplies you need:

>> A tarpaulin. A tarp makes it easier to clean up afterward, but you can do the audit on a concrete driveway or in the backyard if you don't have one.

>> Choose a bin to audit. I recommend starting with your recycling bin.

>> A pair of gloves and a face mask if you prefer to wear one.

>> Long pants and a long-sleeved shirt are also recommended.

>> The waste tracker worksheet provided in the Appendix and a pen.

>> A camera to take photos, or use your mobile phone.

Conducting your waste audit

Choose a day just before your bin's pickup date for your waste audit. You want to ensure there's enough material for a reasonable audit. Make sure to choose a location sheltered from the weather and with good airflow to prevent any rubbish blowing away. Then follow these steps:

1. Lay down the tarp and secure it at the corners.

2. Empty the contents of your bin onto the tarp.

3. Grab your gloves and start sorting and separating your rubbish into different piles.

   Depending on which bin you're auditing, I recommend the following:

   ● Recyclable items: Paper, metal, glass, and recyclable plastic. If there's enough room, make separate piles for each.

- Hazardous or specialist recycling: Soft plastics, e-waste, batteries, or light bulbs.

- Organic waste: Food and yard waste or garden clippings.

- Other nonrecyclables: Paper towels, single-use plastics (cutlery, plates, straws, coffee cups), polystyrene, and mixed materials.

- Items that may still be good for reuse, like clothing or home decor.

4. **Using the worksheet I provide in the Appendix, write down all the items.**

   Note what material they're made from and then tally up how many of each in the quantity column. Refer to Figure 17-1 for an example.

TIP

   Don't worry if you don't know what material an item is made of; just write it down and you can look it up later.

5. **Take some photos to look back over in the next few days.**

6. **Clean everything up.**

REMEMBER

Don't get depressed when you go through your waste; being curious is a great start, and you're already making changes just by being more aware.

WASTE TRACKER

Date: _Oct. 20, 2022_   Which Bin _Recycling Bin_

Item Description (Add a short description of the item)	Material (metal, glass, paper, plastic, organic, hazardous, or mixed)	Quantity (Tally up the number)
Plastic bottles	Plastic no. 1	IIIII
Detergent bottle	Plastic no. 5	I
Toothpaste tube	Mixed plastics	I
Tuna can	Metal (steel)	II
Cardboard box	Paperboard	I
Milk carton	Mixed paper and plastic	II
Food scraps	Organic	IIIIIIII
Take-out containers	Plastic no. 6 — polystyrene	II
AAA battery	Hazardous	III

FIGURE 17-1: An example of how to fill in the Waste Tracker worksheet.

© John Wiley & Sons, Inc.

Analyzing your waste data

REMEMBER

After you've finished your audit, it's time to analyze your results. The information you've collected can reveal a lot and help you come up with many actions to help you improve. I recommend starting small and finding some things you can change easily first. Here are some things to consider when analyzing your results:

>> Focus on the items with the biggest tally. Is there some way you can eliminate or reduce those items?

>> Look over some of the worst offenders in plastic packaging. Are there changes you could make to reduce these items? Could you buy in bulk or make your own? Is it an item you could do without?

>> Single-use plastics: Did you find many items like coffee cups, plastic bottles, or plastic cutlery? Consider swapping these for reusables (find some great single-use swaps in Chapter 15).

>> Soft plastic food packaging: If you are not already, consider collecting your soft plastics separately and finding your local drop-off location (see Chapter 11).

>> Food waste: Have you considered composting? Discover how to start your own compost and ways to reduce your food waste in Chapter 12.

>> Identify items that don't belong. For example, if you're auditing your recycling bin, make note of items that would contaminate the other recyclables. In particular, check for any hazardous items like e-waste or batteries and see whether you can find a local specialist recycler. Look through Part 2 and check your local rules to help figure out what goes in and what stays out.

>> Identify any recyclable items in your general waste bin or regular waste items in your recycling bin.

Make some notes on what you've discovered, and then turn this knowledge into simple actions you can start implementing. You can log these down using the Waste Actions worksheet in the Appendix. Focus on one or two changes you can make easily. Then after you've mastered those, you can look over your data again and set a new goal. Figure 17-2 offers examples of how to record your actions on the Waste Actions worksheet.

TIP

If you're not so excited about getting your hands dirty, another option is to keep the Waste Tracker worksheet and a pen next to your bins. Every time you put an item in each bin, write it down or add it to the tally. Do this for about a week and then analyze your results as described here, using the Waste Actions worksheet. This approach may also be helpful for apartment dwellers who don't have an out-door space to use for a waste audit.

WASTE ACTIONS

RECYCLING	ORGANICS
Things to keep out:	
• food waste	Food waste — do I have a compost service
• toothpaste tubes	
• polystyrene take-out containers	
• batteries	
Things to reduce:	
• buy a refillable water bottle	
• try a refillable detergent brand	
• choose a different take-out place that doesn't use polystyrene	
GARBAGE	**OTHER**
	Find a battery recycling drop-off location

FIGURE 17-2: Using the Waste Actions worksheet to set your goals.

© John Wiley & Sons, Inc.

Setting up a recycling station at home

Having a convenient, organized system in an easy-to-access location can make recycling easy for the whole family. Your recycling station can be a set of large bins in the garage or smaller ones in your laundry room. The most important thing is figuring out what works and makes things easier for you. Check out the following guidelines:

>> **Get to know your local rules.** Find out your local recycling rules to determine how many bins you need and what to separate. Knowing what is accepted curbside or at your local recycling center will help you figure out the best way to set up your home recycling center. (Part 2 can help you get started.)

>> **Work out how big your bins should be.** How often do your bins get emptied? Take note of how much you throw out each week to give you an idea of how big the bins need to be. If you're collecting items that go to a specialist recycler, consider how often you'll drop them off.

>> **Find the right location.** To figure out how much space you'll need for your recycling station, consider the following:

- Choose somewhere that has sufficient space and is easy to get to.

- Make sure there's room to grow. Over time, you might want to add more containers.

TIP

- Keep smaller containers in your kitchen or bathroom that can be emptied into the larger ones in your garage or laundry room.

>> **Find the right containers.** It's best to see whether you've got any containers around the house that you can use. If not, try asking your local Buy-Nothing Group or checking local businesses that may have containers you can have for free. If all that fails, try to buy recycled containers.

>> **Go the extra mile.** You don't need to limit your recycling station to what's collected through your curbside service. Why not consider collecting materials for specialist recyclers like soft plastics or e-waste? You can even sign up for a free TerraCycle recycling program for various items. (See www.terracycle. com/ for details.)

TIP

If you're gathering items or materials that won't be collected through a curbside pickup service, choose transportable containers so you can put them straight into your car when they're full.

WARNING

>> **Clean and dry everything.** Recycling and other trash can tend to attract pests. So make sure your recyclables are clean and dry before you place them in your recycling station containers.

Running a neighborhood collection

Although I've been a bit busy writing this book, I like to run a few collection programs for my neighbors from time to time. I simply put some bins outside my house and let my neighbors know what I'm collecting. Then I take the recycling or waste to the appropriate drop-off point.

If you're interested, here are a few pointers to help get you started:

>> Make sure there's a recycling service that will accept the items.

TIP

Be careful of quantities. Some transfer stations or collection points limit how much each household can drop off. If you go over, you might have to pay a fee. Try contacting the business to explain what you're doing; they might allow you to bring more than the per-household quantity.

>> Select a location at the front of your property that is easy to reach for your neighbors to drop off their recyclables.

>> Start by picking one or two easy items for people to collect. It's wise to start small by choosing one or two items to avoid any unexpected glitches. Then you can add more items later. Examples of items I've collected in the past include pens, toothpaste tubes, and mobile phones.

>> Contact your neighbors.

- Reach out to them in person, if you're comfortable doing that, or maybe by dropping a note in their mailbox. Ensure you clearly advise them of the details, like exactly what and how much you will be collecting and if you need them to wash the items.

- Set a date for when they should drop it off by. You might plan a one-time event or establish a weekly or monthly collection.

Taking Action Beyond the Curb

Our waste issues are endangering the environment. Reducing, reusing, and recycling can immediately benefit the environment, but there are other ways to lend a hand. In the following sections, I list a few examples that you might like to explore.

Joining a local cleanup

In the past, I'll confess, I often stepped over trash on the ground. Sometimes I wouldn't even see it; if I did, I would mumble about how terrible it was and keep walking. But over the last few years, my attitude toward litter has changed. Now I pick it up. It's something I'm proud of. I feel like I'm part of the solution instead of just a bystander shaking my head. You can't undo the fact that it was dropped, but you can pick it up and make sure it doesn't do any more damage to the environment.

REMEMBER

You can pick up litter anywhere, anytime. If you're new to the concept, you might like to join an organized event. Local cleanups benefit the environment by reducing litter, protecting local animals, and keeping toxins from leaching into the water. But joining a local cleanup group can be rewarding in other ways too. You can meet new people, get some sun and fresh air, and even get some exercise (all that bending down can be a pretty good workout).

CLEANING UP THE OCEAN THROUGH ART

Plastic Fisherman is a global project that uses social media and art to call attention to the dangers of marine plastic pollution. It invites action through creativity, turning beach cleanups into a fun activity named #plasticfishing.

Wanna try? It's easy:

1. Pick up five pieces of plastic polluting your beach or community.

2. Use them to make a little fish.

3. Snap a photo of your catch.

4. Share it on Instagram using #plasticfishing.

5. Please clean it up and dispose of it properly.

By leveraging the power of community and an "act-local-think-global" mindset, the #plasticfishing movement has removed thousands of pounds of plastic pollution from beaches and the environment all over the globe, one plastic fish at a time.

Check out the figure here for some ideas to help spark your imagination and join in. After all, the ocean should be for fish, not plastic.

Plastic Fisherman/www.plasticfisherman.com/last accessed February 21, 2023

To find local cleanup events, you can run a Google search for terms like "beach cleanup," "litter cleanup near me," or "cleanup events near me." You can also try local volunteer sites. Here are some examples of local cleanup events or groups to join:

>> Ocean Conservatory's International Coastal Cleanup events (see oceancon servancy.org/trash-free-seas/international-coastal-cleanup/).

>> The Surfrider Foundation (www.surfrider.org/) also holds a lot of events across the globe. Find your local chapter to see what events they have planned.

>> Clean Up the World Day is on the 17th of September every year. Events are organized in most countries across the world. (See www.cleanup theworld.org/.)

If you can't find an event why not get your friends, family, or community together and start your own beach or street cleanup?

Volunteering at your local Repair Café

Repair workshops are a positive outcome of our increased frustrations with not being able to repair our products. It works like this: Community organizations plan a day when locals can bring damaged goods, and volunteers help to fix or repair the items. People can bring any manner of things along, like clothes, electronic gadgets, appliances, dolls and toys, furniture, or jewelry. It all depends on what sort of skills the attending volunteers have.

Today there are more than 2,000 Repair Cafés across the world. Find your local Repair Café at www.repaircafe.org or start your own. And if you can't make it to an event or don't have a Repair Café near your home, you can find repair instructions on their website.

REMEMBER

The idea of the Repair Cafés goes beyond just repairing items and helps us appreciate the value of our possessions.

Supporting local and federal action

Local, national, and international legislation all play an essential role in helping to improve waste and protect the environment. While governments grapple with waste issues and determine the best course of action, what can you do? The best thing you can do is make a lot of noise and let them know that you want better systems.

TIP

Otherwise, you can take action in many ways. Here are just a few ideas:

>> Get in touch with your local representatives and ask a few questions. You may be pleasantly surprised to find out what they are already doing.

>> Write to your local government representatives to let them know you're concerned about the issues: Tell them you want:

- Bans on single-use plastics like bags, straws, stirrers, and cutlery

- Deposit return schemes and bottle banks

- Extended producer responsibility for packaging

- Right to repair laws to protect consumers

>> Ask your local government to establish a Library of Things, a Repair Café (see the previous section), or other community events for education or waste drop-off.

>> Sign a petition to share your voice. Signing petitions can have many positive outcomes. It lets the decision makers know what you think. You can find many petitions in support of cleaning up the oceans and stopping the flow of plastic and other pollution through the environmental groups listed in the next section.

>> Why not start your own petition? Perhaps you want to get single-use plastic bags banned in your area or help remove barriers to repair your gadgets. Simply log into your chosen site (try www.change.org or www.gopetition.com), set up your petition, and share it, and then once you have enough signatures, take your petition to your local representatives.

CATCHING UP TO THE OTHERS

While many other countries have introduced legislation to reduce plastic pollution, the United States is lagging behind, despite ranking second only to China in total plastic waste generated per year. You can help move things along by getting behind the Break Free From Plastic Act, which offers much-needed solutions. This bill aims to strengthen environmental protection, support reuse programs, reduce single-use plastics, and improve the transparency and accountability of companies.

Sound good? You can find out more about the bill at www.breakfreefromplastic.org.

Backing environmental groups

Another way to help clean up our world is to support environmental nonprofit groups working hard to reduce pollution. Here are some organizations doing a tremendous amount of good:

» **Oceana** (`https://oceana.org/`): Oceana promotes greater marine biodiversity and habitat protection on a global scale. They're strong advocates of policy change and offer many ways for you to get involved and take action.

» **The Ocean Conservancy** (`https://oceanconservancy.org/`): Based in the United States, the Ocean Conservancy is working hard to protect the oceans by supporting science-based solutions. They have many campaigns, like keeping microplastics out of the ocean, which you can get involved in.

» **The Ocean Cleanup** (`https://theoceancleanup.com/`): The Great Pacific Garbage Patch isn't an easy problem to solve, but the Ocean Cleanup has risen to the challenge. Through initiatives to collect plastic from the ocean and install waste collection systems in strategically selected rivers across the globe, they've already successfully removed over 2,000 metric tons of waste from marine environments.

» **Ocean Voyages Institute** (`www.oceanvoyagesinstitute.org/`): With the North Pacific Sub-Tropical Convergence Zone as its focus area to date, the Ocean Voyages Institute has removed more than 500,000 pounds of plastic from the ocean. They run regular expeditions to clean up the oceans, raise awareness, and increase knowledge.

» **The 5 Gyres** (`www.5gyres.org/`): They aim to prevent plastic pollution through science, education, and adventure. They have conducted 19 research expeditions studying plastic pollution in the oceans.

There are so many more organizations, big and small, taking action to solve our waste problems and ease the pressure on our natural environment. If you're looking for a local charity group, try searching websites like `www.greatnonprofits.org`, `www.canadahelps.org`, or `www.charitychoice.co.uk`.

Chapter **18**

Considering the Future of Recycling

The recycling and waste industry, as with most industries, has its own unique and complex challenges. As users of this system, we see only the tip of the iceberg, and often this tip is full of negative stories. But there is a lot of positive stuff going on as well. The industry is moving forward quickly and addressing challenges as they arise. They have a vested interest in increasing the likelihood that our waste is recycled and turned into new goods.

Solutions are not always simple, and we must tackle our waste problems from all angles. It's not just the waste industry that needs to evolve continually. To support a circular economic model and reduce waste, we need more focus on designing products to be recyclable from the beginning. Additionally, we should emphasize product stewardship, where corporations are accountable for the full life cycle of their products. These changes may require government regulation to help advance them.

Many exciting things are going on in the recycling industry, from introducing new technologies for collection and sorting to implementing policies to support growth in recycling. In this chapter, I give you a flavor of what the future might hold for the recycling industry. I describe other opportunities for dealing with waste plastic using chemicals and enzymes. Then I explain how policy can boost recycling and recycled products.

Redesigning Products for Recyclability

We spend a lot of effort solving problems like keeping food fresher longer or making convenient packaging to save time. But we've been so focused on making things more convenient, attractive, and marketable that we left the environmental part behind. Everyday recycling is becoming more difficult with the growing complexity of modern products and materials.

It's time we changed that focus. We need to spend more time considering the endgame, what happens to a product or its packaging at the end of its life. Here are some of the concepts that play a part in redesigning for our future:

>> **Making things recyclable:** Designing things that can be collected, sorted, and recycled cost-effectively. This can be achieved in many ways, from simplifying the design to designing modular products for easy disassembly prior to recycling.

>> **Designing single-material products:** Products with multiple layers and materials complicate recycling. By simplifying the packaging design and limiting it to one type of material, you can increase its recyclability significantly.

>> **Eliminating unnecessary materials:** Redesigning products to remove or replace unnecessary plastics is another part of the solution.

>> **Minimizing the use of toxic compounds:** Simplifying packaging can also help remove the need for toxic materials, reducing the risk of them escaping and harming the environment.

TECHNICAL STUFF

At the forefront of the redesign movement is the Ellen MacArthur Foundation (https://ellenmacarthurfoundation.org). It's an international organization working on key issues around the circular economy. In particular, they focus on designing a circular economy to prevent waste and keep materials in use. Among many other topics, they offer education on circular design principles for professionals and students. Here are a few real-life examples of redesigning products:

>> Colgate recently redesigned their toothpaste tubes to use only one type of plastic, high-density polyethylene (HDPE), so that they are more recyclable. Reducing how much multilayer packaging we use is important as these materials are one of the most difficult to recycle (see Chapter 10).

>> On the same topic of toothpaste, Tesco has been running a trial recently to remove the cardboard box from toothpaste packaging. By eliminating this unnecessary part of their packaging, they estimate they can save 680 tons of cardboard annually. Would you purchase toothpaste tubes without cardboard

wrapping if you knew that doing so would help save hundreds of tons of paperboard — roughly 17 trees per ton — and a lot of energy as well? Watch out for this change in your local store if you live in the United Kingdom.

>> Another great invention is the KeelClip by Graphic Packaging International. The new design is made from recycled paper and replaces the typical plastic rings or plastic shrink wrap used for multi-can packaging.

Transforming the Recycling Process

As new materials and other product solutions are developed, recycling technology and accessibility must also advance. Technically recyclable versus actually recycled is an important distinction. Companies may make products that can be recycled in certain conditions; however, a lack of collection or inadequate recycling infrastructure can mean the item never gets recycled.

For example, in the preceding section, I mention Colgate's toothpaste tube, which is now made from one type of plastic, making it more recyclable. The problem is that not all curbside recycling programs accept HDPE (plastic #2), and even if they do, they will likely not accept toothpaste tubes. You see, it would be difficult for them to sort these toothpaste tubes from the regular variety. So although it's a step in the right direction, we need all parties to align for solutions to be truly effective.

In the following sections, I examine changes currently in progress and upcoming developments in the recycling sector.

Improving existing systems

The primary job of recycling services is gathering materials, sorting them, and cleaning them so they can be sold to manufacturers and reprocessors for use in new products. The biggest challenge in recycling is taking a messy mix of materials and sorting and separating them to a standard that allows them to be reused in manufacturing.

The positive is that investment in the recycling industry is increasing, and technology is advancing. In response to the more recent China National Sword policies (refer to Chapter 4) and a number of other market factors, including the accessibility and reduced price of artificial intelligence (AI) and robotics, materials recovery facilities (MRFs) have been investing in various new technologies.

The following is a list of the improvements the sector needs to work on:

» **Standardizing the industry:** It's pretty clear that consistency in recycling is something that everyone would like to see. We can push for global standardization, but to be honest, achieving consistency at a national level would be a pretty good start. As technological solutions are developed and investment increases, we may see more uniformity in material recovery across regions.

But standardization isn't just about what goes in the bin; it's also about everyone having equal access to recycling services. Currently, access to recycling services depends on where you live. Some pay, others receive it free, and many don't have access at all. Our target should be to reach a point where recycling is equally available to all.

» **Taking responsibility for waste management:** It's time we do away with sending waste to other countries and take full responsibility for it ourselves. Fortunately, many developing countries have recognized this and, following China's National Sword Policy, have implemented their own bans on waste imports.

» **Boosting manufacturing in parallel:** Increase investment in domestic manufacturing facilities to be able to process recycled materials in-country.

» **Automating with robots:** The introduction of AI-based robotics, where high-tech robotic arms dart in and pick up individual items to remove contamination or sort items appropriately. (See the nearby sidebar for more about AI and recycling.)

» **Introducing AI technology at recycling plants:** AI-based technology can provide real-time data on material composition and labeling. With this information, recovery rates increase, and contamination rates decrease. Cleaner end products may also be more cost-effective and improve end-market demand. This technology can also increase efficiency and safety, and reduce costs.

» **Capturing the data:** One of the most important changes the recycling industry can adopt is data capture. Data enables recycling businesses and governments to make informed decisions. It also helps build greater transparency where claims can be backed up with data. Here are just some ways that big data can improve the waste industry:

- Help businesses and manufacturers understand what sort of waste and how much they create so that they can implement changes.

- Help governments identify how different communities produce and dispose of waste to enable targeted education and services.

- Enable better sorting and separation through data collected by AI-based technology.

- Improve inefficiencies in waste collection routes through towns and cities.

- Track the source of recycled materials used in new products for transparency and stewardship.

BOOSTING RECYCLING WITH ARTIFICIAL INTELLIGENCE

We've all heard about artificial intelligence — computer systems that can complete tasks that humans would normally perform. It might bring to mind terminators that look like Arnold Schwarzenegger taking over the world! But don't worry, it's a lot less scary than that.

AI has already been around for some time. You've probably encountered it in your everyday life already. Some common examples where it is used include the following:

- Chatbot assistants online
- Google maps
- Face detection software on your mobile phone
- Smart home devices
- Text editors and autocorrect features
- Music and media streaming services

First, AI programs work to gather data and categorize it to learn the different patterns and features. Next, they develop their own algorithm to help them get the desired result. Finally, they continually fine-tune the algorithm to improve their performance. Here are a couple of examples of how AI is already being used in the recycling industry:

- **AI robotics sorting things out:** The introduction of AI-based robotics into recycling has exciting potential. One of the most challenging issues for recycling is the ability to sort materials into different types. With the myriad of plastics and other materials present in the recycling stream at most materials recovery facilities (MRFs), it's an area where they could do with a helping hand, so to speak. Picture high-tech robotic arms darting in and picking up individual items to sort them appropriately or remove contamination. These robots could outperform even the best optical sorters around. Using millions of different images, they can identify and pick up thousands of pieces of waste per hour.

- **Recycling education with AI:** AI is also finding its way into recycling education. Recycle Mate, Australia's first community-driven recycling app, helps Australians recycle no matter where they live. The user simply snaps a photo or types in the name of the item they want to dispose of. The app uses AI photo recognition technology to compare the user's image to a database of more than 5,700 items. Once found, it displays the recycling rules for the user's location on the screen, including ideas for what to do with items not accepted in curbside systems. By collecting this data, the app will continue to grow and improve the more people use it. The best part is that it's free to download and use. You can take a closer look at www. recyclemate.com.au.

REMEMBER

You can be a part of the solution by getting to know your local rules and following them (see Parts 2 and 3 for details). This will keep contamination low and help ensure your recyclables can become new products.

Potentially solving plastic problems with chemical recycling

Chemical recycling is a process where plastics are broken down or depolymerized using chemical, pressure, or thermal methods into their original components. They are typically separated into monomers, polymers, or other chemicals, all of which can be used as feedstock for manufacturing. The process is also designed to remove impurities, contaminants, or additives, leaving components that can then be used to make new plastics, fuels, or other products.

TECHNICAL STUFF

Here are a couple of useful definitions:

>> *Polyermization* is a process of creating the building blocks for plastics. Called *polymers,* these long chains or molecules are made up of repeating molecules called *monomers.* Polymerization is a chemical process that helps bond these monomers to create long-chain polymers. Find out more about how plastic is made in Chapter 6.

>> *Depolymerization* is the process of breaking these long polymer chains back into monomers.

WARNING

Recycling plastic and other material through traditional mechanical means is not always efficient and has limitations. Chemical recycling has the potential to close this gap and recycle hard-to-recycle plastics into useful materials that can be formed into new products. However, it's still early days in the development of chemical recycling, and many processes are still in their experimental phase. Debate is ongoing, with supporters seeing the potential for recovering and recycling many hard-to-recycle plastics unsuited to mechanical recycling, like multi-layer plastic film. Opponents challenge the high energy consumption and the potential risk to the environment of toxic emissions and residues resulting from the process.

Chemical recycling is unlikely to replace mechanical recycling but will more likely supplement these existing systems. The best situation is for mechanical recycling facilities to improve and develop alongside these new facilities. It must also work hand in hand with sustained demand for recycled content in products. And, of course, we all must strive to reduce and reuse to stop plastic waste at the source.

Replicating enzymes to munch on plastic

Could plastic-eating enzymes be the solution to the world's plastic problem? Researchers across the globe are discovering many different enzymes that can process plastic. Proteins called enzymes occur in all living things. They assist in accelerating the chemical processes that occur in the cells of living things. These plastic-eating enzymes are primarily found in bacteria but have also been discovered in gut microbes in superworms.

Researchers hope to replicate these enzymes on a large scale to accelerate plastic recycling. Similar to chemical recycling, this isn't expected to replace the existing mechanical recycling processes but would offer complementary solutions that can deal with some of the harder-to-recycle plastics.

Some of these enzymes can even depolymerize plastics and break them into their original components, similar to chemical recycling. Not only does this provide another avenue for processing hard-to-recycle plastics, but it can also reduce our reliance on virgin plastic.

Driving Change Through Policy

Policy is a crucial ingredient not only in addressing the many challenges of recycling but in the implementation of reduction and reuse strategies. There are many ways that policy can help drive change in recycling. Key types of policies that promote and support recycling include the following:

» Container deposit laws or bottle bills encouraging the return of glass and plastic bottles by providing financial incentives

» Mandatory recycling content laws generating demand for recycled materials by stipulating the level of recycled content that brands must include in their products or packaging

» Banning single-use or particularly problematic plastics to help reduce waste creation and plastics in the environment

» Laws restricting recyclability claims to ensure claims by producers are accurate and not misleading

» Introducing mandatory recycling laws to safeguard the environment by restricting certain materials from landfills, such as electronic waste, and imposing fines on those that don't comply

>> Extended producer responsibility, switching the cost of collection and sorting of recycling material from the taxpayer to the producer

>> Right to Repair laws protecting consumers' right to be able to repair products and keep them in use

Many policies have already been implemented across the globe. In fact, some have been in place for decades, while others are still in development. An effective policy that is put into law could be a key factor in boosting recycling. I list some great examples of existing or imminent policies in the nearby sidebar "Making progress with policies."

MAKING PROGRESS WITH POLICIES

There are numerous examples where policy changes have been implemented that have positively impacted the community. These changes involve everything from recycling legislation to banning specific items or even helping to fund the cost of recycling through extended producer responsibility (EPR; see Chapter 4.) Here are a few examples from across the globe:

- In England, local governments were obligated by the Home Waste Recycling Act of 2003 to offer every household a separate collection of at least two different recyclable items by 2010. The bill was successful, and as a result, the proportion of household waste that was recycled reached 43 percent by 2016. This is a great success story.

- The Australian government is in the process of phasing out eight problematic and unnecessary plastics by the end of 2025. Although most states currently have single-use plastic bans in place, a national agreement will reduce confusion for consumers and businesses.

- The United Kingdom is introducing extended producer responsibility (EPR) for packaging in 2023. This will mean the cost of collecting household packaging will shift from taxpayer to producer. In addition, businesses will be required to provide better reporting. Plus, labeling will be standardized and simplified using the On-Pack Recycling Label (OPRL). You can find out more about this labeling in Chapter 5. Hopefully, these measures will encourage businesses to improve product packaging design using more sustainable and recyclable materials.

- Many states in the United States have passed extended producer responsibility (EPR) laws covering mattress recycling. It's intended to reduce the dumping of mattresses and help establish suitable collection sites. Under the program, mattress producers must join a stewardship organization, pay a fee, and submit a management plan for approval. Mattress EPR laws already exist in California, Rhode Island, and Connecticut.

TIP

If you want to find ways to support recycling and circular economy policies where you live, check out Chapter 17.

Demanding recycled content in new products

REMEMBER

I cannot stress enough that what we need are companies using recycled material in their products. Generating demand for recycled material is imperative for securing secondary markets and reducing our reliance on virgin production systems. Otherwise, all our recycling efforts are pointless. We can help by choosing to buy recycled goods whenever possible. Chapter 16 gives you all the information you need to find recycled products.

Mandates on recycled content can potentially increase market demand for recycled products. This will help create the end market I've highlighted throughout this book as an essential part of successful recycling. Creating a more consistent end market will also hopefully spark investment in recycling infrastructure and promote innovation. I describe a few examples of policies that have been implemented to support recycled content in the nearby sidebar "Boosting recycled content."

As demand for recycled material increases to meet mandated percentages, the collection of good-quality recycled material is imperative. This is where you and I come into the picture. Taking responsibility for our waste and recycling with a mind to keeping contamination at a minimum is our job.

BOOSTING RECYCLED CONTENT

Here are some great examples of policies that promote recycled content:

- The United Kingdom introduced a Plastic Packaging Tax in April 2022. It's a tax on any manufactured or imported plastic packaging that does not contain at least 30 percent recycled content. Its goal is to incentivize recycled content and penalize those who don't adapt.

- In California, the SB 270 legislation mandates a minimum of 40 percent post-consumer recycled (PCR) content in reusable plastic retail bags. They have also introduced a law that sets a minimum of 15 percent post-consumer recycled content in plastic bottles covered by the state's container redemption program. This percentage will increase to 50 percent by 2030.

Following in the footsteps of the European Union

The Circular Economy Action Plan (CEAP) was adopted by the European Commission in 2015. It's a set of actions designed to promote the transition to a circular economy across Europe. Initially, there were 54 actions intended to reduce pressure on natural resources and make sustainable products the norm. It's also a key component of the European Green Deal, a road map toward no net emissions of greenhouse gases by 2050.

The CEAP's actions started at the beginning of the life cycle of products and set goals for more sustainable production and better design. It encompassed all aspects of a better system, from extending the life of products to protecting and empowering consumers. It continues through waste management and the promotion of secondary raw materials with a particular focus on plastics and food waste. But it also addressed issues around funding and, last but not least, tactics for measuring and monitoring progress.

By 2019 all 54 actions were either completed or in progress, so in 2020, the CEAP was updated. The update addressed the following key areas covering the full life cycle of products from design to end-of-life. Those actions were

>> Extending the life of products by promoting durability and ensuring access to upgrades and repairs

>> Minimizing hard-to-recycle and toxic materials

>> Increasing recycled content

>> Improving recyclability by introducing right-to-repair laws and eliminating built-in obsolescence

>> Eliminating greenwashing

>> Reducing carbon footprints

The European Union provides some good examples of how to implement policy to help drive improved recycling and support a circular economy. By focusing on all facets of product life cycles and circular economy principles, the EU is paving the way for the rest of the world. Here are some of the top reasons why the European model is the one to watch:

>> They encompass all facets of a circular economy. Equal pressure and focus are applied along the entire life cycle of products.

- >> Their actions lead to a reevaluation of resource efficiency and the flow of materials.

- >> They promote a collaborative approach sparking innovation as companies try to find ways to comply.

- >> By empowering consumers, they are encouraging them to be part of the solution.

Working Together to Achieve a Truly Circular Economy

A circular economy is one in which waste and pollution are eliminated, products and materials are kept in use as long as possible, and nature is regenerated. It seems like such a natural solution, but we have been moving away from this idea and building a nonregenerative linear system. It's time to flip that on its head.

We have our work cut out for us, but if we stay the course and all parties work together, we can get there. The secret to success is collaboration, and to keep pushing forward on all fronts. That involves finding ways to eliminate the root cause of our issues while working on solutions for everyday impacts. It means giving it everything we've got.

REMEMBER

Some people assume that recycling is the responsibility of industry or the government, and of course they play a part, but in my opinion, we all share the responsibility. And we can all lend a hand in breaking our linear mindset in which we take, make, and waste everything. Let's do this!

5

The Part of Tens

Investigate the answers to the ten most common recycling myths. Recycling works, but wishcycling is out, and so is putting your recycling in a plastic bag.

Explore the ten things you thought you couldn't recycle but you actually can — you might be surprised by what's on this list.

Discover ten things you thought you could recycle but can't — getting acquainted with this list will help reduce contamination in your recycling bin.

Chapter **19**

Ten Recycling Myths Debunked

U nfortunately, there are many myths about recycling that make people wonder whether it is all worth the effort. In this chapter, I debunk the top ten myths about recycling.

Recycling Is a Scam, and Nothing Gets Recycled Anyway

If you've read through the entire book up to this point, you're already aware that this statement is simply not true. The idea that recycling is ineffective and a scam frequently undermines consumer trust in recycling. Many recycling success stories are overlooked by media outlets in favor of more sensational stories of stockpiling or dumping recyclables in landfills. Given these problems affect only a very small percentage of waste streams and are occasionally impossible to prevent owing to contamination (see Chapter 4 to find out more), this negative media does more harm than good. The fact is the recycling industry successfully recycles tons of materials every day; you can find some great success stories in Chapter 4.

Recycling Is Too Complicated

It can seem like there is a lot of information about recycling, but once you take the time to familiarize yourself with it, you might discover it's not as complicated as it initially appears. Here are some suggestions for simplifying recycling:

>> Understand that most curbside recycling programs are only designed to accept one or all of the following common packaging materials (flip to Part 2 for more details on recycling these materials): rigid plastic bottles (depending on the plastic number), aluminum cans and tins, glass jars and bottles (may not be accepted at all in some places), and paper, paperboard, and cardboard boxes.

>> Always check your local rules. Recycling rules vary from place to place because not all recycling facilities are designed the same, and access to end markets varies, so it's important that you check your local rules.

If You Throw It in Your Curbside Recycling Bin, It'll Get Recycled

If you can't work out whether an item is recyclable in your curbside service, sometimes you might decide to put it into your recycling bin anyway, hoping someone else will figure it out. We call this *wishcycling*. But you can't just throw everything in your recycling bin in the hope that it will get sorted and recycled. Curbside recycling services are only designed to handle specific types of materials, as explained in the preceding section.

WARNING

When we place things in the recycling bin that don't belong, we cause what is called *contamination*. This contamination makes it harder and sometimes more costly for recycling companies to extract recyclable material. It can also cause safety hazards and result in a recycling facility having to shut down temporarily. Follow this rule: When in doubt, leave it out. It's better to put an item into the general waste bin than contaminate your recycling bin.

Curbside Is the Only Recycling Option

Many people are unaware that recycling goes beyond the services offered at your curbside. There are many other programs for recycling, including soft plastic, e-waste, and even composting of food waste. In Part 3, I describe several of these recycling programs in detail. I encourage you to seek out more recycling programs to reduce your overall impact.

If There's a Recycling Symbol, It Must Be Recyclable

Many people believe that if an item has the recycling symbol with the three chasing arrows on it, it means that it's recyclable. Unfortunately, this isn't always the case. A good example is when an item has a Resin Identification Code shown. These codes are designed to help identify the different plastic types by displaying a number in the chasing arrows symbol (see Chapter 6). However, because they use the universal recycling symbol with the chasing arrows around the number, many people think it means the item is recyclable. There are seven resin codes, and which ones are accepted through curbside recycling differs depending on where you live. Always check with your local town or city government rules before recycling your plastics.

Materials Can Be Recycled Only Once

A common misconception is that many everyday items can be recycled only once. In fact, most materials can be recycled more than once, although the number of times depends on the material. Metals can be recycled repeatedly and never lose their quality. On the other hand, plastic has a shorter life span and can generally be recycled up to only ten times. The current mechanical recycling methods shred, melt, and reform the plastic, causing degradation of the material.

It Takes More Energy to Recycle Than to Make Something New

Another myth thrown around a lot is that recycling takes more energy than making something from raw resources. Sure, collecting recycling from households, sorting, cleaning, baling, and then transporting it to reprocessors or manufacturers takes energy. However, it's not nearly as much as what goes into making products from virgin resources.

Consider, for example, aluminum manufacturing. It takes a great deal of energy to extract raw minerals from the earth, transport them to a processing facility, extract the metals, convert them into usable materials, and then transport them to a manufacturer to make a can. But by inserting a recycled aluminum can into the last steps of this process, all the energy required for mining and processing is avoided. In fact, recycling just one aluminum can saves enough power to run a TV for three hours.

Waste Decomposes Quickly in a Landfill

Landfills aren't designed to allow materials to break down. They're purposely designed to slow the degradation process to stop waste from decomposing quickly. Slowing down the degradation process lowers the many risks that landfills pose to the environment. It makes it possible to regulate the quantity of methane generated, reduce the danger of spontaneous combustion, and keep an eye on the leachate to ensure it doesn't escape. As a result, it can take up to two years for an apple to break down, and most plastic will take hundreds of years to decompose.

You Should Bag Recyclables

REMEMBER

Many people collect their recyclables in plastic bags and put them into their curbside recycling bins. Other than in some specific locations, bagging your recyclables is a big no-no. Recyclables should be kept loose so the machines can sort them. Plus, plastic bags are a big issue for recycling facilities. They can get stuck in machinery, creating safety issues for workers and potentially causing the entire plant to have to shut down temporarily. Unless your local regulations clearly specify, keep your recycling unbagged and loose.

Products Made from Recycled Content Are Inferior

Many recycled products have long been considered inferior to those created from raw resources. This may have been more likely 20 years ago, but manufacturing of recycled products has advanced significantly, and today these products perform just as well as their virgin counterparts. For instance, many glass and plastic containers meet stringent food-grade-quality standards and you wouldn't know they were manufactured from recycled content. Take a closer look at the many recycled products in Chapter 16.

Chapter **20**

Ten Things You Thought You Couldn't Recycle but Can

Our curbside recycling services don't accept many items we come in contact with daily. Luckily, some unique recycling programs turn these items into useful products. But these items don't belong in your curbside recycling bin. Here are ten items you can recycle that you may not know about.

Batteries

Many materials used to make batteries are toxic if allowed to enter the environment. Once let loose, these chemicals can contaminate waterways and endanger animals and humans. The good news is that almost all the materials in batteries can be recovered and used in new batteries or other products. It's never been easier to recycle your batteries. Many programs are available either through retail stores or hazardous waste collections. Loads of supermarkets and retail stores have drop-off bins to collect spent batteries for recycling, including Best Buy, The Home Depot, Staples, Lowe's, and Officeworks. Check your local stores or find more information in Chapter 13.

Keep batteries out of your general waste bin and your curbside recycling bin.

REMEMBER

Your Mobile Phone

Many people may not be aware, but a mobile phone has many useful materials that can be recovered and reused. You can recycle mobile phones in any e-waste (electronic waste) recycling program, or in some cases with specialist services designed just for mobile phones. Some companies will help you wipe the data from your mobile phone before it's recycled, protecting your personal information and the planet. Find a list of specialist recyclers and other useful information in Chapter 13.

Ink Cartridges

More than 1.3 billion ink cartridges are used worldwide every year, but only 30 percent are recycled. These cartridges contain plastic, metal, and of course, ink and toner chemicals. Many of these components can take thousands of years to decompose and are hazardous to the environment.

Specialist businesses can recycle ink cartridges in most locations. Materials that can be recovered and recycled include plastic, metal, ink, and even the toner chemicals. Drop-off sites and some mail-in programs are available, plus many printer manufacturers like HP, Brother, Canon, and Xerox have take-back recycling programs. Don't send your old ink cartridges to a landfill. Find a recycler near you and keep an eye out for recycled ink products.

Chewing Gum

What does gum have to do with recycling? Chewing gum is actually made with butadiene-based synthetic rubber, a synthetic material, and a type of plastic. More than 100,000 tons of chewing gum is chewed every year across the world. And the problem is it's discarded anywhere and everywhere, leaving behind an expensive mess for governments to clean up. It also impacts animals that eat it or get stuck in it.

You might be surprised to find out that chewing gum can be recycled and made into many different products. Some of the products it's used in include collection bins, frisbees, dog bowls, coffee cups, gum boots, cookie cutters, and even mobile phone covers. Find out more at `www.gumdropltd.com`.

Toothpaste Tubes

TerraCycle offers a recycling program that accepts all your old toothpaste tubes. In fact, they accept other oral care items like used toothbrushes and dental floss containers. All you have to do is sign up for the program and start collecting. Once you have enough, you can post them in or find a nearby drop-off location. You can either sign up and mail them in or check for local retail stores with drop-off bins available.

Coffee Pods

Unfortunately, our addiction to coffee has some pretty bad outcomes. Even if we avoid purchasing coffee in single-use cups, we may find ourselves with coffee pods piling up and wondering what we can do with them. Each coffee pod is made from different materials; some are recyclable, while others are a bit trickier. Here are a few options to check out:

>> TerraCycle has several recycling programs for different types of coffee pods. Check their website (`www.terracycle.com`) for free programs.

>> Look for collection points for the different brands.

>> Check the brand's website to see if they have a mail-in recycling service.

Sneakers

Your average sneaker contains many different materials, including leather, textiles like polyester or nylon, rubber, and plastics. Whether you are a passionate athlete or simply like to wear them while around town, sooner or later your sneakers will wear out. Unfortunately, more than 300 million are tossed away every year, most of which end up in landfills.

TIP

The good news is a few programs take your old sneakers and running shoes and recycle them. If they're in good condition, I recommend donating them to a charity first so they can go to someone in need. You can try One World Running (www. oneworldrunning.com/) or Soles4Souls (https://soles4souls.org/). But if they're no longer wearable, then recycling is your best bet. The most well-known recycling program is the Nike Reuse-A-Shoe program (www.nike.com/a/ recycle-old-shoes). They take any sneaker brand and have drop-off points at many stores. Search your local area or talk to your local sneaker store and see what recycling programs they support.

Wet Suits

Wet suits might not be on the top of your list of recyclable items, but possibly because you didn't know they're made from a synthetic petrochemical rubber called neoprene. When sent to a landfill, this material breaks down into smaller pieces and can leach chemicals into the environment.

Wet suit recycling programs are available, but before using them, it's a good idea to check if any organizations will take your wet suit for reuse, particularly if it's in good shape. Patagonia takes back its products worldwide. Ripcurl runs a program in partnership with TerraCycle (www.terracycle.com) where you can drop off your wet suits. Otherwise, run a Google search for "wet suit recycling" or talk to your local retail supplier.

Stockings and Pantyhose

Whenever I wear a pair of stockings, it takes no time to catch them on something and create a ladder as long as my legs. If only someone could invent stockings that didn't ladder. Swedish Stockings (https://swedishstockings.com/) may not have solved that problem, but they are solving the problems with waste from pantyhose and stockings. They collect them in their take-back program and turn them into furniture. Depending on which country you are in, they have a mail-in service, and they accept all brands and types of stockings or pantyhose. While you're there, check out their new stockings and socks made from recycled nylon yarn.

Skis, Poles, and Boots

Skis can go through some pretty rough treatment, so they're made to last using timber with fiberglass or carbon fiber. But whether you've outgrown them or torn them to shreds on the slopes, sooner or later they will need replacing. The good news is you don't need to send them to a landfill. Plenty of programs are available that take your old skis off your hands. Some will even accept old ski boots too. Although the fiberglass makes it difficult to recover materials from skis and ski poles, they can be repurposed into cool furniture, fences, or sleds.

You might find what you need secondhand and save yourself a penny, or you could try the latest recyclable skis. By implementing circular economy principles, a company in France has designed a recycled ski. Check them out at www.rossignol.com/us/essential.

IN THIS CHAPTER

» Leaving plastic bags out

» Ensuring there's no food waste

» Keeping paper and cardboard dry

» Recycling e-waste elsewhere

» Finding other ways to recycle bulbs

Chapter **21**

Ten Things That Don't Belong in Your Curbside Recycling Bin

When it comes to recycling, there are some common mistakes we are all guilty of making. However, keeping the things in this chapter out of our recycling bins will help keep contamination low and make the recycling process much more successful.

Biodegradable and Compostable Plastics

Compostable and biodegradable products and packaging cannot be recycled through curbside recycling programs. Separating biodegradable and compostable plastics from regular plastics is extremely difficult at a recycling facility, and they can end up contaminating these plastic waste streams. Keeping them out of your curbside recycling bin helps ensure that regular plastics are free from contamination and can be processed and used in new products. Find out more about the pros and cons of biodegradable and compostable plastics in Chapter 6.

Polystyrene Foam

Polystyrene, or Styrofoam as it's also known, is used in many takeaway cups, clamshells, and other containers. It's also used to package products because it's very good at protecting them during transport.

Polystyrene cannot be recycled through curbside recycling programs and should be disposed of through specialist recycling services if available or in your general waste bin. It can't be recovered through curbside systems because it's too light-weight and breaks up in the collection and sorting process, creating litter and contaminating other recycling streams. Flip to Chapter 6 to find out which types of plastic can be recycled.

TIP

Because it's so lightweight, polystyrene can easily blow out of bins into the environment, where it can also easily break into small pieces that animals confuse for food. Always push it far down in the bin or tie it inside a bag to contain it.

Dirty or Wet Cardboard

Not all that long ago, extensive media attention emphasized a great deal of uncertainty around recycling pizza boxes. Lots of articles suggested pizza boxes weren't recyclable, while others said they were. You can recycle your pizza boxes, but you can't recycle dirty, greasy, or wet cardboard. So if your pizza box is covered in cheese or grease, it belongs in the general waste bin or possibly in a compost bin, but if it's clean and dry, you can recycle it. The same goes for any of your paper, paperboard, or cardboard. Find out more in Chapter 7.

Paper Towels and Tissues

Paper can be recycled only around seven times (as you find out in Chapter 7). The fibers are shortened each time it's recycled, and the quality decreases. As a result, it's recycled into lower-quality products until finally it can no longer be recycled. The last products made are usually tissues and paper towels, so as a result they have very short fibers and cannot be recycled again.

The truth, however, is that no one wants to recycle your used tissues. Apart from being pretty unpleasant, they're usually covered with food or something worse, which can contaminate the other recyclables. Put used tissues and paper towels into the general waste bin, or compost them if you can.

Broken Glass

It's common that broken glass isn't accepted in curbside recycling. This seems counterintuitive to some people because glass breaks up during the collection and sorting process. There are two reasons why broken glass can't go into curbside recycling:

» Broken glass can become a safety hazard for workers collecting bins. Intact bottles and jars are much easier to handle.

» Glass tends to continue to break up into smaller and smaller pieces through the sorting process. If those pieces become too small, they can contaminate paper and plastic or fall through gaps in the machinery.

Discover how to properly recycle glass in Chapter 8.

Soft Plastics

Soft plastics like plastic bags, zip-top bags, bubble wrap, shrink-wrap, chip packets, and pasta packets cause some of the worst recycling contamination. Not only do they contaminate other types of plastic, but they get tangled in the sorting machinery at recycling facilities. Workers usually have to shut down the machine and climb in to cut the material away, creating unnecessary safety hazards and a potential loss of income. However, you can recycle soft plastics and plastic bags through specialist services. Drop-off locations are conveniently available in supermarkets and other retail stores. In Chapter 11, find out more about recycling soft plastics.

Food Waste

REMEMBER

Food has no place in your curbside recycling bin. Recycling facilities aren't designed to process it. Paper and cardboard are particularly susceptible to contamination from food waste due to their tendency to absorb liquids and fats. Because of this, they may be needlessly disposed of in landfills.

However, keeping food waste out of landfills is just as important as it can lead to the release of greenhouse gases. The best solution for food waste is to compost it. If you're lucky, you might have access to a separate curbside collection for food scraps. Talk to your local town or city government to find out. Otherwise, you can set up your own compost at home or find someone in your local area to take it. Get more facts about food waste in Chapter 12.

Electronic Devices

E-waste devices cannot be disposed of in curbside recycling bins unless your local area specifically offers this service. They are best recycled through specialist recyclers that are set up to handle it. E-waste is any electronic device or appliance with a cord or battery. It includes things like mobile phones, computers, TVs, household appliances, and toys. See Chapter 13 to discover more about e-waste.

Apart from the fact that it's illegal to send e-waste to landfills in some locations, there are many other reasons to ensure your e-waste is disposed of responsibly, including the following:

>> It may contain toxic materials, like lead, mercury, or arsenic.

>> It has valuable materials that can be recovered and reused.

>> Much of the material can be recycled and reused in new products.

Clothes and Textiles

Textiles and clothing cannot be recycled through curbside recycling systems and are likely to cause issues in the collection and sorting machinery. They are what is referred to as *tanglers*, items that will get tangled in the machinery and potentially lead to a shutdown at the facility. Other types of tanglers include rope, cables, garden hoses, and soft plastics (covered earlier in this chapter). The best options are to sell or donate your clothing or home linens, assuming they're still in good condition. If they are no longer wearable or useable, then look into recycling options. See Chapter 14 for details.

Light Bulbs

Similar to batteries and electronics, broken or spent light globes cannot be recycled in your curbside recycling bin. This is particularly the case for compact fluorescent (CFL) light bulbs because they contain small amounts of mercury. Even LED light bulbs can contain trace amounts of lead or arsenic.

TIP

The materials found in most light bulbs can be recovered and reused in new products when they're recycled responsibly. Head to Chapter 14 to discover how to find your local bulb recycling service. Plus, you can check out all the other recycling programs there.

Appendix
Waste Audit Worksheets

You can use the following worksheets to run your own waste audit; just make copies whenever you need them. In Chapter 17, I provide the detailed steps for running a waste audit. You can use the Waste Tracker worksheet to log your results and the Waste Actions worksheet to record the actions you can implement to help reduce your waste.

WASTE TRACKER

Date: _____   Which Bin: _____

Item Description (Add a short description of the item)	Material (metal, glass, paper, plastic, organic, hazardous, or mixed)	Quantity (Tally up the number)

WASTE ACTIONS

RECYCLING	ORGANICS

GARBAGE	OTHER

GENERAL ACTIONS AND NOTES

© *John Wiley & Sons, Inc.*

Index

A

acrylic (plexiglass), 120

acrylonitrile butadiene styrene (ABS), 120

advanced recycling, 54

air pollution, 24, 43–44

Aldi, 64, 308

aliphatic-polyester bioplastics, 109

aluminum, 64, 182–183, 184, 345–346

Amcor, 231

American Textile Recycling Service (US), 281

ammonia, emission of, 44

anaerobic digestion, 24, 52, 244

Anderson, Gary (creator of universal recycling symbol), 84

A.N.E. (Adopt a Native Elder), 313

apartment living, recycling challenges in, 82–83

apps, 102, 246, 333

Armoire, 296

arsenic, as toxic substance in e-waste, 256

artificial intelligence (AI), boosting recycling with, 331, 332, 333–334

Audi, 65

Australasian Recycling Label (ARL), 91–92, 224

Australia

  aluminum mining in, 182

  Australia Post, 283

  Australian Consumers Association (Choice), 271

  battery recycling locations, 268

  Department of Agriculture, Water, and the Environment (Australia), 160

  DiaperRecycle, 284

  e-waste recycling locations, 265

  on exporting waste, 70–71

  Great Wrap brand, 244

  iron ore mining in, 182

  as lacking consistent bans on plastic bags, 220

  Lids4Kids, 122

  phasing out problematic and unnecessary plastics, 336

  PP5 recycling program for plant pots, 283

  Recycle Mate (app), 102, 333

  recycling options for polystyrene in, 283

  soft plastic recycling facilities in, 228

  website to locate your location's recycling information, 102

Australia Bedding Stewardship Scheme, 282

Australian Consumers Association (Choice), 271

Australian Packaging Covenant Organisation (APCO), 91

B

bad habits, breaking free from, 94–96

baked-on/baked-for date (on food products), 239

baking paper, 138, 147, 148, 152

bales, processing and manufacturing of, 62–63

bananas, use of in making textiles, 244

Basel Action Network (BAN), 259

Basel Convention, 70, 257, 259

Batoko, 313

batteries

  button-cell batteries, 267

  as item that doesn't belong in curbside recycling bin, 99, 150

  lead-acid batteries, 267

  lithium-ion (Li-ion) batteries, 267, 268

  rechargeable ones, 267, 268

  recycling of, 265–268, 347–348

  safe disposal of, 264

  single-use/disposable ones, 266–267, 269

  using fewer, 268–269

bauxite, 178

BBC, report on shipping waste to other countries, 70

E

earthworms, as option for recycling food waste at home, 245–246

eBay, 295, 298

eddy current separators, for separating recyclable materials, 96

electrolysis, 180–181

electronic devices, 262, 271, 356

Ellen MacArthur Foundation
  on plastic in ocean, 10
  on redesigning products for recyclability, 330

end markets, finding of for recycled material, 69

energy
  making of from timber waste, 137
  reducing consumption of through paper recycling, 139
  used in making food, 236
  used in making glass, 157
  used in making metals, 179, 185
  used in making paper, 135
  used in making plastics, 106
  used in making soft plastics, 215
  waste of, 51

England, Home Waste Recycling Act of 2003, 336

envelopes and mailers, 150, 209, 311

environment
  helping of by recycling e-waste, 254–256
  impact of food production on, 237–238
  preservation of with metal recycling, 185–186

environmental groups, support of, 327

environmental pollution
  air pollution, 24, 43–44
  from plastics, 37–38, 38–41, 42, 213, 218
  in soils, 43

enzymes, use of to munch on plastic, 335

EPEAT (Electronic Product Environment Assessment Tool) certification, 271–272

e-Stewards certification program, 71, 259, 263

Ethical Consumer, 272

ethylene-vinyl acetate (EVA), 203

ethylene-vinyl alcohol (EVOH), 203

e-Trash Transparency Project (Basel Action Network), 259

Etsy, 295, 298

European Packaging and Packaging Waste Directive 94/62, 86

European Union (EU)
  Circular Economy Action Plan (CEAP), 338–339
  on exporting plastic waste, 70
  Green Dot system, 73
  on right to repair, 263
  Single Use Plastics Directive, 76
  steel production in, 182

Everyday Recycler (website), 65, 67, 131, 308, 313

e-waste (electronic waste) (WEEE)
  categories of, 252
  dangers of informally recycling of, 258–259
  defined, 251, 252
  examples of, 199
  as items that don't belong in curbside recycling bin, 99, 256, 356
  percentage of that gets recycled, 253
  reasons for recycling of, 254–256
  recycling of, 257–273
  reducing your overall e-waste impact, 269–270
  responsible disposition of, 261–265
  as specialist recycling service, 65, 66
  tackling problem of, 253–256
  toxic substances in, 255–256
  as world's fastest-growing waste stream, 251, 253

expiration dates (on food products), 239

extended producer responsibility (EPR), 72, 73–74, 86, 336

extraction (of natural resources), 30, 31, 32, 107

F

Facebook
  Buy Nothing group, 173, 230, 298
  Marketplace, 298

Fair Wear, 313

fashion textiles, recycling options for, 280–282

neighborhood recycling collection, running of, 322–323

Nestle, 231, 309

new home for items, finding, 298

New York City

    Department of Transportation, success in recycling plastic, 64

    putting recyclables in clear plastic bags in, 100

newspapers/newsprint, 138, 147

nickel-cadmium batteries (NiCd), 267

Nike, Reuse-A-Shoe program, 350

nitrogen, emission of, 51

nitrogen oxides, emission of, 43

nonferrous metals, 182, 191, 199

nonrenewable resources, as compared to renewable resources, 106

North Atlantic gyre, 38

Nuuly, 296

nylon, as plastic #7, 120

O

Ocean Cleanup, 327

Ocean Conservancy, 49, 325, 327

Ocean Conservation Namibia, 40

Ocean Voyages Institute, 327

Oceana, 327

oceans

    cleanups of through art, 324

    plastics in, 37–38, 111

    role of, 36–37

The Ocean Cleanup, plastic tracker, 36

OEKO-TEX certification, 313

Office Depot, 283

Office National, 283

Officeworks, 283, 348

1% for the Planet, 312

One World Running, 350

On-Pack Recycling Label (OPRL) (UK), 89–91, 224, 336

open-pit mining, 180

ore, 178, 179

organic waste, 20, 21, 23, 24, 34, 319

Organisation for Economic Co-operation and Development (OECD), 70

other household waste, 20

oxygen, emission of, 51

P

packaging

    delivery packaging, 209

    encouraging companies to make changes in, 301

    food packaging. *See* food packaging

    of materials and products, 31, 32

    multilayer packaging, 201–209

    paying attention to size in recycling of, 101

    personal product packaging, 207–208

    with recycled content, 309

    simplifying of, 204

    soft plastics as fastest-growing material for, 216

Packaging Recyclability Evaluation Portal (PREP), 91

paper. *See also specific paper products*

    amount of sent to landfills in US and UK, 139

    buying certified timber products, 153

    coated paper, 138

    composting of, 144

    curbside recycling of, 144, 151

    defined, 134

    degradation of, 34

    examples of for recycling, 94

    items that don't belong in your bin, 148–149

    items that go in your curbside bin, 147

    items to check with local rules about recycling of, 150

    keeping it free from contamination, 143

    knowing what can and can't be recycled, 144–151

    majority of as recycled, 133

    making new paper, 134–137

    number of times waste paper can be recycled, 140

    per person usage annually, 133

    purchasing recycled paper products, 153

    recycling of, 63, 133–153

transportation, of materials and products, 31, 32

Trash Is for Tossers, 300

Trendpac, 64

TRESemmé, 309

trona, defined, 156–157

U

Ultrapolymers, 64

underground mining, 180, 186

United Kingdom (UK)

  battery recycling locations, 268

  e-waste recycling locations, 265

  on extended producer responsibility (EPR), 336

  Horizon (app), 102

  milk bottle top recycling in, 122

  On-Pack Recycling Label (OPRL), 89–91, 224, 336

  paper and cardboard recycling in, 133

  percentage of mattresses recycled in, 282

  Plastic Packaging Tax, 337

  recycling clothing in, 281

  recycling of soft plastics in, 221

  recycling options for mattresses in, 282

  recycling options for polystyrene in, 283

  on right to repair, 263

  on shipping waste to other countries, 70

  soft plastic recycling facilities in, 228

  website to locate your location's recycling information, 102

  Which, 271

United Nations (UN), on plastics treaty, 71

United States (US). *See also specific states*

  access to recycling services for multilayer packaging in, 204

  adoption of EPEAT ecolabel by, 272

  American Textile Recycling Service, 281

  as among top waste-producing nations, 20

  amount of plastic waste in landfills, 111–112

  battery recycling locations, 268

  Carpet America Recovery Effort (CARE), 285

  Consumers Union, 271

  e-waste recycling locations, 265

  as having no federal laws addressing e-waste, 257

  as lacking consistent bans on plastic bags, 220

  as lagging behind other countries on legislation to reduce plastic pollution, 326

  landfills as third-largest source of methane emissions, 139

  producer responsibility laws for mattresses, 282

  recycling of soft plastics in, 221

  recycling options for polystyrene in, 283

  on right to repair, 263

  on shipping waste to other countries, 70

  soft plastic recycling facilities in, 228

  soft plastic waste in, 216

  statistic about waste production, 20

  website to locate your location's recycling information, 102

universal recycling symbol, 83–85. *See also* inverted Mobius loop; Mobius loop

upcycling, 281, 307

Upparel (New Zealand and Australia), 281

U.S. Environmental Protection Agency (EPA)

  on e-waste, 253

  on food waste, 238

  on glass recycling, 160, 161

  on global food production, 235

  on paper recycling and energy, 139

  on plastic waste in landfills, 111

  on recycling of cell phones, 254

  on soft plastic waste, 216

U.S. Society of the Plastics Industry, 117

use-by date (on food products), 239

V

VarageSale, 295

vegan leather from pineapples, 244

Veolia, 65

Vietnam, on acceptance of low-quality waste, 70

Visy Industries, 64

Viva, 309

Volution Group, 64

"voting with your wallet," 304

W

Walmart, 228, 283, 308

waste. *See also* e-waste (electronic waste) (WEEE); food waste; hazardous waste; organic waste

biohazardous waste, 99

consequences of burning waste, 52

environmental costs of too much waste, 35–44

global initiatives on restriction of international trade of, 70

global production of, 35

as harmful to environment, 10

as harmful to humans, 10–11

hazardous waste, 20, 21

as litter, 23

organic waste, 20, 21, 22

other household waste, 20, 21, 22

pathways of pollution, 36

per person daily generation of, 35

percentage of household packaging in, 79

preventing old clothing from going to, 281

recyclable waste, 20, 21, 22

shipping it abroad, 81

social costs of too much waste, 44–45

supporting local and federal action to improve, 325–326

types of, 20–22

understanding the problem with, 29–52

use of term, 19–20, 20

what happens to it, 22–25

waste actions (worksheet), 321, 361

waste audit

analyzing data from, 320

conducting of, 318–319

use of, 230, 292, 318

worksheets, 16, 359–361

waste hierarchy, 26–28, 32

waste management

as disproportionately affecting low-income communities, 45

hierarchy of, 26–28

landfill as one aspect of, 35

primary purpose of, 22–23

recycling as one aspect of, 12, 35

waste-to-energy as one aspect of, 35

waste tracker (worksheet), 319, 320, 360

waste transfer stations, 58

waste-to-energy plants, 23, 24, 28, 52

water

amount needed to make one pound of plastic, 106

amount needed to make one sheet of printer paper, 135

lowering consumption of through paper recycling, 139

used in making food, 236, 237–238

used in making metals, 179

used in making soft plastics, 214

Waterhaul, 314

waxed paper, 138, 143, 147

websites

Everyday Recycler, 65, 67, 131, 308, 313

for getting local recycling info, 102

www.crayoncollection.org (UK), 284

www.crazycrayons.com (US and Canada), 284

www.gumdropltd.com, 349

Wegmans, 228

wet suits, recycling of, 350

when in doubt, leave it out, as important guideline, 96, 149, 205

Which, 271

Whole Foods, 308

wildlife, plastics as endangering, 38–41, 111

Wishbone, 314

wishcycling, 69, 71, 95, 169, 344

Wolven, 314

worksheets

glass recycling worksheet, 169, 170

metal recycling worksheet, 195, 196

waste actions, 321, 361

waste audit, 16, 359–361

waste tracker, 319, 320–360

worm farms, as option for recycling food waste at home, 245–246

About the Author

Sarah Winkler is the founder of Everyday Recycler, an educational website that offers its readers simple and actionable recycling tips (https://everydayrecycler.com/). She has been passionate about environmental issues all her life. Her mission is to create a world where recycled products are commonplace and waste is scarce.

Sarah holds an honors degree in science and postgraduate training in business analytics and the circular economy. She has spent more than 25 years working in various facets of project management, where her aptitude for developing reports, procedures, and training manuals has helped set many projects up for success.

Through her varied project and life experience, she has developed an entrepreneurial style with strong conceptual thinking and problem-solving skills — skills she now applies to solve the world's recycling questions.

Sarah spent the first half of her life living and working in many different countries. Now based in Melbourne, Australia, she still loves traveling for fun, whether locally or internationally. She is an avid hiker and loves exploring the outdoors with her husband.

Dedication

I want to dedicate this book to all the amazing educators, environmental advocates, innovators, circular thinkers, scientists, and researchers who dedicate their lives to expanding our understanding of environmental issues and how to solve them.

Their passion is contagious. I recommend you seek them out, support them, and let some of it rub off on you.

Author's Acknowledgments

My passion for the subject of recycling led me to write this book, but it's thanks to the team at Wiley for recognizing that passion. Thanks to Lindsay Lefevere for guiding this project and Georgette Beatty, Kristie Pyles, Amy Handy, and Kelsey Baird for their valuable guidance throughout. Finally, a big thanks to the remaining crew behind the book, including the editors, illustrators, and everyone who helped pull it together.

My incredible husband and partner in life, Daniel, has supported and encouraged me throughout the whole process. He has also taken on all the chores while I sit and write — shopping, cooking, cleaning, and maintaining our home. I am so lucky to have such a wonderful partner, and I have a bit of catching up to do, I promise.

A special thanks to my amazing Mum and Dad. They are a big part of who I am today, instilling in me the belief that I can do anything. My Dad also read over the many chapters and offered helpful criticism and suggestions.

I am fortunate to have a loving family and an amazing group of friends — thanks to everyone for encouraging me and sharing my excitement. A special thank you to Janet, my closest friend, who was there every step along the way.

I would also like to acknowledge the countless industry professionals who have provided input into the book. Writing such a comprehensive book on recycling has required extensive research, something I have only been able to complete with the assistance of many committed professionals across a broad range of subjects who have shared their research on recycling and the environment. Thanks to all of them for their hard work and passion. Also, many thanks to those who shared their extensive knowledge through discussions and first-hand tours of facilities.